THE NEW STATESMAN

The *New Statesman* has been published for fifty years. It has become an essential part of intelligent opinion. It has attained this position both by the quality and by the integrity of its journalism. Many of the century's most stimulating personalities have been concerned with the *New Statesman*'s operation right down to our own day—Bernard Shaw, the Webbs, Desmond MacCarthy, Arnold Bennett, Maynard Keynes, Kingsley Martin, C. P. Snow, John Freeman are some instances; indeed, there are few famous names who have not written for it. 'New statesmanship', the attitude of mind which found—and still has—its expression in the journal, started in the parish and expanded to the constituency, the nation, the Empire, the Commonwealth and beyond.

This authoritative and readable history, together with its companion NEW STATESMANSHIP : An Anthology, has been planned to coincide with the fiftieth anniversary. It tells the story of the journal's varying but always magisterial role, of the exceptional people involved and of the editorial policies which have given the *New Statesman* its unique character. This is a book which everyone interested in the Britain of the twentieth century must read.

Clifford Sharp 1913-30

Kingsley Martin 1931-60

John Freeman 1961-

The New Statesman

THE HISTORY OF THE FIRST FIFTY YEARS

1913-1963

BY EDWARD HYAMS

with an Introduction by John Freeman

1724

LONGMANS

LONGMANS, GREEN AND CO LTD
48 GROSVENOR STREET, LONDON W 1
RAILWAY CRESCENT, CROYDON, VICTORIA, AUSTRALIA
AUCKLAND, KINGSTON (JAMAICA), LAHORE, NAIROBI
LONGMANS SOUTHERN AFRICA (PTY) LTD
THIBAULT HOUSE, THIBAULT SQUARE, CAPE TOWN
JOHANNESBURG, SALISBURY
LONGMANS OF NIGERIA LTD
W. R. INDUSTRIAL ESTATE, IKEJA
LONGMANS OF GHANA LTD
INDUSTRIAL ESTATE, RING ROAD SOUTH, ACCRA
LONGMANS GREEN (FAR EAST) LTD
443 LOCKHART ROAD, HONG KONG
LONGMANS OF MALAYA LTD
44 JALAN AMPANG, KUALA LUMPUR
ORIENT LONGMANS LTD
CALCUTTA, BOMBAY, MADRAS
DELHI, HYDERABAD, DACCA
LONGMANS CANADA LTD
137 BOND STREET, TORONTO 2

Printed in Great Britain by
The Camelot Press Ltd., London and Southampton

Contents

Acknowledgments

I SHOULD like to record my thanks to a number of people who patiently and generously gave valuable time to talking to me and answering my questions about the *New Statesman*. For the early years I had help from the late G. D. H. Cole and the late S. K. Ratcliffe. I shall not try to name everyone who helped me in this way but I must say how grateful I am to Mr. Leonard Woolf, Mr. Richard Crossman and above all to Mr. Kingsley Martin. I must also say thank you for permission to quote from certain letters written by Lord Keynes, granted by his Trustees, to Mrs. Sylvia Blelloch for a letter by Robert Dell, the Public Trustee and the Society of Authors for an extract from G. B. Shaw's *Manifesto* and a letter from him to Mrs. Beatrice Webb, and to Mr. Julian Symons and Mr. Arthur Koestler whose enlightening works I have made use of. I have been unable to trace the Executors of the late Clifford Sharp for permission to include his letter to Mrs. Beatrice Webb, and I should welcome any information which would enable me to do so. The portrait of Clifford Sharp is from a photograph by Bernard Shaw and that of John Freeman is from a BBC photograph.

Introduction

THIS is a book about the *New Statesman*. But it is not one of those monumental 'house' histories which big firms sometimes bestow on themselves with the same cynical indifference as they bestow gold watches on their aged employees. It is an independent, and in part critical, study, written by an author of distinction, whose repute is enough to assure the reader that what follows is not advertising matter.

How did the book originate? First, with the feeling that a history of the *New Statesman* ought to be written while it was still possible to consult some of the people who remembered its early days. The idea was obviously a good one. The story of the paper would necessarily involve much of the political and social history of the first half of the twentieth century; inevitably, it would turn out to be, to some degree, an evaluation of the British Left since the First World War. Then it became clear that such a history would be a most appropriate way of marking the fiftieth anniversary of the founding of the *New Statesman*. And so some time in 1957 it came to be accepted that our Jubilee—in April of 1963 —should be celebrated if possible by the publication of a History. If possible. How could the project be realized without turning the historian, who would have to depend on us for most of his material, into a *New Statesman* hack?

The integrity of the book would depend on finding an author and publisher whose personal integrity was sufficient proof of independence without elaborate guarantees and written safeguards. Obviously such an author must be a man or woman qualified to handle the raw material of political and social history; well versed in the communications of the Left; catholic in outlook and taste; experienced in the wider world outside Britain; confident and independent in his judgments; in the most general sense sympathetic to the paper; and above all a good writer. He must be, in other words, 'with' the *New Statesman* but not 'of' it. Eventually it was decided that Edward Hyams was the man—and Hyams jumped at the idea.

Long an outside contributor to the *New Statesman* and generally sympathetic to its dissenting view of the world, Hyams had never been involved in the internal workings of the paper, always saw himself as a reader of the *New Statesman* rather than a writer for it. The fact, however, that he seemed to embody about the right mixture of sympathy and detachment was neither the only nor even the principal reason why he seemed a particularly appropriate historian. Hyams is one of the most widely-talented and underrated men of his generation. Novelist, scholar, gardener, traveller, he has an international reputation both as a French scholar and as a grower of fruit. Less well known but equally real are a passionate interest in politics and a totally original, maverick judgment. He is a Socialist who fits into no regular mould, a *bon viveur* with a conscience and highly developed critical sense, a critic and writer with a strong affection for the French satirists. He seemed to represent as wide a range of New Statesmanly sympathies as would be found in one person; and no one could doubt his integrity and independence.

In May of 1958, then, Hyams was invited to undertake this book. The arrangement was a simple one. The *New Statesman* made available to him both the whole of its records and a sum of money (not over-generous, it now seems!) to cover what in another context might be called the 'loss of earnings' occasioned by a considerable period of research and writing. Longmans undertook the publication of the book, and work started. Were any special directives given to Hyams in return for the money he was paid? None at all. Kingsley Martin, then Editor, explicitly refused to establish any editorial right to censor or suppress anything which Hyams might write. This therefore is a book which the *New Statesman* sponsored, but the work has been Hyams's and the opinions and judgments are his alone.

I make this point specifically and categorically for two reasons. First because the reader is entitled in a book of this kind to be told with candour how far 'sponsorship' has gone. Secondly because it must not be assumed that the author's opinions in every case coincide with the views we hold about ourselves, or that his interpretation of particular actions invariably coincides with the memory of the individuals concerned in them. The truth is that his method has been that of the historian rather than the journalist. He examines the available evidence and, wherever possible, he includes in that evidence the personal recollection of the individuals concerned. Having scrutinized it all, he then makes his own judgment, which may or may not coincide with the rationalized 'memory' of those who have provided him with verbal recollection. It follows, therefore, that we who are personally involved in the events he describes occasionally prefer our own (perhaps more apologetic) interpretation of particular episodes than Hyams, with the historian's cool and uncommitted appraisal of evidence, has chosen to place upon our actions. This is true of me, who features comparatively little in the pages which follow. It must be far more true of Kingsley Martin, whose story this book so largely is. And it must be true to a greater or lesser extent of every living character who appears.

None of which is to say that the portrait which emerges of the *New Statesman* or its personalities is inaccurate or tendentious, but merely that this is Hyams's view of the *New Statesman* seen in the perspective of one man's judgment. Other and more personal verdicts about some of the individual episodes which make up this History are perfectly possible on the evidence which exists. We have, however, deliberately chosen to expose ourselves to the critical judgment of an independent recorder and we make no complaint about the thoroughness or fairness with which he has examined us. Indeed, lest the very fact of dissociating the *New Statesman* and those who have served it from the opinions presented in this book should seem to imply some dissatisfaction, I should perhaps state in terms that I regard this portrait of the paper which I now have the honour to edit as being fair and true in all its essentials—and by no means ungenerous in its terms. If there are interpretations here or there which I should myself have rendered differently, or assessments of motive which seem to me, as an interested party, to attach too little weight to the personal testimony of the individual concerned, or judgments about literature or politics which differ from those of the *New Statesman*— well, what blushing sitter ever looked upon his own portrait without an ambivalence of feeling, in which the comfortable glow of self-esteem is chilled at points by a draught of personal chagrin that the artist has seen something less than agreeable behind the best face which has been presented to him?

If Hyams has done less than full justice to any salient point in the *New Statesman*'s history, it is that he has perhaps not sufficiently emphasized the extraordinary influence which Kingsley Martin's 'irresponsible' journal of dissent had upon the weight and gravity of the British Establishment. The essence of Martin's editorial achievement (which ensures that he will always be considered among the handful of great editors) is not simply the style, quality and honesty of the journal he produced; not that he took over an ailing and insecure fledgling in 1931 and thirty years later handed over to his successor one of the lustiest and most self-confident voices in journalism; but that over these three decades the *New Statesman*, unceasingly jibed at for its 'irresponsibility', its 'querulousness', its 'pessimism'—in fact for all the pejorative attributes which the guilty and cynical can attach to the voice of conscience—has nevertheless played a crucial role in shaping the thought of a generation. Again and again it has brought authority to accept its point of view. It is, in fact, difficult to deny that, had Martin's *New Statesman* not existed, public opinion on such varied and momentous issues as anti-fascism in the Thirties, war aims, the Welfare State, and—perhaps above all—the anti-imperial revolution of India and the British colonies would for the three decades of his editorship have been very different from what it was. When historians of a later generation than Hyams come to consider why the opinion-forming public of the Thirties, Forties and Fifties lived and thought as they did, they may well conclude that one significant and enduring influence was an angular, argumentative, exuberant nonconformist called Kingsley Martin, who never acquired the good taste and discretion to keep quiet in the face of injustice and folly, and the journal in which he weekly wrestled with the doubts and proclaimed the convictions of a whole generation. It seems to me that, in properly paying tribute to the material and technical success of Martin's *New Statesman*, Hyams may not fully have understood that the true measure of that success (and anyway the only standard of measurement for which Martin himself would give a damn) was the success of the causes which the *New Statesman* backed.

What of the future? At some point in this book Hyams expresses the opinion that the present Editor (only the third in fifty years) belongs more to the school of Clifford Sharp (the founding father of the *New Statesman*) than to that of Kingsley Martin. That is for others to judge. What I am certain of is that the man who has to face the challenge of succeeding Martin will not in fact succeed merely by copying. If Martin is a preacher by temperament (which he is), none the less the fundamental reason why his *New Statesman* preached to its readers week by week was because he was able to face his world with a measure of certain assurance. The political and social course of the Thirties and Forties had been mapped out in advance with astonishing accuracy by the Socialist thinkers of the inter-war years and the prophets of that generation were confident that they knew the answers. Their problem was to knock the truth into thick or inattentive heads.

Today's *New Statesman* preaches far less—and this is only in part because the present Editor is an ineffectual preacher. More deeply it is because in face of the problems of the Fifties and Sixties there is no certainty. British Socialist practice and precept has, so to speak, come to the end of the homework done by the early new statesmen, and a period of intense disputation and inquiry is now needed to relate basic Socialist morality to the exigencies of the modern world. The Left in Britain has for some years been divided between those nostalgic fundamentalists who whistle in the dark by annunciating the slogans of an earlier generation and those super-pragmatists who, unable without trouble to reconcile their principles with the acquisitive world they experience, cynically abandon principle. Both sides—no doubt unwittingly—dishonour the Socialism whose name they take in vain. The function of the *New Statesman* in the next few years is to help the British Left to rethink its attitudes to the modern world and to undertake a fresh analysis of the problems of welfare capitalism and the Cold War. In so far as it succeeds, it will play an honourable part in recreating the element of certainty upon which the self-confidence of any political movement must be based and in charting the course along which Socialists can walk together in unity. Socialists, I say, because the *New Statesman* is and always has been a Socialist journal. The purpose which Sidney and Beatrice Webb had in mind fifty years ago for their new paper was, to quote Edward Hyams, 'to preach the introduction of scientific method and scientific efficiency into social management. It would preach the substitution of social salvation for personal salvation; and the State, being in the hands of socialist philosophers who had seen the light of reason, would be a State which could be trusted to respect liberty as well as promote well-being.' I have already explained why today's *New Statesman* has some reservations about that word 'preach'; but, that apart, our purpose is the same as the Webbs' was. This does not, of course, mean that we are in any sense a party journal. Naturally a paper which seeks to identify and apply the principles of scientific Socialism will not infrequently find itself supporting the Labour Party— simply because Labour is the organized political group most likely to give effect to the ideas which we strive to propagate. I should like to be able to give that support more consist- ently—and I should like the Labour Party to be a more consistent and conscientious exponent of Socialist principles. These, however, are aspirations which hang on events. In the meantime, let us be clear that the *New Statesman* is independent of party. This position of commitment to principles and independence of organizations is not without its pitfalls. 'We did not merely profess to have no political affiliations,' said Clifford Sharp. 'We had none. We were soon to discover, however, that a great many people who profess to admire independent political thought are apt to be both puzzled and shocked when they come across it.' From time to time in its history the *New Statesman* has found itself at loggerheads with the Labour Party. I have no doubt that this will happen again. It may cause less resentment and misunderstanding when it does if I say now to our friends in that Party: 'We have many ideals in common, but our immediate purposes must necessarily be different. Yours is to win a tactical battle for your Party; ours is to seek and proclaim the truths which we think all political parties ought to heed. In so far as the Labour Party listens to us it will have our support—as would any other political group. But we owe nothing of deference or loyalty to any Party organization as such, or to any group of leaders, and you must never count on us to toe your Party line.'

The *New Statesman*, in fact, will be party to no Establishment—political or literary. It deliberately sets out to be a journal of dissent, of scepticism, of inquiry, of nonconformity. It has never in the past been afraid to speak the awkward or unpopular truth; I hope it never will be. It has never in the past been content to accept either men or events at their face value; I hope it never will be. It has never in the past been corrupted by the rewards of prosperity or praise; and I hope it never will be. The battles it will have to fight in the future will no doubt be different in detail from those of the past, but they will be concerned with the same ultimate objectives. The men who control the *New Statesman* today write and dispute in what is superficially a different idiom from that of either Kingsley Martin or Clifford Sharp, but they are equally the representatives of dissent and individual responsibility in their generation, and their fundamental purpose is the same. If I had to express that purpose in a single sentence, I should say that it was to show men by analysis and reason how they may apply to public affairs and great issues the standards of personal morality and common sense which civilized men take for granted in their private dealings with one another. That individual men and women should take personal responsibility for asserting that principle at the level of national and international affairs is the fundamental proposition upon which democratic Socialism must be based. And more than anything else it is the business and purpose of the *New Statesman*.

JOHN FREEMAN

I

The New Statesmanship

HIPPOLYTE TAINE, most observant and sensitive of nineteenth-century French thinkers, and the historian of English literature, paid much attention in those *Notes on England* which he wrote after his several visits in this country in the 1860s and 70s to the sense of responsibility of the English gentry. Not merely of the landed gentry, and not merely to that traditional sense of responsibility manifest even in so disagreeable a woman as Lady Catherine de Bourgh. He found the same spirit in what, on the analogue of the *noblesse de la robe*, we may call the gowned gentry, the rich professional people including the Church of England clergy; and in the Radical businessmen. He remarked, moreover, how this serious-mindedness in the ruling classes had its response in the self-respecting and self-helping aspirations of the upper working class, such as the men who formed the first Rochdale Co-operative, and the non-revolutionary Trade Union leaders. This is in strong contrast to the English *canaille*, whom he found greatly inferior in spirit to the French, being so pusillanimous that they could be cowed by a handful of police; and so contemptibly submissive that they consented to wear the cast-off clothing of the people they acknowledged as their betters. All the more remarkable, then, that middle and upper class people were so determined to help these wretches, to give them some education, to raise them out of the drunken brutality in which they lived—except, presumably, while they were doing their twelve or fourteen hour stint in a mill, or dying of starvation as unemployed.

These observations led Taine to some reflections on the nature of those political and social means whereby freedom and justice are best achieved, established and defended. These reflections throw some light on the hostility to the democracy manifest in such diverse lovers of freedom as Dr. Johnson, the novelist Frederick Marryat, Edmund Gosse and many others. Taine perceived that political freedom, impartial justice and social progress were much more nearly accomplished in England, where the suffrage was very restricted but the voters responsible, than in France, where a national referendum under universal male suffrage established the tyranny of Napoleon III by an overwhelming majority.

Political freedom and the higher social progress are things you can be interested in only if you have enough to eat, clothes to wear, a roof over your head, and a measure of security. It must always, therefore, be the concern of people who have a high enough standard of living and freedom to be concerned for other people's, and not merely for their own. The majority—the underfed, ill-housed and shoddily clad— will make a revolution to get bread, but will not organize social and political evolution towards a condition of general welfare in the widest possible liberty; whenever the democracy is roused to force violent changes the outcome is invariably some kind of Caesarism. In the century since Taine noticed that a gentleman elected to Parliament by a handful of comfortable burghers, or for that matter by half a dozen drunks in a rotten borough, could be more truly 'representative' of the people, more concerned with reconciling the well-being of the citizen with the minimum loss of liberty, than an imperial politician supported by nine out of nine and a half million votes, history has largely confirmed his observations and conclusions. And it is true to say that if the *New Statesman* was, in its early years under Clifford Sharp, the first Editor, concerned chiefly with persuading the governing class to give the people a fair deal, it was, in its maturity under Kingsley Martin, obliged, almost as often, to persuade the people to give themselves a fair deal. For universal franchise settles nothing much: there is substance in the permanent implied threat of insurrection which inheres in an unenfranchised mob; and it is possible by exchanging it for a shadowy vote to give up all power whatsoever, notably the power to impose the will of the people by force.

What was peculiar to the English, in Taine's opinion, which I adopt as my own because it seems to me valid, was the singularly serious-minded method which they brought to the business of winning new rights and privileges, of broadening the basis of their democracy, of advancing towards the good life. They formed societies, they joined together in 'movements', founded magazines and reviews, infiltrated established institutions, bored from within, propagated their ideas on every possible occasion, a method subsequently often imitated with good results by the Communist parties of the world. Gradually, they won over more and more people to their cause until they could put such pressure on the governing minority that the revolutionary idea—the repeal of the Corn Laws for example, or reform of the franchise—became the law of the land, part of the constitution. It is curious that Edward Pease, in his history of the Fabian Society, refers to this method as an invention of Henry George. It had been going on long before George's *Progress and Poverty* was written; but that book revived interest in the method.

In short, the English had a gift for constantly reforming their State to suit new conditions by writing, talking and voting, not by insurrection and *coup d'état*. And by founding and carrying on journals to propagate their ideas. Taine had a great admiration for the serious purpose and painstaking methods of English political journalism, especially as practised by women of the middle and upper classes. In England in the Sixties and Seventies women were engaged in writing valuable studies of the condition of the industrial poor and advancing practical plans for the education of poor children. Whereas in France, alas! women in equivalent situations read frivolous fashion magazines. Is it a measure of the triumph of the kind of unchecked democracy which Taine feared but thought England safe from, that the number of frivolous women's papers has enormously increased and their circulations risen to many millions, while those of the serious weeklies have, relative to the rise in population, fallen catastrophically?

Not only did Taine admire the way in which a certain number of English people were ready to give their time and spend their money for the advancement of liberty, justice, knowledge. He admired their readiness to suffer boredom in the transaction of public business. The preparation of their articles, speeches and campaigns entailed very tedious study of statistics, figures, collation of facts and opinions, the reading of dull pamphlets and dry-as-dust reports. Ordinary, rather slow-witted English gentlemen and businessmen, he notes, will, out of their sense of duty, submit themselves to such mental tortures as hardly a Frenchman living could be brought to support. The French paid officials to suffer these pains: and by so doing they placed their liberty and their justice at the mercy of the bureaucracy in the service of a tyrant, and were then frequently driven to some measure of disorder and violence in order to restore their rights.

This is not the place to study the reasons for this difference between the two most brilliantly successful peoples of modern Europe. It will be enough to suggest that it is to be found in their different religious experiences. Taine himself, with his admiration for the political and social genius of the English, was greatly attracted to the Church of England; its clergy, he thought, were men of education trained to teach ethics, and not peasants trained to serve a superstition, as in France. Their sermons were lectures in ethics built on a solid foundation of classical and biblical scholarship, by which a man of sense, albeit a sceptical rationalist, could be interested and edified. The Protestant is accustomed to bear the burden of a sense of responsibility to God for his soul and conduct; the Catholic delegates that responsibility to his Church, his confessor, in short to a sort of ecclesiastical bureaucracy. The Protestant is in less danger of being driven by irrational and therefore unacceptable dogmas into agnosticism or atheism, both dangerous to the masses because they are negative opinions. It is perhaps in their religious differences that the difference between the English and French attitudes, in Taine's time, to political and social business, is to be found.

But although the English Protestant in the second half of

the nineteenth century was apparently not being driven into agnosticism and atheism, as were rational men in Catholic countries, by the Roman dogmas, he was in great danger of the same fate precisely by reason of his independent approach to religion. For it made him apt to read religious criticism, first German, later English. Bishop Colenso's is the classic case: asked point-blank by an African convert whether he believed the Bible to be literally true, instead of dismissing the question, he considered it, apparently for the first time; and discovered that he did not.

There was another aspect of the English character, manifest in all classes, but striking in the upper-middle and middle classes, which tended, likewise, literally towards godlessness: a practical empiricism. The English were attracted by applied science: it was, in the form of industrial growth, hourly transforming their society, creating immense wealth, concentrating that wealth in relatively few hands. It had brought into existence an enormous class of industrial poor, rapidly growing larger; and this in itself was a challenge to solve social problems in economic terms, and not by reference to a problematical hereafter which the victims— ultimately heirs of industrialism—were much less inclined to accept than a poor peasantry.

It cannot, of course, be said that the English governing classes, seduced by scientific rationalism, suddenly found themselves godless; and that they set about dealing with this situation, rendered dangerous by the fact that good conduct was thought to be impossible without divine sanction. The outward show of religion and a vague inner faith, persisted. It is none the less true that by the end of the century, and certainly a decade or so later, it must have been obvious to any man able to think at all, that man was going to have to find sanction for good social behaviour in his own common sense and common goodness; that while lip-service was still paid to religious arguments for good social conduct, such arguments no longer had any real force. In fact this state of mind was fairly widespread much earlier. Higgins, the tragically intelligent agnostic working-man of Mrs. Gaskell's *North and South*, was probably a quite representative figure.

There seem to be two conditions in which 'good'

5

government, within the limits of any community's means, may be expected: the religious, when the god's wish that men behave well towards each other has influence; and the irreligious, when the king is a philosopher, for example Marcus Aurelius. But until the nineteenth century of our era philosopher-governments had always been absolute monarchies. The peculiar problem confronting the twentieth century was to govern parliamentarily, democratically, and *nevertheless* to govern by the highest lights; and all without religious sanction. That, at least, must have seemed to be the problem: it cannot have been apparent in those simple terms. But it was (and is) none the less real for not having been clearly stated.

Pompous though the claim may sound in 1963, the *New Statesman* came into existence to propagate the idea of good government by the light of reason. And since the minds to do this difficult work must be those formed by what was best in the thought and feeling of the times, it was, from the beginning, a journal not only of politics but of art, letters and science.

Although I have said that I adopt Taine's opinion as to the sense of responsibility to the lower orders peculiar to the English upper classes, and of the best of those lower orders to themselves, it is of course impossible to be convinced by the impression that powerful thinker conveys, that of a whole upper class composed of such admirable people. But it is perhaps true to say that the most able and conscientious men of both Conservative and Liberal parties were of that kind. Both were willing to introduce, from time to time, social welfare legislation to lessen the suffering of the destitute masses. The Liberals, and liberals of both parties, went further, being willing slowly to broaden the franchise so that more and more people should have a say in the matter and manner of such legislation; and so that fewer and fewer should be tempted to insurrectionary action to redress their wrongs. It would not, even, be absolutely true to say that the idea of the State taking responsibility for certain economic parts of the national life, for social reasons, was entirely abhorrent to them as a matter of principle. It was less

6

abhorrent to the Conservatives than to the Liberals. The old-style Tory, with a sort of class-memory of feudalism, is nearer to being a socialist, in spirit, than the old-style Liberal. The modern, fiercely capitalist Tory is really a Liberal (i.e. a businessman, not a squire). True, the idea of interference by the State between employer and labour was abomination to the new industrialists of the midlands and the north. But it would be truer to say that the larger idea, that of a planned economy to get rid of mass destitution by deliberate State action on scientific lines, had simply not occurred to the old political parties. When the idea, namely Socialism, was brought to their attention, it does not seem to have been regarded by the educated men of either Party with horror, though there were many who thought that, the so-called laws of economics being immutable, Socialism must be impossible. To some extent, no doubt, this was a rationaliza- tion in the service of their interests. It seemed possible that Liberals and Conservatives could be persuaded to adopt an increasing measure of Socialism and to give it effect by Acts of Parliament. It was thus as an organ for the introduction of Socialism into the existing political Parties' programmes that the Fabian Society was to function during the first twenty years of its career.

The Fabian Society was typical of those social movements, peculiar to England, which Taine had admired. It was founded in 1882 by a group of middle-class people, led by Edward R. Pease, under the influence of books like Henry George's *Progress and Poverty*, of the Christian Socialist move- ment, of that powerful entity the Nonconformist conscience aware of injustice in the world, and more immediately of Thomas Davidson and his Fellowship of the New Life. It was following the reading of a paper written by Davidson that Pease's group resolved:

> That an association be formed whose ultimate aim shall be the reconstruction of society in accordance with the highest moral possibilities.

Probably the Fabian Society as it was later called would have remained at the do-gooding level implied in this resolution had not Bernard Shaw attended a meeting, decided that something could be made of the Society, and in due course attracted other members of the toughest and finest intellectual fibre. Shaw blew away the cobwebs of religiosity and set a new tone, manifest in his Pamphlet No. 2, written for the Society. This pamphlet took the form of a *Manifesto* asserting that the opinions which Fabians were associated to spread were, to quote only some of them as an example of the style later to grace the *New Statesman*:

That under existing circumstances wealth cannot be enjoyed without dishonour or forgone without misery.

That the most striking result of our present system of farming out the national land and capital to private persons has been the division of society into hostile classes with large appetites and no dinners at one extreme and large dinners and no appetites at the other.

... That nationalization of the land in some form is a public duty.

... That competition has the result of rendering adulteration, dishonest dealing, and inhumanity compulsory.

... the State should compete with all its might in every department of production.

That the State should compete with individuals, especially with parents, in providing happy homes for children so that every child may have a refuge from the tyranny and neglect of its natural custodians.

... that the sexes should henceforth enjoy equal political rights.

That the established government has no more right to call itself the State than the smoke of London has to call itself the weather.

That we had rather face a civil war than such another century of suffering as the present one has been.

Shaw was elected to the executive committee of the Society in January 1885 and in March he brought Sidney Webb to a meeting. In a private letter, written when he was eighty-eight, to Kingsley Martin, Shaw explained that he had thought Webb the man the Society needed. Webb was elected a member at his third attendance.

By 1893 the Fabian Society had created the politico-social instrument since called Fabianism out of the materials

provided by such diverse thinkers as Robert Owen and Karl
Marx, Frederic Harrison, Henry George, Davidson and a
score of others, not to mention the Fabians themselves. In the
next twenty years (and thereafter) it was first to force this
new statesmanship, by a manifold programme of research,
report and propaganda on the two existing political parties;
and, when they proved insufficiently flexible, to give its
whole support to the young Labour Party which it succeeded
only partly in turning into a political instrument of Fabian
Socialism.

But the Society had found, and for the next three decades
was to find, its expression in Fabian Tracts and Pamphlets,
in the famous Fabian Essays, in the Reports of its committees
or the committees on which Fabians served; and in action. It
had no organ of publicity regularly published, and read
outside Fabian circles. (The *Fabian News* was read by
members.) Nor did the *New Statesman*, when it was founded,
come into being as a direct result of a Fabian Society
activity. It was fathered by the Webbs on a sort of Fabian
by-blow called *The Crusade*.

Webb, as we have seen, was an active and soon a leading
member of the Fabian Society from its early days. Beatrice
Webb did not join it until 1893 and she took very little part
in its work until 1906. The Fabian Society as such had nothing to do with her famous work on the Royal Commission
on the Poor Law. But when the Minority Report, historically
so much more important than the Majority Report which
was promptly forgotten, came out, the Fabian Society
adopted it because it was excellent Fabian Socialism. The
Webbs reprinted the Report, with an Introduction and
Notes; the Fabian Society issued an edition of its own from
the Webbs' type.

In order to propagate the idea that the findings of the
Minority Report, '. . . a comprehensive and practical scheme
for preventing unemployment under existing conditions and
for coping with the mass of incompetent destitution which for
generations has been the disgrace of civilization', Beatrice
Webb set up the National Committee for the Prevention of
Destitution and managed its activities for two years. One of
the instruments created to gain wider support was *The*

Crusade, edited by Clifford Sharp—a Fabian, a founder of the Fabian Nursery, a member of the executive committee since 1909, who married Rosemary Bland, the daughter of a founder Fabian, Hubert Bland and his wife, who was to be better known by her pen-name of E. Nesbit. In the autumn of 1912 when Beatrice Webb concluded that since Government and people were not going to swallow the Minority Report whole, the National Committee could serve no further purpose, *The Crusade* ended its brief life.

Meanwhile, however, the idea of a weekly paper expressing the policy of Fabianism while not formally Fabian (though it could be, among other things, a vehicle for carrying the results of Fabian research) had been in the minds of the Webbs, Bernard Shaw, and some of their friends, for some time.

The strategy of the Minority Report campaign and the tactics of *The Crusade* can be described in one word, permeation. The potentially responsible, educated middle and upper classes were to be permeated with a new sense of duty. They were to be persuaded that it was their duty to study the idea of a scientific reorganization of society behind which, as driving force, was to be a moral idealism dissociated from the usual religious rewards and punishments. The aim was to be production of the best possible conditions of living for the largest possible number of people. The thinking and feeling behind the weekly journal which was to come into being as the *New Statesman*, were the same. In so far as they were Marxists, English socialists believed that you could only improve human beings, and might improve human nature, by improving the environment. Even many religious people were at this time coming to the conclusion that until you had given all the people decent living conditions, food, clothing, shelter and a measure of social security at least sufficient to keep them self-respecting, you could not expect them to take much interest in God. This line of thought can be followed, for instance, in the life of a minister of religion like Basil Martin, father of the man who was to become editor of the *New Statesman* in the Thirties, and described by himself in *An Impossible Parson* (George Allen & Unwin). And in so far as they were Fabians these same Socialists thought that the way to accomplish their ends was not by violent revolution but by rousing the old sense of social responsibility in the upper- and middle-class élite by making them aware of the vile conditions in which so many of their fellow citizens lived. That done, this small élite could be trained to take the leadership of the working class in the move towards economic Socialism. Thus the spirit of new statesmanship was that of Victorian morality, Christian ethics, but with science taking the place of religious faith and with rational self-helping action taking the place of prayer.

How did this differ from existing movements for social improvement and from the policies of those journals already in being which spoke for these movements? We need to glance at only two of these.

The dominant wing of political Liberalism in Britain was no longer Radical. The new Liberals were imperialists whose sense of responsibility towards the proletariat at home and towards the colonies overseas led them to think in terms of gradual but steady betterment of the proletarian lot at home —though it was not at all clear how this was to be done— and of evolution of the colonies towards self-government and independence. In foreign policy these Liberals believed in self-determination, the rights of small nations to be free and masters in their own frontiers. Typical of this Liberalism's leaders were men like Edward Grey, Asquith, Haldane. And their enemy was *The Nation* whose brilliant, high-minded editor was the famous H. W. Massingham. What, in one word, Massingham and *The Nation* stood for was Freedom.

Deeply concerned, on the other hand, with economic distress was the most active Socialist movement in Britain apart from the Fabian Society, that Guild Socialism which had G. D. H. Cole for its young and brilliant prophet, A. R. Orage and the *New Age* for its herald. Guild Socialism was the English manifestation of Syndicalism, and it appealed to many minds because it pointed out a way of getting the means of production, distribution and exchange out of the hands of private capitalist exploiters into those of the workers, but without putting them into the hands of the State. Syndicalism and Anarchism came into being because many men who were of the same mind as the Social Democrats, the original Marxists, about the tyranny and dangers of Capitalism, did not believe that the State should be trusted with economic power, for it would inevitably abuse it to the destruction of the individual's liberty. As this has, in fact, happened under Communism, it is clear that the Syndicalists were perfectly right. The aim of Guild Socialism was to transfer ownership and control of industry to the Trade Unions. It was international in outlook and it made a stirring appeal to many people who were far from being Socialists because of its analogues with medieval trade guild organizations. As a consequence the movement led by Cole and propagated by Orage, and which we can call Libertarian Socialism, was supported by some men of the Right and cut clean across ordinary Party lines.

Neither the *New Age* nor *The Nation* was doing what the Webbs' new paper was to do. The paper they had in mind was to preach the introduction of scientific method and scientific efficiency into social management. It would preach the substitution of social salvation for personal salvation; and the State, being in the hands of socialist philosophers who had seen the light of reason, would be a State which could be trusted to respect liberty as well as promote well-being.

2

Sharp and Shaw

THE *New Statesman* was founded at the Old Rectory, Liphook, in the course of a number of the week-end parties to which the Webbs invited their friends and such actual or potential associates in their work of reshaping British society on rationalist, socialist lines as could be drawn upon—generally during long, conversational walks—for information, ideas, expert help, moral support, and even money. Such walks might be over Beachy Head, since become, like so many of England's beauty spots, a car park and thus revealing one of the social problems the Webbs did not deal with: once you have made the people free of the land their heritage, how do you prevent their mere number from spoiling it? Or the stimulating walk might be under Beachy Head, like the one Lord Beveridge refers to in his Introduction to Beatrice Webb's *Diaries* for the years 1912-24 (Longmans Green, London, 1952), a walk which took place during one of the week-ends devoted to discussing the foundation of the *New Statesman*. It was probably later, rather than at the time, that Lord Beveridge formed the opinion that the Webbs possessed two qualities among their many others which enabled them to accomplish that most difficult feat, the successful launching and maintenance afloat of a new political weekly: namely, their practicality and their freedom from creators' vanity. 'Both were illustrated in the founding of the *New Statesman* and in the free hand they left to successive editors.'

That editors would be left such a free hand was not the impression of many who, among the outsiders unfamiliar with the selflessness of Beatrice Webb's aristocratic purpose— the quality so admired by Taine in upper-class English reformers—were as journalists closely or remotely interested in the projected new weekly. S. K. Ratcliffe, one of the earliest contributors to the paper and among the few who, as he told me just before his death, were considered as possible editors before Sharp was appointed, did not believe that the Webbs would allow any editor a free hand and was convinced that the editor, whoever he was, would be tied to their opinions.

Ratcliffe, trained as a journalist on the Calcutta *Statesman*, editor of *The Echo* in 1900 and writing regularly for Massingham's *The Nation* at the time of the new foundation, was summoned to Liphook in the late summer of 1912. It is impossible to tell what weight the Webbs gave to the many and diverse opinions they solicited: they had a ruthless way of calling the possibly useful to their house, feeding them merely adequately, walking them off their feet, boring the more frivolous with their serious-mindedness, and keeping to themselves the values given to the material thus accumulated when they came to collate it. Ratcliffe told the Webbs that the projected weekly could not possibly succeed. This was likewise the general Fleet Street opinion, based on the persuasion that any paper run by the Webbs must be dogmatic and doctrinaire and that in journalism dogma and doctrine are fatally repulsive.

Whether in fact any journalist other than Sharp was ever seriously considered for editor does not appear. It seems possible that certain journalists whose opinion was considered worth having had to be given the impression that the job might be offered them, as a matter of courtesy, and that this could be done with very little danger of becoming involved, since all such journalists were quite sure that the new paper must fail. So was H. G. Wells, who told Beatrice Webb that only a completely un-engaged weekly had any chance of success.

Among the experts who prophesied disaster was Massingham, a Fabian whose radicalism was, however, emotional, and who was openly contemptuous of the whole project, and particularly of Clifford Sharp as soon as he heard that Sharp was being spoken of as the probable editor. Massingham had met Sharp and knew something of his work and his attitude to it; he disliked the man so acutely that he would not willingly stay in the same room. 'Massingham', Ratcliffe told me, 'had a strongly moralistic attitude to his work and to life itself; whereas Sharp gave the impression of being cynical and was certainly immoral.' Ratcliffe himself preferred working for *The Nation;* he liked its high moral tone. All this did not prevent Massingham from writing for the *New Statesman* later.

Beatrice Webb's own account of the experts' view of the project's chance of success bears out all this pessimism. The lowest weekly sale at which the paper could struggle along was 3,000 copies; the highest it could expect was 5,000. Something between these two extreme figures could not be achieved unless several different groups of readers were attracted to and held by the new paper. These groups could be considered under the heads of potential contributors' names and followings: thus, Bernard Shaw would attract and might hold between 500 and 1,000 readers; the Webbs themselves between 300 and 500; and J. C. Squire, who was to be a founder-contributor and Literary Editor, not more than a hundred. The maximum sale to be expected, therefore, was 1,500 a week, a figure which must mean failure.

Moreover—it is Beatrice Webb citing the opinions she had collected—the paper will be one-idea'd. The Webbs only know the social and economic questions and they will always be hammering at one idea exactly as Belloc and Chesterton hammer at the one theme of political corruption in the *New Witness.* 'The paper would be the Webbs flavoured with a little Shaw and padded with the contributions of a few cleverish but ignorant young men. . . .' It is not an attractive prospect, and there is at least a possibility that had the Webbs not been so thorough in canvassing opinion the new paper might indeed have been what journalistic experts thought it would be. The Webbs were probably among the very few people in the history of the human race who were capable of correcting themselves before, and not after, the mistake had been made. It is significant that Beatrice, in her Diary entry touching this question, says,

There is truth in this criticism. . . . But I think Sidney and I are not quite so one-sided as we look—we have never written on other questions, but Sidney has an encyclopaedic knowledge and we have seen a few things. G.B.S., if he really throws himself into it, has a far larger public than is thought by the Liberals, and I believe we can attract around us able persons of quite different interest and outlook and in harmony with our general position. And though we are wholly inexperienced on the business side we have initiative, persistency and audacity, which more conventionally experienced persons lack. So I think that our friends . . . may be unpleasantly disappointed. However, they are obviously better judges than we are and the chances are they are right. In that case we shall have spent our money and our time, not exactly in vain because we shall have raised the standard of Socialist journalism. If I were forced to wager, I should not back our success.

The Webbs were, in fact, clear from the start that the project was speculative. This appears in the very first reference which Beatrice makes to it, an entry for 10 October 1912: there is a clear call for leadership in the Labour and Socialist movements; they feel they must respond to it; one of their responses is to be the starting of a new weekly in the spring: 'The planning of this organ of Fabianism is largely devolving on Sidney. It is by far the most risky of our present enterprises. . . .'

Some time towards the end of 1912 the appointment of Clifford Sharp as Editor, if there had ever really been any question of another man, was decided; and capital, to a total which Beatrice describes as quite insufficient, was subscribed. The sum was £5,000, four contributions of £1,000 each from Shaw, Edward Whitley, Henry Harben and Ernest Simon, and another £1,000 made up of smaller sums. A private company was formed in December. A name for the paper had to be found and the subject was discussed by the Board. The name ultimately decided upon was suggested by Balfour, an old friend of the Webbs and at that time leader of the Conservative Party Opposition, and to whom the original Fabian plan of pressing Socialism on the existing political parties instead of the later plan of backing a specifically socialist party, had been applied with some success.

The first Board Meeting of the newly formed company was

held at the offices of the National Committee for the Prevention of Destitution, in Norfolk Street. At the first of these the name adopted for the new paper was *The Statesman*, Sharp and Squire were officially appointed as Editor and Literary Editor, the former with £500 and the latter with £300 a year, and Sharp was voted £50 'to visit Paris, Berlin and elsewhere', presumably to arrange for foreign correspondents. It was at the second meeting, in February 1913, that the paper's name was changed to *The New Statesman*, and that rent of £10 was voted to the National Committee for the use of their offices, and another £5 for the use of a secretary. At the same time Mr. George Radford, an advertising agent, was appointed to sell the paper's advertisement space on commission; he was to be allowed to sell the space in guineas and to account for it in pounds less 15 per cent.

Capital, Editor, a name, money and an administrative organ having been conjured into existence, it remained to drum up subscribers and contributors. It was in the existence of a known body of potential subscribers that the great advantage of the new paper lay. The machinery for the National Committee for the Prevention of Destitution was still in being. Its supporters were circularized with a special offer, a one-guinea annual subscription to the new paper which was to last the subscriber's lifetime. The same offer was sent to what Beatrice Webb called the Fabian Society 'clientele'. The total mailing list was of the order of 20,000 names. Despite the experts' opinion that a weekly sale of 3,000 was the minimum requirement for survival, the promoters believed that if they could get 2,000 postal subscribers the success of the paper was assured. 'If we get only 500 it is extremely doubtful whether it can survive two years', Beatrice Webb recorded in her Diary (Christmas 1912). Personal letters from Beatrice Webb were sent to all the most promising National Committee supporters, manifolded ones to the less promising. Shaw and Sidney Webb dealt in the same way with the Fabian Society nominal roll.

The result was gratifying. The new paper started with 2,300 postal subscribers, a number which later rose to 2,600. At the end of the first year 1,600 of these were renewed. Of these guinea-a-year subscribers, a thousand were still on the

New Statesman books twenty-one years later. A promise, strictly kept, never to renew the offer was made in the course of the initial promotion, but the saving in money, 5*s*. a year, can hardly have been a serious inducement to subscribe.

The *New Statesman* directors did not rely solely on the National Committee lists and the old *Crusade* readers for its initial circulation. A Mr. Hogg had been appointed after the first Board Meeting to do the rounds of the bookstalls. He evidently had some success, for at the second meeting he was given a small bonus for his 'keen and successful' canvassing, and reappointed to work three days a week selling the paper to the bookstalls, for which he was paid 30*s*.

A weekly subscription sale of 2,600 copies plus casual sales of 500 or 600—the paper's sale during the first year fluctuated between 3,000 and 4,000 a week—did not, however, mean that the *New Statesman* was launched as a paying proposition. To make a profit, at least 5,000 a week would have been necessary, a figure which was not attained until 1916, by which time costs had risen. But it did mean that consumption of capital would be slow enough to ensure the *New Statesman* a run for its money and a chance to establish itself. A weekly paper has, in the way of trade—that is, apart from any question of subsidy—two sources of revenue: income from sales of the paper itself, and income from advertisements, the sale of advertising space. Today the second source would as a rule be given far more consideration than the first. The *New Statesman* founders, although no doubt they gave some consideration to revenue from advertising, do not seem to have given it much weight; and in fact, during the first sixteen months of the paper's life, advertising revenue amounted to something less than £1,000.

While these steps to ensure circulation were being taken, Clifford Sharp was engaging the services of writers. It went without saying, of course, that Shaw and the Webbs were to be regular contributors; theirs must be the features on which sales of the paper largely depended. For dramatic criticism Sharp turned to an old friend, Desmond MacCarthy. It had been decided to have a City page dealing with financial and commercial matters, for it was, of course, the stock- and share-owning middle class, which new statesmanship did not look upon as the enemy but as the only class likely to possess the common sense and the goodwill to bring about the changes Fabianism looked forward to, to which the paper was appealing. For this page Sharp chose a fellow officer on the executive committee of the Fabian Society, Emil Davies. He was subsequently a Labour Party alderman, the creator of the Supplies Department of the L.C.C., and author of *The Collectivist State in the Making*. In 1936 he was to become Treasurer of the Fabian Society, and his son Ernest, in due course a Labour M.P., was the first Secretary of the Fabian Nursery. In some unpublished notes for an autobiography* Davies says: 'The financial articles of that day were lengthy and technical and completely devoid of interest to the general reader unless they happened to deal with one of his own investments. . . . I determined to link up my weekly comments with everyday life, in other words to make them more human.' Davies, a stockbroker as well as a Fabian, presumably succeeded, for his page ran for a long term; re-reading it now it is impossible to judge whether he succeeded in his good intention; it is probable that no form of journalism is so devoid of interest a month after publication—except perhaps to historians of company finance—as a City page. Given the convictions, ideas and beliefs of the people he was working for, Davies's task was not an easy one. At one point in his career as City Correspondent of the *New Statesman*, two directors (the letters touching this matter do not reveal which two) conceived the idea that Davies was using his page to puff the shares in certain shipping companies in which his own firm was interested financially; and that these shares were not really a good investment. He was able to show Sharp that there was nothing in this and the unpleasantness passed over. Davies resented the implications of the complaint, but not actively. One wonders if his advice was taken about investing the company's capital. £1,000 of it went into Hungarian Government Bonds which soon became and remained completely worthless.

MacCarthy, Squire, Davies and of course Sharp himself composed the permanent staff of the paper when the first

* For which I am grateful to Mr. Ernest Davies, M.P.

number appeared in April 1913. Robert Lynd contributed to the first number, but he did not become its most regular staff-writer (and famous as the essayist 'Y.Y.'), until later.

The first number of the *New Statesman* reveals one thing of great interest to journalists and newspaper publishers: that the physical 'personality' of the paper was established without any fumbling from the very beginning; its look and feel were, at birth, what we who have known it in its maturity have been familiar with. Editorial typography and layout are startlingly modern, a fact which a glance at the advertisement pages emphasizes by contrast. These make the same impression as the half-century-old pages of a family photograph album, whereas the editorial pages make the same impression on the eye as this week's issue. This physical smartness, well in advance of its day, was as much owing to Sharp as were the paper's intellectual and moral tone; he was a gifted, albeit amateur, typographer, whose work in that field could probably not have been surpassed by any professional in 1913.

The first four pages of the paper are devoted to 'Comments', short paragraphs dealing with current affairs and written, unsigned of course, by Sharp, Sidney Webb, J. C. Squire and others. In these the tone of the paper, a tone which has not been lost and which may be described as one of didactic and brisk common sense, was set. In Number 1, I find Sharp suggesting that Press comments on the coercion of Montenegro in the matter of who was to have Scutari support the view that the British are a people of sentimentalists in foreign affairs because they are so abysmally ignorant in that field that they can be guided by nothing *but* sentiment. In another paragraph he is giving a rather patronizing pat on the back to the United States Government for lowering tariffs and imposing an income tax, apparently for the first time, of $2\frac{1}{2}d.$ in the £ on incomes between £800 and £4,000, and on a rising scale which took no less than tenpence in the £ from those whose income exceeded £20,000 a year. This, says Sharp, seems rather 'tender' towards large incomes. (*The Times* comment was that the tax 'seems likely to be levied in a more generous spirit than our own'.) Webb makes a snide comment on Lord

Curzon's 'jog to the Mandarins of his party'—Curzon had told his audience at the Junior Imperial League that no party which had no social programme deserved to have a political future; and he goes on, in the next paragraph, to point out that the Labour Party already had such a programme. The Miners' Federation, with one million members, had just put forward a Bill for the nationalization of the Coal Supply; and the National Federation of Railwaymen one for the nationalization of the railways. It was to take thirty-three years and the bankruptcy of both industries to accomplish these aims. Squire's paragraph is a comment on Mr. Justice Joyce's judgment in a case brought against the Palladium by the police, that a theatre queue constituted 'an unreasonable use of the highway'. Both Ratcliffe's paragraphs deal with social measures before the House of Commons. Whether in pointing out that the weak are not always and automatically the virtuous in international politics or in advocating the advance booking of all theatre seats, the note is one of brass-tacks and no nonsense, in sharp contrast with the high moral tone of the rival *The Nation*. Sharp himself explains:

> We did not merely profess to have no political affiliations. We had none. We were soon to discover, however, that a great many people who profess to admire independent political thought are apt to be both puzzled and shocked when they come across it.

This was to become very apparent later when the paper's attitude to the war was made clear. But the matter was not so simple as Sharp claimed; it was complicated by his own nature, and it was by that nature also that the paper's success was assured. Either by a remarkable piece of luck or by that kind of judgment which, being unconscious, is called intuition, the Webbs had chosen as Editor the one man who, at a high intellectual level, could satisfy the Toryism of English Socialists and the Socialism of English Conservatives. His own statement of his position in the first number is revealing:

> In common with every thinking man and woman of today we recognize that vast social changes are imminent and for

our part we welcome them. That we welcome them is our bias. But it is not in any sense whatever a party bias. The world movement towards collectivism is altogether beyond and above party. . . .

Later he writes:

We shall strive to face and examine social and political issues in the same spirit in which the chemist or the biologist faces and examines his test-tubes or his specimens.

Social problems, he adds, can never be satisfactorily solved unless something of the detachment of the scientific spirit be applied to them:

The cultivation of such a spirit and its deliberate application to matters of current controversy is the task which the *New Statesman* has set for itself.

Such scientific detachment was, however, apt to exclude the heart from political decisions, which may be a very good thing to do but which could not fail to offend those 'feeling' liberals to whom the paper was bound to look for some and perhaps most of its support. Scientific examination of the problem of imperialism, for example, did not lead to the conclusion that Africans and Asians should be liberated. The Empire should be maintained because, since the progressive thinking was being done at home in England, the correct scientific policies produced by it would not, then, be confined to one small European country but could be applied to a worldwide dominion. Sharp, like the Webbs, was quite as ready to shoulder the white man's burden as any Kiplingesque empire-builder.*

In the same spirit, scientific examination revealing that nationalism is a great evil, Sharp was not interested in the 'rights of small nations' and was bound, for example, to be anti-Zionist. The thing to do was to get rid of all nations, not create a lot more. And when, in little more than a year from the foundation of the paper, the question of winning the

---

* See, for example, 'What is Socialism', XVII. The Webbs do not consider that any part of the Empire composed of what they call the non-adult races will be ready even for self-government within the Commonwealth [sic] for 'many generations'. And for some parts 'conceivably never'.

war had to be considered scientifically, the policy which Sharp imposed on the *New Statesman* was of the same kind. If sinking enemy merchantmen would reduce the Central Powers to submission by starving their women and children, then sink as many as possible and make the blockade as efficient as it could be. This policy, much nearer to a Tory than to a Liberal or liberal point of view, was to lose the paper some readers but, on the whole, to win it more. Socialists of the Webb stamp were never sentimental: having found answers to social or political questions by scientific examination, their aim was to put the policies thus arrived at into practice everywhere, persuading the people to like them if possible, but certainly not to reject them on emotional and therefore absurd grounds. There was, in this, much to appeal to the aristocratic Tory of the Balfour stamp, with his tradition of aristocratic paternalism; but little to appeal to the conventional liberal with his respect for every man's and every nation's right to be as silly as he or it liked, in the sacred name of liberty. It was this complete and rather provoking assurance which was the strength of new statesmanship and of early twentieth-century Socialism generally; it is the want of it which is Socialism's weakness today.

Clifford Sharp was not a nice man. It is very doubtful whether a nice man could have made a success of a paper dedicated to plain common sense, which is what it amounts to. It is an illusion that the English are a sensible people; they are highly emotional, sentimental, deeply romantic. But they are, as Orwell pointed out, remarkably gentle; and they are therefore, contrary to the accepted notion, self-critical. Consequently, a tough can make them behave reasonably by jeering at their soppiness, provided he can avoid the charges of cynicism and heartlessness—a very difficult thing to do when the majority of the Press is indulging its own and its readers' emotions at the expense of their sense, and counting this fraudulent conversion of facts as merit. It was Shaw's method, and it was Sharp's, but Sharp had none of Shaw's charm. We have already seen that Massingham of *The Nation*, a man of rather vague but strongly held ideals, an *homme de cœur* if ever there was one, literally and rather excessively shrank from him in horror. Such of

Sharp's correspondence as survives reveals him as arrogant, even ruthless, an imperialist, slightly inclined to such conventionally Right-wing attitudes as anti-Semitism. I have not been able to find many among those who knew him to say a good word for him as a man or a bad word as an editor. As to that 'immorality' which Ratcliffe complained of, although a measure of discretion saved Sharp from coming a cropper over his numerous adventures with women—which seem to have been as clinical, so to speak, as his attitude to social questions—discretion could not, in the nature of things, cover up his drinking which, however, did not become such as to impair his powers of mind for another fifteen years.

Bernard Shaw, who was 'proprietor, director and contributor' rolled into one, understood Sharp better than Sharp understood himself. He constantly quarrelled with Sharp's conduct of the new paper. That, journalistically speaking, Shaw was as constantly wrong as Sharp was right, does not alter the fact that Shaw was (nearly) right when, provoked by one of Sharp's decisions, he wrote to him (November 1915):

> The difficulty with you personally is that you are a Tory in grain. You are shocked and irritated by stupidities or abuses, but not in the least by violation of liberal principles. You have no patience with principle when a war is on and very little when a war is off. . . .

It was with Shaw as contributor, however, that Sharp had most difficulty. The Editor was determined that contributions to the paper should not be signed. His object was to give the *New Statesman* a consistent tone and style from cover to cover, not to edit a weekly symposium. He believed, and he was no doubt right, that only so could the paper impose itself as an entity, an integral journalistic 'personality', and so succeed not merely for one or two of its contributors, but for itself. The difficulty was that the paper had really been brought into being by means of the promise of regular contributions from men who were well known and who had their own followings, Shaw, Webb, Squire. This was covered by Sharp in the last of the 'Comments' in the first number:

It is not usual for a journal to communicate to the public the names of those of its staff who contribute unsigned articles. We feel, however, that, in view of the promises which have been made, and which have possibly induced many persons to subscribe to *The New Statesman*, we owe it to our readers to explain that Mr Bernard Shaw and Mr Sidney Webb will as a rule write editorially in our columns, and that the present issue includes, in fact, more than one contribution from each of these gentlemen.

But when every contributor to a paper is using not his own name but the editorial WE, it is obviously necessary that all express the paper's policy and not their own private ones. It is true that reading any issue of the *New Statesman* during the first year, it is quite impossible not to recognize Bernard Shaw's contributions; but they were not signed and readers were therefore free to take Shaw's often outrageous and flippantly expressed views for *New Statesman* policy. Although Shaw was always generous in his dealings with Sharp and never really questioned the Editor's right to the last word, yet since they saw eye-to-eye on nothing but 'Ireland, Municipal Trading, and the Death Duties', Shaw's contributions were a source of embarrassment to an editor who was, after all, young and inexperienced; and who was dealing, in Shaw, not simply with a contributor, nor simply with a contributor who was a great man, but also with one of his proprietors.

Sharp's obvious way out of this difficulty was to break his own rule and ask Shaw to sign his articles. This Shaw flatly refused to do. He now had, he said, his first chance to use the editorial WE and he was going to make hay while the sun shone. As Sharp was forced to edit some of the more outrageous nonsense out of Shaw's contributions, Shaw accused him of inserting 'nots' into his sentences: he was quite right; Sharp had to. But they could hardly go on in that way and the dispute between them came to a crisis when Shaw, having been asked to write on the subject of Godfrey Isaacs's criminal libel suit against Cecil Chesterton,* turned in an article which was based on a complete misapprehension of

* The case was a by-product of the unsavoury Marconi shares scandal in which members of the Government, including Rufus Isaacs, later Marquess of Reading, and Lloyd George, were caught speculating in shares over whose price they might be supposed to have some influence.

both facts and law. Asked to rectify it, he only made it worse. With half an hour to go before the piece was due at the printer's, Sharp and Squire rewrote it. Although Shaw admitted over lunch next day that the Editor had been right over facts and law, he was far from apologetic: facts were tiresome; he had been right in spirit.

The final outcome is best summed up in an answer by Shaw to Israel Zangwill who had written to him complaining that Sharp would not print a letter from him criticizing Desmond MacCarthy's review of his latest play:

My Dear Z,
    You complain that Sharp will not print your letter. That's nothing. You're not a proprietor; I am; and he won't print my articles.

After the Marconi shares article, Shaw wrote less and less for the paper. His withdrawal as a contributor was to be a relief to Sharp, but it had required courage and remarkable self-confidence to let him go. For a young editor of a new and struggling weekly to allow a man of such reputation and following to cease writing for his paper rather than compromise his own editorial policy and authority, shows that kind of assurance, almost of effrontery which, to an experienced journalist, might have been clear evidence that the Webbs had done well to appoint Sharp as Editor; for obviously he knew the kind of paper he wanted and he knew how to get it. The parting, described in its place, entailed no open row, only mutual recognition of incompatibility. But squabbles about minor points, and Sharp's difficulties with Shaw's irresponsible exuberance of expression if not of opinion, covered a deeper and more serious difference. Shaw was not really a true Fabian; Sharp was. Sharp, following the Webbs, or at least Beatrice, was not in the least impressed by or interested in the overtly Socialist leaders, whether working class or middle class. He believed that much more could be done to advance the cause of rational, scientific government by influencing the responsible, intelligent upper-class leaders, men like Arthur Balfour, with their tradition of service to the State. He did not always conceal his contempt for, on the other hand, men like Ramsay MacDonald, or his indifference to men like Ponsonby. Shaw was offended when the *New Statesman* failed to support these people in their strife with the Establishment, and their determination to give the working class a voice. Nor did he approve of Sharp's way of dealing with current political affairs; he accused the editor of 'contriving a political crisis every week to make the paper interesting', but claimed that even this policy was not succeeding. Sharp, with characteristic Sharp-ness, records that 'we did not even agree about the Income Tax'. (Shaw, with magnificent disregard for logic, believed that author's royalties ought to be counted as capital increment and not as income.)

There is no doubt that Sharp was right, but the loss of Shaw was a blow; records of weekly sales figures are not sufficiently detailed to reveal the effects of his withdrawal, but it must have been noticeable, though recovery was swift. For even now, as one reads through the first year's numbers of the paper, and astonishingly good though most of the contributions are, one looks forward all the time to the periodical firework displays of Shavian wit which must have had a considerable influence on circulation. If his opposition to the general policy line of the paper and his perversity of expression could have been kept within bounds, it would have been immensely valuable. It is at its best in his contribution on the subject of the Belgian General Strike in April 1913, at the very beginning of the paper's life. The strike was over the franchise controversy and Sharp handled it by getting an article from Shaw in the form of a letter, unsigned, the answering letter being an article by Webb, also unsigned, in which Sharp collaborated. Shaw's condemnation of the idea of the General Strike is brilliant and amusing; but it is also superficial. It is obvious that he has refused to bore himself by thinking it out. Sharp needed contributors who were prepared, as it were, to bore themselves in the service of the cause but without boring his readers. Shaw's 'letter' is full of 'good theatre'. Good theatre is not good serious journalism, although it may well be good bad journalism, of the kind which has become a major industry, as witness the fabulous success of that combination of melodrama and three-ring circus, the *Daily Express*.

Modern civilization is fed by rail; and the strike which paralyses the railway service at once plays the supposed trump card of the general strike—famine. Famine expresses itself at first in high prices for provisions. The railway strike, therefore, begins by preventing anybody but the rich from feasting, and ends by preventing anybody at all from eating.

Then can a General Strike do no good? Anything on earth can do some good: the recent earthquake in San Francisco 'usefully demonstrated the superior stability of steel-framed skyscrapers'. Shaw's piece is full of this sort of thing; Webb's answer full of careful reasoning from facts and notice of social phenomena which it had suited Shaw simply to ignore. Here, in this one feature, the incompatibility between Shaw and the *New Statesman* as Sharp was bringing it to life, is apparent; but also apparent is the value of Shaw's stuff as sheer entertainment.

On the question of female suffrage which was at a crisis in 1913, Sharp's, and therefore the paper's, attitude was coldly reasonable. (It is significant in this connection that Beatrice Webb had never been much interested in it and had difficulty in considering it important.) Women should have the vote, no doubt, but militant suffragism was a mistake; the behaviour of the suffragettes was damaging both to their own cause and to the community and it would not advance the date of their enfranchisement by one hour. This po-faced attitude is another example of Sharp's Toryism. Shaw's attitude was much more influenced by his rage at the Government's barbarous handling of the militant women; it was a disgrace to civilization. When McKenna, as Home Secretary, arrested Mrs. Pankhurst before instead of after the funeral of Emily Davison, so as to prevent her from attending it, Shaw characterizes this as a 'coarse blunder', approves the adjective 'filthy' which he claims is being widely applied to it, and concludes '*Quem deus vult perdere, etc.*'.

As we have seen, one of the rare matters on which Shaw and Sharp agreed was the Irish question; so that it is possible to express the paper's policy on that, which, again, was at a crisis in 1913, in half a dozen lines of Shaw:

So far, we have on one side the determination that whatever Ulster wants she must go without, and on the other that whatever the three other provinces want they are not to have on any account. It would be wiser to define what Ulster wants: and then ask her whether she really wants it. Also whether the other provinces seriously object to her having it.

But here, too, is evidence of what Sharp was losing in entertainment value when he made up his mind not to give in to Shaw:

> The worst difficulties of the situation are the result of the gross moral cowardice and vote-serving of the cultivated classes both in England and Ireland. They have allowed the children of Ulster to be brought up without remonstrance or rebuke in that blasphemous irreligion which consists in believing that all those who worship by a ritual different to that used by the child's parents are abhorred of God, and will, on their death, be burned throughout eternity in a literal hell of burning brimstone. If an Ulster Protestant child expressed the smallest scepticism as to this it would be beaten as severely as if it had done its Christian duty by asking God to bless the Pope.

Any other journalist working for the *New Statesman* would have found it necessary to say something of the other side. (What *they* were preaching to children may be found in that shattering passage of Joyce's *Portrait of the Artist as a Young Man* in which Stephen Dedalus is driven into temporary piety by a Retreat sermon on hell which arouses stark terror, as well as aesthetic horror, of his own adolescent lust.) But this Shavian exuberance was at least useful in such tasks as baiting Massingham and *The Nation*:

> Mr. Massingham complains that all official Liberals are not Liberals. Whoever supposed that they were? Is any man nowadays so simple as to believe that the actual constitution of our cabinets, or even of our Parliamentary majorities, has much to do with the political principles they have been labelled with at the polls by their election agents?

This is the kind of realism which simply is not good journalism in Britain, and Sharp knew it. There is a degree of honesty and fact-facing which the English will not tolerate; unlike the French they do not enjoy seeing their leaders stripped naked, and they prefer to believe that a man is mistaken rather than that he is a hypocrite or a rascal. English literature and journalism are very poor in political satire. Swift at one level, Malcolm Muggeridge at another, are singular, not representative, men. Thus, Massingham would have called this stuff cynicism, a pejorative word in his vocabulary; and his hatred of Sharp and contempt for the *New Statesman* were not likely to be softened by such Shavian jibes as: 'Mr. Massingham emphasizing his attachment to the Liberal Party always reminds us of Mr. Belloc who emphasizes his attachment to the Catholic Church by keeping us wondering how soon he will be excommunicated.'

The final breach with Shaw came over an incident of the kind which no editor, even a man with much less assurance, much less confidence in himself than Sharp, can tolerate. Shaw sent in an unsolicited review of a book about the war, by E. D. Morel. At the same time the *New Statesman* received a quarter-page advertisement for the book from its publisher, with a note saying that this was 'to be printed on the same page as Mr. Shaw's review'. Apart from the impertinence of this, the review itself expounded views diametrically opposed to those which had been *New Statesman* war policy for a year or more. Nevertheless, Sharp was willing to print it if Shaw would sign it. Shaw refused to do so, the review was not printed, and a few weeks later Shaw resigned from the Board.

3

Quickening

I CANNOT prove it, but I fancy that infant mortality among periodical journals has, since they first began to appear, exceeded 75 per cent. of live births, not to mention the ones which never really showed any sign of life at all. What goes wrong? The infant journal fails to quicken. Just what this means is hard to explain, but an attempt must be made.

When a journal is started, a number of minds combine under the dominion of one, the editor's, to bring it into existence; it begins as a sort of weekly or monthly symposium. But a symposium in print is not a journal. What the editor and his colleagues have to do is contrive to make such disparate material as news, views, fiction, criticism, poetry, even competitive word-games, 'jell' into coherence and reflect a single and particular state of mind and spirit towards life. If this be done successfully then, after a certain lapse of time, a certain number of issues, the new paper takes on a quality which is indefinable, and which is apparent, for example, in a work of art or a well-designed machine: call it integrity, its own integrity. At that point the paper, to exaggerate a little, becomes a being. Some philosophers, at a loss for a word to express the essence of an object which its physical nature first brings into existence but which thereafter has a validity of its own, for instance the chairness of a chair, have written of the *whatness* of things. The *whatness* of a periodical paper which has quickened has so strong an influence over the men, the minds, which have brought it about, that in due course it is this attribute of life, for it is almost a kind of life, which decides what is and what is not appropriate to itself. Put it like this: the editor of an

unquickened paper—they do not live long without subsidies—
receives an article or a story which is a good piece of work;
he has nothing to guide him in deciding whether he will or
will not use it but his own taste and opinions or those of his
editorial board if there is one. In the case of a quickened
journal, the problem is much easier. The contribution
offered either is or is not, usually quite obviously, appropriate
to the *whatness* of the paper in question.

The 'born' editor brings about this quickening by knowing,
almost at a glance, if a contribution will contribute not
simply to the pleasure and instruction of his readers, but to
the life of his paper. Consequently, no paper can come to life
unless it has such an editor. I do not know what it is that he
does, how he does it, any more than I know what a painter
does to make a picture in the way he makes it. At its simplest,
this is a matter of having and conveying style. I do know that
the power to bring a paper to life is very rare; there have
been fewer great editors than great composers. But once
the trick has been turned, once the paper is quick of its own
life, it becomes extremely robust; it can, for example, stand
a change of editors without flagging; for it imposes itself. A
new editor may change its contents to some extent, may even
modify its policy, but he will kill it only with difficulty.
Quick papers tend to survive financial anaemia, a common
disease of periodical publications; whereas unquickened
ones tend to die even when money is pumped into them like
blood into a case of haemorrhage.

It is no longer possible to tell, simply by reading the first few
hundred numbers of the *New Statesman*, when it quickened
—for this reason: that one has long been familiar with the
live creature and it is impossible to feel that it was ever not
alive. The integrity, the whatness, of the *New Statesman*, now,
seems to have been present from the first number. It was not,
of course; Sharp himself, writing two decades later, says he
was aware of a time if not a moment, when the paper
quickened. He says, vaguely, that this was after a year or two.
So that in the time of the first fifty to a hundred numbers life
was being pumped into the paper. It was not a free being, but
still an embryo.

Sharp disclaims credit for giving the *New Statesman* life.

We can discount this modesty; it is amiable hypocrisy and I do not believe him when he says that the job was done by a team. But he was certainly well supported, notably by J. C. Squire. Yet the paper as we know it is not 'like' J. C. Squire, nor is it like Sidney Webb or G. D. H. Cole or Frederick Keeling or Lynd or Lloyd or 'Lens' or anyone else who was in and out of the offices at 10 Great Queen Street. It *is* like Sharp at his best.

Of Sharp's team Squire was the Admirable Crichton. He was, for one thing, constantly available; and he was almost incredibly versatile, so that in an emergency there was no part of the paper which he could not write, though he was never called upon to turn in a City page, Emil Davies being thoroughly reliable. Squire wrote 'Comments', he wrote political leaders, he dealt as critically and amusingly with the great men of cricket, which then as now was in a state of decline, as with the great men of the political or literary worlds. His Solomon Eagle page became famous and there were certainly many people who took the paper for that alone. He wrote, too, that series of literary parodies which became known, and was published in a volume later, as *How They do It*. Sharp thought him the best parodist in the language since Calverley; Squire was quite capable of dashing off one of these parodies in a few minutes, at the printer's, in order to fill an unforeseen gap. Or, if such a gap occurred, he would sit down and write a Letter to the Editor of just the right length, signing it H. de B. Winton. The first of his parodies appeared in Number 1 of the *New Statesman*. The series eventually stopped because Squire took himself seriously as a poet and felt, no doubt rightly, that the public would not do likewise if they knew him well as a literary clown.

It was Squire's influence rather than Sharp's own taste which led to a certain amount of poetry being printed in the *New Statesman*. This policy has been maintained for half a century, so that a good anthology of modern poetry could be put together very easily from the pages of the *New Statesman*. In the first number appeared W. H. Davies's 'Thunder Storms'. In the second, Squire's parody of the same poet, whose work appears at intervals throughout the first year;

while other poets of England's golden evening, for it is as such that 1913 appears in retrospect, whose work was printed, were Rupert Brooke, Squire himself, who is not as good a poet as he is a parodist, D. H. Lawrence, Walter de la Mare, James Elroy Flecker, and some whose names have been forgotten but whose claims to be remembered do not always, upon reading them now for the first time, seem any less good than those of the poets whose names endure. It would seem that Time sifts the poets but that the sieve he uses is a mystery. F. T. Marinetti, the Futurist *chef d'école*, was represented by two long poems in translation.

Squire was probably also responsible in a large measure for the literary prose contributions, although both Shaw and Desmond MacCarthy had their say, as in the literary supplements which, beginning with the first number, made what seems a desperate effort to catch up on the arrears of unreviewed books. They were not particularly profitable; probably the standard was too high and advertising support from publishers was not enthusiastic.

Present readers are familiar with 'Books in General' as a two or three thousand word critical essay whose form and style were fixed by Desmond MacCarthy and modified by Raymond Mortimer and by V. S. Pritchett, whose long series of such essays constitutes at once the most lively, the most readable and the most enlightening work of literary criticism of our time. This feature of the paper did not begin life in that form. It began and long continued as a page of paragraphs of literary and publishing gossip, written by Squire as Solomon Eagle. Some of these paragraphs read half a century later contain matter chastening to literary pride. Here, for example, is a list of names which appeared in one of them: Mistral, Sully-Prudhomme, Fuken, Hauptmann, Heyse, Carducci, Maeterlinck, Sienkiewicz, Lagerlof, Kipling, Tagore. At a guess, I should say that only about half these names of Nobel Prize winners from 1901 to 1912 mean anything to anybody. The Shakespeare Memorial Theatre is to be built in Bloomsbury, and will be ready to open in 1916. But will it present Shakespeare? Shaw, not to mention Tolstoy, is saying that Shakespeare is bad theatre. Squire writes of books to come, books which ought to come, publisher's plans, peculiarities of the language; he makes a collection of bad verse, most of it sent in by readers: the Laureate Alfred Austin is, of course, the best source for this material, but even that fountain of ineptitudes can produce nothing to equal the magnificent contribution sent in by one reader, which laments the fate of a sick gipsy woman:

> There we leave her
> There we leave her
> Far from where her swarthy kindred roam
> In the Scarlet Fever
> Scarlet Fever
> Scarlet Fever convalescent home.*

Occasionally Solomon Eagle would devote his whole page to one new book; even then he did not write an essay on it, but by retaining the form, gossipy paragraphs, was able to pick out and concentrate upon those parts of the work which gave him something pertinent or amusing to say. It is a method which might be revived with advantage.

The very high standard and richness of the literary prose contributions as compared with the poetry, reflects no bias on Sharp's part and is, if anything, in opposition to Squire's personal taste. It looks very much as if poetry was already withdrawing, like a sick beast, to undergo its long death agony in a decent obscurity. But prose remained hale: the 'creative' writing contributed to the *New Statesman* in 1913 and 1914 is for the most part of a very high quality indeed. A study of the paper's literary half for half a century reveals quite clearly a decline in the quality of such writing coinciding with an improvement in the quality of critical writing. It is tempting to see in this a more general tendency: creative writing, in poetry or prose, is a work of art; critical writing, of science, at least in its old, broad meaning. At all events, the process is unfortunately quite clear; and if the present editor of the *New Statesman* would find it impossible to fill his pages week after week with work of the quality which was maintained by Shaw, Lawrence, Gorki, E. Nesbit, and others, he would, on the other hand, consider it out of the question to print novel-reviews as flabby and pedestrian as commonly

* Attributed to Andrew Lang.

appeared over the signature of Hubert Bland. Bland was a founder Fabian and a very successful popular journalist, star man on the *Sunday Chronicle*. He was an extraordinary mixture: that he gave his mind and time to serious matters is obvious from the fact that he was not only a Fabian but for twenty years Treasurer of the Society. He was one of the authors of the Tract, *Government Organization of Unemployed Labour*, and, of course, one of the Fabian Essayists. Yet it seems that he was an unscrupulous womanizer and *bon vivant*, and that he was extravagant in his pleasures. Indeed, he was an active and noisy member of the Anti-Puritan League; and his appearance, with his heavy moustache, marked eyebrows and ribboned monocle is that of the ha-ha-me-proud-beauty stage-villain of melodrama. All of which does not change the fact that his work for Socialism was valuable, and that although Margaret Cole calls him a Tory Democrat in her Fabian Society history, it was he who, at a Fabian meeting, proposed the foundation of an active Socialist Party, which gave rise to such a noisy row that the manager of Anderton's Hotel, where the meeting took place, refused to let the room to the Society thereafter.

Old reviews are fascinating in cases where time has crowned a book. In the first half year of the paper's existence Bland had to review, among others, Leonard Woolf's *The Village in the Jungle*, placed third to a Jeffrey Farnol and a Mrs. Belloc Lowndes: reading this was 'a sombre and poignant experience'. Jack London's *South Sea Tales*, which is treated with gentle mockery, probably quite appropriate to its juvenile level. *Trent's Last Case*, ' . . . a good detective story as detective stories go'. Anatole France's *The Gods are Athirst* is treated with respect, but there is a suggestion of eyebrow-raising in the passages chosen for quotation; too much blood and violence, surely? It is, by the way, interesting to note by how much the price of books has fallen since 1913; in other words by how much publishing and printing have improved in efficiency. *The Gods are Athirst* was published at 6s., at a time when the £ was a golden sovereign. That is, at the equivalent of 24s. Yet today it would be published at 16s. Bland does not seem to me to have been a good reviewer, although he gave satisfaction to an increasing band of readers over a long period of time; at least, however, he knew a good book when he got one, and sticks the tip of his nose out of his usual cloak of caution. Thus, Lawrence's *Sons and Lovers* is not only 'noteworthy', it 'would have been noteworthy at any time during the last dozen years'. But Bland is sure that Lawrence did not know what conclusion the book would lead to when he began to write it, nor what he was going to write on the way to that conclusion.

Then, as now, 'general' books were, for some reason connected with editors' illusions about social values, given more, and more serious, attention than fiction. Probably the most important work of philosophy reviewed in the first year was Sigmund Freud's *The Interpretation of Dreams*, which did not appear in English until after the third German edition. (But the *New Statesman* often, in its early years, reviewed German or French books of importance without waiting for the translation.) Robert Lynd was the reviewer, and he used his gift of giving a clear and perfectly fair idea of a book while making it quite obvious that he was inclined to shrug his shoulders over its claims. This salutary mockery of the 'heavies' is something which has been lost and it is a pity. In 1913 Sharp, or Squire, never hesitated to give a work of philosophy or science or scholarship to a real journalist for review; the practice of giving such books to specialists has meant that general criticism from the point of view of the ordinary intelligent man has almost disappeared from the Press, with the result that 'great' thinkers tend to be too great by half. Lynd, adapting new statesmanship to the literary pages, tells one exactly what Freud's ideas are, he gives one a very complete notion of the book he is reviewing, but at the same time he is entertaining at the expense of a theory which he clearly considers rather silly, rather pretentious, and definitely 'rickety'.

If a partial failure to achieve whatness from first to last page of the paper be apparent, it is in the reviewing of books. The literary pages appear much less new statesmanly than the front half of the paper. This failure was to continue for a very long time. I shall have more to say about it. That it was less harmful to the paper's success than it might have been seems to me owing to one thing only: although most readers of the *New Statesman* probably read all of it, there were two large minorities which bought and read the paper either for its political half or for its literary half, but not for both. What was the difficulty? I think it is to be found in the fact that the Fabian, the Webbian, the Sharpian method, the cold penetration of appearance to the reality, is much less effective when the object of study is a work of art or letters than when it is a work of social science or politics. Charm, style, are even more beguiling in works of art than in personality, and the mind which penetrates a social or political or economic disguise to the miserable reality, may be quite incapable of doing as much for a book.

When Sharp was asked to describe his policy in the literary half of the paper he said that the *New Statesman* had no policy; it had a state of mind. Later, when Kingsley Martin was reproached for not making the literary pages of the paper as Left as its political pages, he declared, and rightly declared, that art and literary critics require 'a wider window' on to life.

Lynd, Gerald Gould and Desmond MacCarthy set a much higher standard than was common in weekly journalism at the time. MacCarthy set and maintained that standard in dramatic criticism over several decades, an astonishing achievement, so that his play reviews have become classics in this minor branch of literature, if that is what it is, and need not, therefore, be discussed here. A point indicative of Sharp's editorial flair is worth making, however: a study of MacCarthy's writing over three decades shows that, although he improved as a craftsman and as a writer, he did not as a critic have to grow, but sprang fully armed with the necessary penetration, sensibility and love, straight from the brain of whatever god is responsible for critical journalism. His writing is as sophisticated in the beginning as at the end.

From time to time an entertaining diversion was introduced into the drama page. In May 1913, after Forbes Robertson's revival of *Caesar and Cleopatra* at Drury Lane, Shaw reviewed his own play on the ground that 'I don't think the critics who have reviewed it worth a cent.' Walkley, 'whose ignorance of history is a disgrace to *The Times* and a joy to its readers' insists that *Caesar and Cleopatra* is 'a comic opera invented by myself'. Only two critics, Mr. Massingham and Mr. MacCarthy, 'knew that what they were looking at was a chapter of Mommsen and a page of Plutarch furnished with scenery and dialogue'. Shaw was Shaw whichever half of the paper he was writing for. As a journalist he applied that immensely profitable discovery he had made as a playwright about the British people: that they greatly enjoy, and will pay generously for, being abused for certain failings of which they are proud. The discovery has since been exploited by lesser men; there are half a dozen of them working veins of this rich seam even now, but Shaw alone knew how to say something important while thus indulging the social masochism of his readers. He flogged for high spiritual reasons; the others just flog.

The ground covered in the front half of the paper during its first year was vast; it is clear that Sharp aimed to cover the entire field of national life and international relations. Overt preaching of Socialism was more or less confined to the Webbs' weekly instalment of the didactic serial 'What is Socialism?' and it should be emphasized that this Socialism had nothing whatever to do with political parties, but was put forward as a policy which might be espoused by any Party. The opposite point of view was, as I shall show, put forward in the Letters from Readers page. On the other hand, the Webbs might be supported from time to time by a technical contribution, for example the articles of very unorthodox economics contributed by Leo Chiozza Money, who demonstrated, among other things, that there was no need whatever to hold interest, usury, sacred and that by ceasing to do so an enormous saving in the financing of such things as rural housing could be effected. This was the sort of thing Sharp liked to print; it was looking hard at the reality of an institution, not its mask. Much of what he printed was, of course, of this socially important kind: 'The English Countryside', another 'serial', set out to make known the real situation of the rural worker, the farmer, farm finance, rural housing, and to suggest means of improving the lot of the agriculturalist and his contribution to the national wealth. Of course, other papers, *The Nation*, *The Athenaeum*, also dealt with such topics; but their way was to express high aspirations and waffle about means; the *New Statesman* did not waffle, it used the Fabian technique—find out the facts and interpret them in the light of reason, of science.

Natural science was not neglected; Sharp wanted to present to his readers a sort of State of Science report in weekly or fortnightly articles; the trouble was to find a man to write them; it remained the trouble for Sharp and all other Editors for several decades. However, in June 1913 a contributor known to readers by the pen-name of 'Lens' began an ambitious series of the kind the Editor had in mind, beginning with an article magnificently entitled 'The Nature of Life'. 'Lens' was partly of Syrian origin, a Fabian, a graduate of Edinburgh Medical School, C. W. Saleeby by name; he was introduced to Sharp by Dr. Letitia Fairfield. Saleeby wanted to sign his *New Statesman* work with his own name, but Sharp insisted on the pseudonym. This had nothing to do with his general policy of anonymity which was applied only to matter of opinion and political policy and not to instruction or entertainment.

The fact is that with Saleeby, Sharp had to solve a problem which was to face *New Statesman* Editors for the next fifty years and will probably continue to face them. There is a certain kind of writer whose main stream of thought and writing is deep and clear but whose course is beset with backwaters, eddies and cross-currents of what is called crankiness; the *New Statesman* was not afraid of cranks, for Sharp, but above all Squire, recognized the great value of the crank in his function of correcting the complacency of the orthodox. But Liberal and Socialist editors have to be more wary of cranks than those who toe the Establishment line, for by printing their work they run a serious risk of having their whole paper shrugged off with a smile. Saleeby was a man whose writing was sound and founded on reading which was both wide and fairly deep; but he seems to have had one of those personalities, perhaps because he was part Syrian, which first attracts a following of the sillier kind of cranks, and then tends to be corrupted by them, since by following him they put him under a sort of obligation to be what they thought and think he was and is. Sharp did not want his science writer's work to be read only by the rather whimsical followers of Dr. Saleeby; it was possible that the name Saleeby might alienate the majority of readers who had perhaps a vague idea that it was that of a crank. Hence the pen-name; later, signed articles from Saleeby were published, as well as the 'Lens' series.

Although science in general—with a chemical and biological bias—was dealt with by Dr. Saleeby, and handled as well as anyone did handle this troublesome subject until the advent of Mr. (now Professor) Ritchie Calder, 'Lens' was not the only contributor in this field. An essay by Bertrand Russell, printed in two parts (24 and 31 May 1913) is of particular interest. Entitled 'Science as an Element in Culture' it makes a point which, to the great damage of the scientist's status, had been lost sight of: the real work of science is thinking, not mechanical ingenuity; the scientist is a creative artist, not an industrial operative. The vulgarization of science has led, since Russell wrote that piece, to the vague and careless equating of a mechanic like Marconi with a scientist like Clerk-Maxwell, of a handyman like Edison with an original philosopher like Hertz or Einstein. Clearly, Russell had foreseen this and, moreover, foreseen it as a danger. His warning did, alas, nothing to check the process, so that today any industrial operative with a degree in science who happens to work in an electronics or nuclear physics factory instead of a jam factory, is called a scientist. In this, as in other fields, the present *New Statesman* accepts what the young one would have deplored; it is evidence of that 'loss of nerve' by the educated class which I shall come to below.

In sport, then as now, the *New Statesman* was not very interested. From time to time Squire wrote something about cricket, more or less facetious; in those days intellectuals sometimes played that game. Squire clearly regretted the rise of football over cricket as the national game. Sometimes an article, again then as now, studied the English at play, generally as a means of demonstrating some attribute of the English 'character' of which English, if no other, readers seem never to weary. But there has been a change, whether for the better or the worse, in the paper's attitude to the people's amusements. It was characteristic of that educated, serious-minded section of the upper class and middle class from which the Fabians were recruited and from which therefore new statesmanship derived, that it had the courage of its convictions, but also of its tastes and standards; high ones. It made no 'democratic' concessions to vulgarity, it did not play down to the masses, it was more inclined to reproach them for being like that and to teach and encourage them to be something better. One of the necessary evils of the spread of democracy has been the proletarianization of taste in almost all fields of work and play. A present-day *New Statesman* editor may personally deplore, but he will hesitate roundly to denounce, such national pastimes as filling in Pools coupons, because he is on the side of the millions; he may not be able to swallow Bingo, it is true, but even there he will seek some way of avoiding what would have been the Sharpian conclusion, that the ordinary common people are thoroughly stupid. The educated class of professional people has, in short, lost not its taste, nor its convictions, but its nerve. There is, too, another point here: Sharp belonged to the upper-class élite; Kingsley Martin, who shaped the paper as we now know it, did not; he had more sympathy with the popular. Freud and Marx having succeeded in exposing the thinking man to himself, he no longer dares to say 'be like me', and he seeks in the masses good qualities which he may humbly emulate. Unfortunately, he has not always been successful in finding them. It is this failure of self-confidence which has been the stumbling stone of Socialism at least on the intellectual plane. But in 1913 this 'leader' class was still tolerably sure of itself—witness the optimism of H. G. Wells and even of Bernard Shaw. In the *New Statesman* for 19 July of that year, S. K. Ratcliffe wrote a long article, 'The Englishman's Lottery', on the prize-competitions run by certain weekly papers (none is named, but *John Bull* was the principal offender) as a means of buying circulation. It was possible to win as much as £500. There is no need to give examples of imbecilities which Ratcliffe or possibly Sharp, who edited the article, characterizes as 'mind-destroying': 'Bullets' was the prototype. The attitude taken to 'Bullets' and 'Thinklets' [*sic*!] is wholly contemptuous as well as censorious. The editor's influence is visible in the conclusion: the English are all gamblers; let their gambling be rationalized to serve some purpose; the obvious way to do this is to run a State lottery and cut out the hypocrisy. It is no wonder that Ratcliffe preferred Massingham as an editor; preferred, that is, to write for *The Nation*; no such coldly reasonable conclusion would have been imposed on him. A modern editor of the *New Statesman* might come to the same sensible conclusion; but he would tend to reach it without passing through the phase of contempt for the gamblers, he would be gentler, more tolerant of stupidity, would, if he could manage it, condone a practice beloved of millions with the uneasy smile of a Hugh Gaitskell being folksy. And this not only because of that loss of nerve manifest on the Right as well as on the Left, but because the Left itself is ambivalent. It is no longer a question, as it was then, or seemed to be, of imposing Socialism from above; and whoever would lead is obliged to seem, if not of one mind with the masses, at least of one heart and one taste with them. Sharp's conclusion to that article has a French touch about it which is wholly offensive to the English system of double-think: gambling is deplorable; but, let's face it, we *are* deplorable creatures. How the liberals detested the man!

It was some time before Sharp was able to organize notes and articles from abroad, and to begin with only France received adequate attention. Later, Ratcliffe's *New Statesman* pieces from the United States were considered by Fleet Street pundits to be the best thing of their kind ever written. Northcliffe was of this opinion. The French contributions from Pierre Chavannes began early in the paper's life, with articles describing the Catholic revival and the *Action Française* royalist movement. Later, Sisley Huddleston wrote Paris notes, and these were so good that Northcliffe snaffled Huddleston for *The Times*. In between these two, Robert Dell, *Manchester Guardian* Paris correspondent, wrote for Sharp on France; but Dell was a pacifist and, as we shall see, the time came when Sharp had to refuse to print the rather hysterical articles he was sending, and even his letters to the editor.

From the beginning of the paper's life its correspondence

page was important. The Webb serial, 'What is Socialism?' drew a great many letters, but there was hardly a feature which was not hailed with fury, sorrow or applause. It was not possible to read the paper with idle indifference. In August 1913 a letter from Hilaire Belloc on the subject of property distribution was printed; it occupied nearly two pages and was an attempt to show that Webb Socialism, collectivism of any kind, was not the only alternative to the capitalism which Belloc deplored as much as the Webbs. The better alternative was a Property Owning Democracy. The letter is brilliantly argued; reading it in the light of present-day Conservative Party policy, or at least Conservative Party propaganda, one can fairly conclude that the *New Statesman* has provided not only the Labour Party but also Mr. Macmillan and his friends with their ideas.

During the first years of the paper's life Sharp really did take a lot of trouble with the correspondence, but in the late Twenties, when his drinking became serious, he once dumped half of it into the waste-paper basket and G. W. Stonier, who was at the time as much *de facto* editor of the paper as anyone else, had to sit down and write some letters to the editor to fill the yawning gap which Sharp's cavalier way with his readers' opinions, ideas and protests had left.

The policy of the *New Statesman* during this first year of its life was deliberately eclectic. It can be summed up as a penetrating of the appearances of any problem, to its reality, without regard to shibboleths. This is nowhere more apparent than in the Blue Book reviews: these were published in separate Supplements in which Government publications were treated as 'books'. Sixteen pages once a month were devoted to this purpose. Ratcliffe edited it for six months, after which it was taken over by Frederick Keeling. Sharp describes him as the most industrious man he had ever known, and industry, with integrity, was what the job needed. Keeling was lost to the paper when he joined up in August 1914 to be killed as a sergeant in the Battle of the Somme. The Supplements continued for three years, cost the paper money, but won it great authority, a solid prestige among the governing class, regardless of party. It constitutes the clearest evidence that Fabianism, new statesmanship, consisted in imposing collectivist ideas on the 'natural' ruling class of England, not educating the masses to overthrow or replace that class. In fact it is almost true to say that only the traditional ruling class was equipped to tolerate *New Statesman* toughness. The cry of 'Property is theft!' may be used by demagogues but to add 'But let us not forget that we are *all* thieves' was the very reverse of the demagogue's method. It was the sort of truth which is highly offensive to the traditional kind of English reformer or revolutionary or radical who liked to found his politics in self-righteousness. Yet its honesty made a strong appeal even to him and, moreover, he was tempted by it, by the chance it gave him to strike a self-critical attitude soothing to his sense of guilt. The English Left has always been and still is ambivalent: on the one hand intellectual, Fabian; on the other emotional, self-righteous, 'religious'. The *New Statesman* forced both halves of every progressive mind to listen to its voice; it offended each in turn, but never quite alienated either. It was a powerful weekly stimulant to both.

4

The War Years: The Shavian Crisis

BY the end of July 1915 the *New Statesman*, having been in existence for sixteen months, had established for itself a position of authority and, with a weekly sale of something over 3,000 copies, was second in circulation only to *The Spectator* among the sixpenny weeklies. It was, of course, losing money, but it was alive, growing, and its backers were not losing heart; for what it said was being attended to.

In the issue for 1 August 1914 appeared four paragraphs on the 'Comment' pages, written in this instance by Sharp, on the imminent danger of the war which did not yet seem inevitable. Sharp's very new statesmanly comments must have annoyed a large minority of readers even of the kind the *New Statesman* appealed to, for it blamed nobody for what was happening. But for once the Editor abandoned the severe analytical method when he wrote:

> The chain of events that we have to fear, the dragging first of one country then of another into the conflict, until practically the whole white race in the Old World is involved, seems to have all the inevitableness of ancient tragedy, where persons and events are controlled not by reason but by the spell of an ironic fate.

In this, however, he may have been leaning over backwards to avoid becoming involved in the popular war-fever which might be generated, although he denies that 'even the utmost efforts of the Press' will succeed in generating such fever in a people so pacific as the British. When a week later the Press, provided by Sir Edward Grey with the F.O. correspondence with the German Government about Belgium, had in fact succeeded in generating a very considerable war fever, Sharp left Comment to his colleagues.

But on 1 August he was still hoping that the British might not be involved in the coming tragedy: there might be a slight feeling in the country favouring France above Germany, but nothing to signify. Maybe the Government would be unable to avoid being dragged into the war at the heels of France and Russia, but it had and would have no popular mandate for making war. The people are pacific; moreover, they have been assured time after time by both Grey and Asquith that the nation is under no obligation to fight by the side of any Continental power. The *New Statesman* did not go as far as *The Nation*: Massingham, H. N. Brailsford and J. A. Hobson were at one in their belief that the enemy of peaceful and civilized mankind was Tsarist Russia and that it was Russia which, in the end, dragged us into the war; in due course, however, Sharp and his contributors were to take much the same line. Doubtless the nation would support the Government in the event of war, but the responsibility for that war would be the Government's, not the people's. To this statement the *New Statesman* remained consistent until the end of the war: we really should not have been in the fight at all, but since we were we must win it by all means short of one—conscription.

This opposition to conscription can serve as a useful example of the ambivalence of the British Left and all the institutions of the Left, including the *New Statesman*, an ambivalence which, curiously enough, strengthens its sense of acting according to true lights, but which weakens its political sector in crisis after crisis. These crises always derive from the same question: by which of the two principal lights is the problem before us to be examined? It is the argument which follows the repeated posing of this question, often taking the form of a noisy controversy, which makes the people as a whole nervous of entrusting the Left with power.

It is probably impossible to resolve this problem of ambivalence because it is at bottom a matter of conscience. The moralists, as opposed to the scientists, of the Left, cannot think that they may be mistaken because their conviction is really a religious one. Anyone who wants to understand the real origins of English Socialism, of Fabianism, of new statesmanship, without reading social history, can do so by re-reading George Eliot's *Felix Holt*, attending particularly to Holt, Lyon and Transome. In so far as the Left, in Britain, derived an important proportion of its driving power from traditions of Radical Liberalism, and its conscience from Dissenting Protestantism, it is bound to be distrustful of the State, must even regard the State as the enemy, at times the Devil, and must therefore refuse to concede it certain powers over the citizen whose responsibility is to a higher power than the State's. Above all, the Left must be reluctant to concede to the State the power to make every citizen a soldier. The Protestant sees every man as an individual face to face with and responsible to God; and subservience to any lesser power is tantamount to whoring after strange gods. This sentiment is an Old Testament, a Jewish, derivative. But on the other hand Socialism implies Collectivism, and the only viable executive organ of a collective which is nation-wide must be the State. In so far as the Left derives its ideas, as opposed to its feelings, ultimately from Hegelian, more immediately from Marxist, arguments, it must concede the State's right to call upon every citizen to serve it not only as a worker but as a soldier. Those kinds of Socialism which tried to avoid this rather comic dilemma were also to find a voice in the *New Statesman*: G. D. H. Cole's; but not yet.

Sharp, as a Fabian, as one of the creators of new statesmanship, was, by deliberate duty, a rational, scientific man. But Englishmen, like English institutions, have never been able to be worshippers of logical consistency; never, therefore, Marxists even in their economics. The opposition to conscription, which was to be sustained to the end, or almost, whatever its real origin, could be and was explained as if it were a thought-out position.

The paper for 8 August had to face an entirely different situation, and 'Comment' was taken over by Squire, Webb and Frederick Keeling. It was as if Sharp found it impossible to reverse his position of the previous week and had to leave it to his colleagues to explain why the whole nation had done precisely that. But acceptance of the view that the violation of Belgium's frontier was the reason for that *volte-face*, is not evidence that the paper was relaxing its sharply critical attitude. Despite what has been written since August 1914, for the ordinary people Germany's behaviour to Belgium *was*, in fact, their reason for their sudden belligerence. *New Statesman* opinion did not, in fact, differ materially from that of the country at large, and we find Squire writing editorially that England had never gone to war with cleaner hands; that Sir Edward Grey could not have done more to prevent or localize the war; and that we entered the fight reluctantly. But that is the limit of agreement with the general cry, unless perhaps Robert Dell's very emotionally francophil articles can be called representative, which I doubt. New statesmanship emerges in a wish-fulfilling statement that 'we are waging war in cold blood and without hatred'; that being so, if Germany and Austria can be beaten to their knees, we must not exercise the extreme of vengeance against them. For what would follow? Probably the collapse of both empires; the paramountcy of Russia, therefore, in the Balkans and Asia Minor; her consequent command of the routes to the East. And that, writes Sharp, 'would be as disastrous to British interests as any German triumph'. In this he was following Massingham's and Brailsford's lead.

The *real* enemy, in fact, is our ally Russia; there is an uncanny feeling of *déja vu* in reading, for the first time, the *New Statesman* war comments for 1914 and 1915.

> We all know, and it is of crucial importance that we should never for a moment forget it, that in the present war the three most enlightened and illustrious communities in the Old World are tearing at each other's throats under the eyes of a vast Power, medieval in thought though modern in its appliances of war, that might, should they exhaust each other, threaten them all, the ideals they stand for and the culture that through painful centuries of development they have evolved.

'*Plus ça change . . .*' Bernard Shaw's 'Comment' paragraph (unsigned, of course) shows the same distrust of our ally, the same assurance in regarding the Franco-British-German civilization as what really mattered. It looks beyond the war to the treaty in which the three will realize their responsibilities as the trustees of civilization. The war will not alter the real problem. The sooner the peoples resolve to tackle it, acknowledging that their diplomacy has reduced itself to an absurdity, the better for themselves and humanity at large.

Nevertheless, the paper noticed the collapse of the peace parties all over Europe with sympathetic if not regretful comment. Frederick Keeling was responsible for that example of new statesmanly common sense. The C.G.T.* has done well, in France, to call upon the workers to defend their country, though it might, under Marxist influence, have been inclined to hold that a worker has no country. But if one could approve the French worker's determination to defend his country against Germany, how, even using the most adroit new statesmanship, could one disapprove the German worker for defending *his* country by rallying to the Junker Imperialists? Modern Socialists have a vague idea that there was bitter disappointment in Left circles with the failure of German Socialism, doyen of Socialisms, to maintain its pacifism. I find no trace of this in the *New Statesman*: for, 'in Germany the Socialists cannot refuse to countenance the defence of Teutonic civilization against the Russian peril'. In England the whole Labour movement had been on the side of peace until Grey announced the German refusal to respect Belgian neutrality and France's agreement to do so. Mr. Ramsay MacDonald, although admitting that this made unconditional pacifism impossible, remains a pacifist and has, therefore, resigned the Chairmanship of the now belligerent Parliamentary Labour Party. The *New Statesman* regrets his resignation, but the regret, one senses, is a mere courtesy.

For Webb, the task of the *New Statesman* now as always was to draw attention to the needs of the wage-earners. It is a curious injustice of history that the Webbs are remembered as social scientists as cool about their human raw material as a metallurgist about iron, and are roundly abused for it by tough-shelled, soft-centred critics. But Sidney Webb was one of the extremely rare men who are not hypnotized by the words *England, France, Germany, freedom, democracy,* into considering those geographical, social, political and philosophic entities as Beings. Their components were people who suffered and Webb could not fail to see that the war might be a social ally, forcing, for example, the settlement of

* Confédération Générale du Travail.

industrial disputes in the men's favour, at least in some industries. Nobody foresaw the nature of the war and consequently one great fear was of unemployment. Webb, backing the Labour Party, proposes what seems very like G. D. H. Cole's suggestions for solving the economic crisis in 1930 and like Roosevelt's New Deal programme. Then there is a danger that shopkeepers will take advantage of the war to charge extortionate prices; rationing is neither foreseen nor suggested, it was not dreamed of as a coming necessity; but the influence of the Co-operative Societies would hold prices steady; they, alone, have not, for example, raised the price of bread.

That, by late 1914, the *New Statesman* had quickened is very apparent from the early wartime issues. No special conference was required, no dramatic editorial orders, to allot each principal contributor his duty for the duration, for it had by then become quite clear to each principal *New Statesman* writer not only what part he must play but how to play it in the *New Statesman* manner, a manner already apparent. Thus the task which he had begun in the first weeks of the war was continued steadily by Sidney Webb until the end: it became his business to draw attention tirelessly to the war-generated miseries of the working people, not only in Britain but, for example, in Belgium and in India; to criticize what little was done to relieve such distresses; to refuse to be silenced, or roused into flag-waving like the rest of the Press, by the British equivalent of the *Union Sacrée* so successfully used by the French to keep the poor poor and the rich rich. Webb was fertile in suggestions; they were not grand, heart-stirring, idealistic schemes of the kind which might earn a sociologist, a journalist, an editor, the paper itself, a reputation for nobility of heart; they were sound, new statesmanly plans all well within the country's political and economic power. It was Webb who drew attention to the way in which the I.C.S. was squandering priceless Indian goodwill by snubbing the movement of generosity towards England in all classes of the Indian people. It was Webb who patiently drew attention to the need for unemployment pay when, at the beginning of the war, some industries, notably cotton, looked like being ruined; and when the new war industries, the monstrous casualties, had not yet started to absorb and later to exhaust man-power. All danger from unemployment had long disappeared by 1916, and then it is Webb again, in the *New Statesman*, who is insisting that release of labour from all but essential industries is necessary, and that the Government is behaving like a fraud in pretending that it would accomplish this by persuading the wage-earners to save instead of spending, since nothing whatever is done, for example, to stop the big drapers from urging the people, in Press advertising, to spend their money on clothes. Webb suggests that Unemployment Insurance can be made a means of thrift by raising contributions. The Fabian pamphlet *How to Pay for the War* gave him a chance to urge, in the *New Statesman*, nationalization of the coal-mines to the great advantage of the miners, the consumers both industrial and private, and the nation, and at the cost, merely, of checking the ferocious rapaciousness and indifference to all interests but their own of the coal-owners, who had exposed themselves on several occasions as mere exploiters of the war situation. But for the coal-owners' greed, coal at 1s. a cwt. was a perfectly economic proposition. In 1917 we find Webb still at it, patiently and sensibly analysing the causes of the strike in the engineering trades, exposing the imbecilities of bad labour relations and the exploitation of the workers' decent loyalties by profiteers. Typically, Webb was not even aware, as far as one can judge, that he seemed to be arrogantly ignoring the cry that the factory operatives were betraying the soldiers. Webb's wartime contributions are new statesmanship at its soberest.

The voice of Shaw is raised in quite a different manifestation of this same spirit. His contributions, too, were expressions of common sense; he, too, insisted on keeping his head when all about him were losing theirs. But whereas Webb is never lively, Shaw risks offending in every paragraph by what sometimes amounts to a flippancy of expression which, while it makes his points vividly with the alert and imaginative reader, perhaps fails to do so with the literal-minded. In November 1914 his 'Common Sense about the War' was published—because of its length, as a Supplement. It drew a large number of letters from readers with a slavish regard for facts or who did not recognize as common sense what was sometimes put over in the form of verbal clowning and may have looked rather like cynicism. Shaw, following Wells, was ready enough to admit that German militarism, 'this drilling trampling foolery in the heart of Europe' (H.G.W.), this 'swank and domineer and guff and bugaboo calling itself blood and iron and mailed fist and God and conscience and anything else that sounded superb' (G.B.S.) was an offensive nuisance. But he insisted on putting the other side. We, too, had our Junkers; we, too, had been guilty of diplomatic blundering. The kind of thing which infuriated some readers, which gave Sharp endless trouble, and which seemed to put the paper in danger, was this: 'Mr. Asquith himself, though serenely persuaded that he is a Liberal statesman is, in effect, very much what the Kaiser would have been if he had been a Yorkshireman and a lawyer instead of being only half English. . . .' It is in Shaw that we can see the extreme of that Fabianism which was so captivated by the Platonic notion of the philosopher-king— that is, of absolute power in partnership with scientific expertise—that it had little patience with democratic politics. Sharp, as I have said, was of this school, and it was not really until Kingsley Martin became Editor a decade and half later that the *New Statesman* modified its *de haut en bas* attitude to the people and the politicians it wished to direct.

Sharp was to have quite a different kind of trouble with his Paris correspondent, Robert Dell. There is an ominously un-newstatesmanly note even in Dell's first war dispatch, an article which appeared on 8 August 1914. The writer's quivering excitement is apparent in every line; the piece is highly emotional and excessively francophil. Dell, like Sharp and Shaw, detests our Russian ally, unless his 'the time may come when we shall have to defend Germany against Russia' was written-in by Sharp; but he is passionately certain that '. . . our present duty is to defend against the unprovoked aggression of Germany not France alone but the cause of democracy in Europe. I cannot believe that England will act otherwise; if she did I would renounce my nationality and become a naturalized Frenchman at the earliest opportunity.'

This fervent bearing towards the war did not last; it was Fabian coolness, not warm-hearted indignation, which proved to have staying power. Dell was a *Manchester Guardian* man and a Fabian; his hatred of war had been briefly overcome upon seeing his adored France assaulted. The spectacle of his beloved being despitefully used by the Germans, however, was more than he could bear; and he certainly had a vision of not only France but all civilization going down into the mire if this horror was not stopped at once. As we know, he was probably right, except that there was no practical way of stopping the horror, men, even Fabians, being what they are. Dell turned pacifist, defeatist, in a matter of months. As such he imagined that the better sort of French, leaders and led, were of his own mind; and that those who were not were either stupid or wicked. This was not, of course, true, but he believed that it was and he began sending articles tending to show that unless a peace was made at once and at any price, even concession of victory to Germany, France would be utterly destroyed. What would a world be without France? Dell gave the impression that an influential minority of Frenchmen thought as he did. Sharp's judgment rejected all this without hesitation.

I believe that it might be possible, in 1963, to defend the opinion that Dell was right. If, in fact, victory had been quickly achieved by, conceded to, Germany before much bitterness had been generated, then the victor would have been a more civilized Germany than any we have since known, and a Germany with a powerful and growing Socialist movement. The gravest casualty of two world wars has been the internationalism of Socialism; in the case envisaged it would not have perished. Nothing so mellows the character of a nation as success; it is at least very possible that the best in Germany, which was very good indeed, would have come to the top instead of the atrocious worst, which was what actually happened. Europe, chastened but undamaged, might have learnt under a milder Germany whose social legislation was well in advance of anyone else's, to create a Welfare State on a continental basis. Evolution would have replaced revolution in Russia. There would have been no Fascism, that hideous disease of the body politic, no Nazi-ism, that extreme and mortal stage of the disease, and probably no Second World War, possibly no further large-scale war of any kind. It is even conceivable that scientific research would have been orientated towards peace instead of war. In short, it is arguable that the real, the great tragedy of the twentieth century was Germany's failure to win her 1914 war in a matter of months.

However, nobody but a German could have entertained such an idea in 1914 or 1915, although Dell came near to doing so. (Did Asquith, in his heart of hearts?) For Sharp, of course, it was out of the question: he was an intellectual, he was extremely intelligent, but he was very much an Englishman and perhaps a bit of a Junker himself. Social progress, by all means; but under British management. In November 1915 he received a letter from Dell which is worth reproducing in part; it had been preceded by others of the same kind:

Dear Sharp,

I trust that in spite of its portentous length you will be able to publish the enclosed letter. It is long because the subject is a large one. There are particular reasons for its publication just now. More and more I see symptoms that France and England will be mortal enemies after this war. The feeling that England wants to drag on the war regardless of what happens to France, in her own interest, is spreading very much. . . . The patent desire of England to keep the German colonies has caused great indignation; the German colonies are the only security the Allies have and if England refused to give them up, negotiation would be impossible. . . . I feel sure that the insistence in Briand's speech on the 3rd on the disinterested motives of France and her repudiation of an 'egoist' peace was intended partly as a hint to England in this regard. . . . I know nobody who believes that England went to war for the sake of Belgium. The general belief is that, if the war, as far as its immediate causes are concerned, was primarily a war between Russia and Germany, it was, as far as its ultimate causes are concerned, primarily a war between England and Germany.

It is also desirable that some hint should be given in England as to the real situation here. Briand has taken office with the intention of opening peace negotiations as soon as

possible. He has made that known to the pacifist section of
the Socialist party, which is now the larger section, and that
was the chief reason why the Socialists were allowed to stay
in the government. Briand has taken in all the old men like
Freycinet, Combes etc. so that they may share with him the
responsibility for making peace. . . . Poincaré is said now to
be in favour of peace. . . . Britain wants . . . to let Germany
know that France asks for nothing but Alsace-Lorraine
(which means of course that she will make peace without it
if it cannot be made otherwise). You can depend upon it, no
French government can long resist the demand for peace
which is becoming too general and too obvious to be
disregarded, especially in the army. . . . I have not exagger-
ated French losses. They were enormous in the recent
offensive: the regiment of a man of my acquaintance was
reduced to 38 men out of 3,000. . . .

There is much more in the same spirit. Dell concludes by
hoping that when peace begins to be openly talked about,
Sharp will not continue to take an intransigent attitude in
the *New Statesman*.

In my opinion . . . the N.S. and all war Socialists in France
and England have done untold harm and have a great responsibility for the prolongation of the war which could have
been finished last February. . . .

Although Sharp rejected this letter and did not, of course,
print the Letter to the Editor expressing the same spirit, he
had too much respect for Dell as a journalist not to take
seriously the suggestion that there did exist a not incon-
siderable pacifist and defeatist party in France. He therefore
sent the letter to Sir Edward Grey, pointing out that '. . . in
my experience of him Mr. Dell is peculiarly careful about his
facts, as distinguished from his surmises'. Dell continued to
send letters and articles; Sharp refused to print them.

The already established literary features of the paper were
carried on during the war in what I can only describe as a
refined version of the national business-as-usual spirit. A
serious loss, less felt with the closure of so many theatres, was
that of Desmond MacCarthy. He had very swiftly become a
part of the paper while retaining that detachment from the
new statesmanly spirit which makes his original association

with the paper so odd, and the making of his great name as its Literary Editor no less so. That MacCarthy was ever engaged by Sharp is a tribute to the Webbs' policy of non-interference with the Editor, or perhaps an example of their indifference to imaginative literature. But Sharp, after all, was as Fabian as the Webbs, or almost; and he was not quite indifferent to imaginative literature.* MacCarthy's first theatrical criticism was written for a weekly called *The Speaker* which paid him 15s. a thousand words. When, under Massingham, *The Speaker* became *The Nation*, MacCarthy was sacked: this was the kind of mistake Massingham was apt to make and which Sharp had a talent for avoiding. MacCarthy then wrote for *The Eye-Witness*. His account of that stage in his career is entertaining:

> We were all of us, Belloc, the two Chestertons, Maurice Baring and I, paid at irregular intervals, and we tried to think of an explanation which would account for these incalculable but blessed spates of money. Oddly enough, they seemed to coincide with our employer's buying yet *another* paper, or with his starting a publishing business, or with abrupt disappearances abroad—in fact with moments when you might have expected money to be tight. We entertained the idea that he must be the illegitimate son of a Russian countess of immense wealth living on the Riviera, whom he could periodically tap or blackmail. He was an open-handed man. The only benefit he ever got himself out of feeding us that I could see, was one review of his own book of verses which all other papers had ignored. It was a difficult review to write. Still, we had three men of genius (they were poets too) on the staff, and between them, and with Cecil Chesterton also pulling his weight, it got written. However, the real explanation of the money-situation proved different. Suddenly, our employer was charged with bigamy and embezzlement. I was left with a stumer of thirty-odd pounds (two months' earnings).

Fortunately for him Shaw admired MacCarthy's dramatic criticism and introduced him to Sharp, who took him down to Sussex for one of the famous week-end parties with walks over or under Beachy Head. MacCarthy, vaguely liberal but

---

* But Leonard Woolf, in a private communication, tells me that Sharp was equally indifferent.

on the whole politically innocent, felt himself to be a fish not exactly out of water but in a strange tank. Yet there were large compensations. 'The *New Statesman* was out to improve the world, to correct the injustices of the social system, to stick up for the have-nots. I had, and have, the vaguest notions of the best means of accomplishing these ends; but provided I am not asked to help myself, I like to associate with others intent on them.' Besides, the new paper would pay him two guineas a thousand words and ten shillings extra for each attendance at a theatre. 'A beautiful prospect!' Then, too, MacCarthy's uneasiness in Fabian company was dispelled by an exchange of remarks overheard during his first week-end at the Webbs'.

> H. G. Wells, as we were all aware, had guyed the Webbs in *The New Machiavelli*, and he had recently published another novel. I remember Beatrice Webb saying cheerfully, 'I'm in it; I'm the woman whose voice is described as "a strangulated contralto", but *you* are not, Sidney.' 'Oh yes, I am', said Webb, speaking from a sofa on which his legs and feet looked absurdly small in comparison with his broad brow and head, 'Oh yes, I am, I'm described as one of those supplementary males often found among the lower crustacea.'

This smiling serenity made MacCarthy feel that he was in 'high and good' company. But his continued detachment from the new statesmanly spirit makes his comment on the paper's character from its beginning of particular interest.

> The *New Statesman* invariably emphasised the least gratifying reasons it could for any generous policy. In this respect it contrasted with its rival, the *Nation* . . . while the *Nation* supplied arguments which encouraged its readers to believe that they were the salt of the earth, the tone of the *Statesman* in arguing the same point would be, 'If you *want* to escape being a short-sighted fool, this is the line you must take.'

In 1914 MacCarthy could still write the 'Miscellany' features late in October. Thereafter he disappeared to serve in the Red Cross, on which he contributed a series of articles. His loss was not total: he continued to contribute from time to time, and later returned to the paper.

'New Novels' which, appalling thought, has reviewed something like 8,000 works of fiction in the past half century, remained in Bland's hands until August 1914, his last review being of Viola Meynell's *Modern Lovers*. There was a short-lived difficulty about replacing Bland, for Sharp reviewed the novels himself for the next two weeks; he was not very good at it, but it is a *tour-de-force* which no subsequent Editor has repeated and at least his criticism was—the double pun imposes itself—sharper than it was bland. Years later his rave-notice of Margaret Kennedy's *The Constant Nymph* is said to have 'made' that best-seller. He was followed by Gerald Gould and later by Cyril Connolly and Rebecca West.

For political and foreign news commentary, in brief under 'Comment', and at greater length in articles, Sharp, and during his absence later on military service, Squire, made increased use of Robert Ensor. Ensor was a veteran Fabian, a member of the society's élite, by trade a journalist on the *Daily Chronicle*, and later an Oxford don. He was, unlike many of his journalist colleagues, a Germany hater: Beatrice Webb describes him as '. . . complacently convinced of the imperative need not only for beating Germany but of dismembering the German empire'. *New Statesman* writers began to pay attention to the problem of peace terms. A stimulus to such thinking was given by President Wilson in May 1916 in a speech which was presumably the first sketch for the League of Nations. Leonard Woolf, who had returned from Ceylon in 1911, and had contributed occasionally to the paper since its foundation, dealt at length in the *New Statement* with the President's suggestions, with his laying down of 'certain general principles of international relationship which may fairly be claimed to embody the British ideal of what the foundation of international society should be'. The important point, on which Sharp, as well as Woolf, seized at once, was that Wilson offered, explicitly, 'the alliance of the United States with any association of nations which may be formed to secure these principles against attack or violation'. It was this speech, and Woolf's article, which gave Sharp the idea for a series of articles on the ultimate peace at a time when everyone else was thinking of nothing but the war. In August 1916 he wrote the first of, or rather an introduction to, the series, 'The Need for the Discussion of Peace Terms'. Both Leonard Woolf's article and Sharp's were the essence of new statesmanship: but the Tory, too, came out in Sharp, in his fundamental assumption that peace terms could be discussed only on the basis of a complete Allied victory. In other words, terms, albeit reasonable ones, were to be imposed on Germany. As to those terms, it was important to begin discussing them at once, for the tide of war had turned; victory, although it might be long delayed was now a definite probability, and unless the 'liberal common sense of the nation'—did he really believe in that or did he mean 'of men like me'?—was given time to assert itself we might fall into one of two equally undesirable extremes, revenge or quixotry. Twenty years later Sharp was to claim that his articles embodied a remarkable forecast of the terms actually made; a careful reading of them does not support the claim. In broad outline, it is true, the articles may be read as such a forecast: Germany was to be completely disarmed as the only alternative to a permanent and crippling arms race and another war; the map of Europe was to be redrawn on the only possible basis, that of nationality, but nationality was not to become a fetish and its claims must sometimes be overruled where greater interests were at stake, for example in South Africa where, unfortunately, it was out of the question to allow the Boer's claim to his own Republic. The most new statesmanly of Sharp's suggestions is not to be found realized in the Treaty of Versailles: we had, he argued, no right to retain Germany's colonies, but also no right to give them back. But come to that, neither we nor the French had any better right in Africa and Asia than Germany herself. On the other hand there could be no question of withdrawing, the native peoples were quite unfit to be self-governing. The only possible answer was an international 'trust' for all colonies, dedicated to the welfare of the natives and, commercially, to an Open Door policy. The articles of this series were reprinted as a pamphlet and widely read. They were condemned in Britain by Liberals and liberals as proposing terms so humiliating to Germany that they would force her to fight to a finish; and in Germany by the Right

Wing, for example in the *Deutsche Tageszeitung*, as an obvious attempt to convince the Germans that if they gave in they would be treated generously.

J. C. Squire's achievement during the war years was an astonishing one. He continued to write Solomon Eagle and to contribute largely to almost every section of the paper, front and back. Moreover, he kept this up after Sharp was called up under the Derby Scheme at the beginning of 1917, so that Squire became the temporary acting-editor of the paper. Yet it would be quite wrong to say that Squire *was* the *New Statesman* for two years; by that time the *New Statesman* has achieved its whatness, of which Squire was the sensitive and responsive servant.

It is possible that had Sharp been called up sooner, and left Squire in charge, Bernard Shaw would not have been lost to the paper until Kingsley Martin brought him back to it; it would never have consolidated its integral being; it would have become simply the voice of Bernard Shaw and died of that grave disease of weekly journals, incompatibility of parts. As it was, the breach with Shaw came in 1916 before Sharp's call-up. It did not entail the withdrawal of Shaw's financial support, which would have been as fatal to it as, in Sharp's opinion, too much of Shaw's editorial support was apt to be. For, financially, the paper was thoroughly unsound, and in August 1914 Beatrice Webb had recorded in her Diary:

> The *Statesman*'s financial position, with no advertisements, the rising price of paper, is serious. The young men are naturally intent on keeping alive their source of livelihood, but our four available capitalists are not likely to want to pay up. . . .

If Shaw's breach with Sharp had entailed, as evidently seemed likely, the withdrawal of his financial support, the paper would probably have ceased publication. Sharp knew this: his persistence in having his own way is all the more remarkable. But Shaw's attitude to this aspect of the matter was impeccably generous: he never used his money power in his rows with Sharp. Moreover, when Arnold Bennett joined the Board and put up money at a time when it already seemed likely that Shaw would sever his connection with the paper, there had been a proposal that Shaw should sell his shares to Bennett. He refused to do so on the ground that if the shares were worthless he would not dream of taking Bennett's money for them; if they were potentially valuable, he would prefer to keep them. As a result, Arnold Bennett's support came as an additional financial prop, not as a replacement merely.

The final breach between Sharp and Shaw came in October 1916. Beatrice Webb's Diary entry (November 3rd) reads:

> G.B.S. has definitely severed his connection with the *New Statesman*. The immediate and real reason—not mentioned to the Press—is an adequate one—Sharp's refusal to insert his articles, signed or unsigned. Clifford is a hard-minded conservative collectivist, who obstinately refuses to condemn either measures or men unless he has an alternative plan or an alternative Government to propose. He is also a materialist, a despiser of all ideals which cannot be embodied, in the near future, in social machinery to improve the conditions of life. Sentimentality is said to be the Emotion of the Un-imaginative—but Sharp has neither imagination nor emotion. Unless he can see through a question and all round it with his intellect he refuses to admit that the question exists. Above all, he loathes the professional rebel. When he does not see the collectivist solution he remains stolidly conservative. Possibly Shaw's prophecy that Sharp will presently dispense with Sidney may be fulfilled. Arnold Bennett is the one Director with whom he seems in complete sympathy, and A.B. is just starting a weekly article of the hard pro-liberal-minister type. But if the paper succeeds we do not grudge Sharp his independence. The new generation must take its own line—it is useless for the older generation 'to cut up rough'. We shall watch the *New Statesman* cutting itself loose from us as we watched the London School of Economics going its own way—with placid content.

So much for the forecasts that the Webbs would be intolerably interfering with their editors. Yet the entry is not quite fair to Sharp; he was all that Beatrice said he was; but a study of Shaw's contributions to the paper shows him quite clearly as much too flippant and much too confident that he was putting forward practical solutions to questions when what he was really doing was showing-off. His letter to Beatrice explaining his resignation is full of the very spirit which made him an impossible contributor:

My dear Beatrice,

It cannot be helped: it was bound to be, in the nature of things. My working relations with Sidney have always been those of a ticket-of-leave man who has forced himself on a benevolent employer by making himself useful. The benevolent employer appreciates the usefulness; but he can never trust the ticket-of-leave man, and is always surprised when his accounts turn out correct after all. This didn't matter in our Fabian work, because he never had to trust me: he had only to accept the finished work from me and wonder at its being so sensible instead of being what he expected. But a paper cannot be run on those lines. I might have wrecked the *New Statesman*: and it was psychologically impossible for Sidney to conceive that a man with my sort of mind and character, and an Irishman to boot, could do anything else. If he, as Chairman, felt this after nearly forty years' experience of me, how could novices like Simon and Bennett have any confidence in me?

A mere disagreement would not have mattered in the least: it would have been all the better, as we should have argued our policies out, and have thereby greatly improved them and arrived at a committee policy which would have strengthened and enlightened Sharp. But this would have involved our throwing aside all our work for three months after the declaration of war, and concentrating ourselves on the very knotty problem of how to encourage recruiting, give the war the character of a democratic crusade, rally even the sporting Jingoes to our side if they had any popular sympathies, and yet make the war achieve the political destruction of the worthless people who have been blocking us for the last ten years, and have at last, by a sort of judgment of God, brought the avalanche down on their own wretched heads. Well, I did that. I threw everything aside to sweat at this job for three months, almost in despair all the time because it urgently needed doing in three weeks. I solved the problem. I not only produced *Common Sense About the War*, but gave Sharp a model, in the *Lion* article, of the way to rally Old England in the interests of New England: a model which delighted the Jingo in him, though he could not work up to it. For a time my stuff went into the paper because Nature abhors a vacuum; and as nobody else had put in the work and solved the problem my solution had to be accepted without understanding or sympathy. But in the end the Reign of Terror became so formidable that my line could not be taken without the conviction that only a hard stretch of work and a winning through to daylight can produce. This being lacking, the alternative was to trust me. And that alternative was, as aforesaid, psychologically impossible. I have therefore to take my solution and my policy elsewhere. And there is no elsewhere except in a book doing at long range what should be done by a journal at short range. My articles in the American papers are doing something; but there are disadvantages in attacks coming from America.

When I tell Sidney that the sword we forged has broken in my hand, he says in effect 'So much the better: you are not to be trusted with a sword; and the broken-off point will come in handy for me as an oyster knife. I can only reply that he will not be allowed to open oysters with it. Northcliffe, who, after seven months' hesitation, followed my example by going for Kitchener and bringing down his man, besides achieving one of the great historic triumphs of the Thunderer* in the matter of ammunition, will not let him. The *New Statesman*, after its little Shavian spurt, has come to heel; and that is the end of our influence on Cabinets.

As to Sharp, you must bear in mind that this conscription business is exceedingly trying to the nerves. Men of military age have to pretend to take it nonchalantly; but I have observed it pretty closely for some months and found that the suspense of playing for exemption is far worse than actual service. Sharp is a man of late hours and plenty of strong coffee; and he is ten times a better man in peace than in war. He is not very good at the technical business of literature: that is, he cannot bring all his personal qualities to literary expression: for instance, nobody who knows him personally would say that he is destitute of humour and generosity; but he cannot get these qualities into the paper, though he may later on, when the strain of war is over. Meanwhile, he is a shaken man; and it was really this that determined me not to sit at the Board as a deadhead and make the nervous strain worse for him. His fundamental opposition to

---

* *The Times* belonged to Northcliffe for a while.

you will develop *unless you exercise his support of you strenuously*.

As to the financial position of the paper, you may leave that confidently to Providence. Like the old Thames Steamboat Company or the *Westminster Review*, it will struggle on long after all creation shrieks for its interment. But if you and Sidney put a violent end to it I shall not be greatly grieved. The longer I live, the more I perceive that Napoleon's rule of six years as the effective lifetime of a general applies to all public bodies and all papers. Three years ago the *N.S.* was young; today it is about eighty: a comfortable age for the directors, but not a promising one for the paper. A paper, unless it is to be frankly a dull paper for dull people, like *The Spectator* (which now suits my elderly taste remarkably well) or an ungenerous paper for ungenerous people like the *Saturday*, must live by adventures. The amazing journalistic feat of sacking Bernard Shaw does not indicate much taste for that sort of thing at Great Queen's Street. . . .

It is perhaps needless to say that Shaw had in fact solved no problems, that the 'Lion' article which he referred to did not and could not accomplish anything and is not even good Shaw; that Sharp knew what Shaw never did, that tiresome truth about politics being, at least in an old Parliamentary oligarchy, the art of the possible; and that his letter is not free from a certain and surprising touchiness of the kind which derives from outraged self-esteem. Beatrice Webb did not show Sharp this letter, of course, but she evidently made use of it in writing to him and presumably (her letter is not extant) reproaching him for losing Shaw. His answer is as Sharpian as Shaw's letter is Shavian:

Dear Mrs. Webb,
     Your letter rather demands an answer. It is one thing to be criticised by Shaw, another to have *you* supporting him. I don't think I have failed to do justice to Shaw's 'lack of practical egotism' (as you call it—though *I* shouldn't). I have always been amazed by his willingness to go on supporting a paper which obviously represented his views in scarcely a single particular, and, of course, he has always been extraordinarily nice to me personally—so much so that I never felt inclined to resent in the least the good-humoured contempt which he never concealed. I think he is much the most generous and sweetest-tempered person I ever came across.

65

But that does not affect the fact that he is intellectually the most grossly egotistical and unreasonable of beings. I cannot imagine anyone more perverse than he has been in his dealings with the editor of the *N.S.* He has never shown the smallest sympathy or understanding of the difficulties of the job of maintaining a coherent line in the paper, but, on the contrary, he has always apparently made it a point of honour or dignity not to compromise on the smallest point. A tentative criticism of mine on a particular sentence of his, for example, has always meant that the sentence would be underlined and strengthened in the proof. His appreciative article on Morel owed its existence, I believe, mainly to the fact that he knew from a conversation of a few weeks before that the personal value of Morel was a point on which he and I differed strongly.

And when a man solemnly writes that he does not expect anyone else to see as far as he does—egotism has surely become a disease. However, that's all done with now. I only refer to it because I gather from your letter that, owing to your own relations with Shaw being of such a special character, you may not quite have realised the extent to which his practical generosity has always been accompanied by the most utter and discouraging intolerance in other directions. His money leaves one liberty, but his personal attitude refuses one not merely the liberty of criticism but the right even to possess any view of one's own at all. I believe that you and Mr. Webb are probably the only people in the world towards whom his intolerance is modified—by, as it were, a long inbred habit of affection and respect.

But what I really wanted to take this opportunity of saying was this: you speak of not having protested, because the paper is more my affair than yours. I think you've really gone farther than 'not protesting' and let me suppose that you *actively* agreed with me in most of my dealings with Shaw. But it's the latter part of the sentence I'm particularly concerned to reply to. *I* do *not* consider the paper is more my affair than yours (meaning you and Webb of course). I have always looked on it as a co-operative concern in which the policy is decided by common agreement. In the event of disagreement I should expect my policy (i.e. my interpretation of the 'entity' referred to just below) to prevail in some matters, yours in others. I do not regard the paper as representing my personal views, but rather the views of an indefinable composite Fabian entity which it is my business to interpret. It often happens that a matter presents itself thus: 'I think so and so, but *The Statesman* ought to think so and so.' Of course such differences of opinion (or more probably feeling) between C.S. and the editor of the *N.S.* are comparatively rare and small, but they are not altogether unimportant. And the point is this: that it is very difficult for me at times to discover, as it were, what the opinion of the *N.S.*— that is the 'common' opinion—really is without discussion. And if you are silent about differences of opinion because the paper is more my affair than yours—well, it *will* become more my affair than I think it ought to be. I've no desire at all to have a *personal* organ, my whole object has always been to express a policy which shall command the widest possible measure of agreement amongst our supporters (the Board on the one hand and the readers on the other) —and, as a matter of fact, I should have been very glad to have incorporated in the policy and personality of the paper a dash of Shaw—such as has run through so much Fabian work. But it has not been practicable because he would not co-operate. I daresay it would have been possible if we had met every week, because he might have been induced to meet one half-way. But as it was, his stuff has always been quite incompatible with the rest of the paper—and all the more troublesome because it attracted so much attention. . . .

The Fabian entity evoked by Sharp was, of course, that whatness of the *New Statesman* evoked in Chapter 3. That it was something real and even more independent of individuals than Sharp implied, is clear from the fact that Sharp's two-year withdrawal by the War Office did not impair or alter the character of the paper. I doubt whether Squire had to make a special effort to keep it so; by the end of 1916 the *New Statesman* was alive of its own life. And there were those with axes of their own to grind who recognized this and considered whether they might not make use of it. The *démarche* —recorded thus by Beatrice Webb: 'Graham Wallas called on Sharp the other day with a message from Herbert Samuel and Montagu: would the *New Statesman* become the organ of H. M. Opposition? . . .'—was recognition of a striking kind. Sharp lunched with the prime movers, but nothing came of the meeting, either because Sharp would not harness the paper to any party or because, called up for service, he was unable to follow up the proposals. The Webbs did their best to get Sharp exempted from service—they had succeeded with G. D. H. Cole and others—but failed, possibly because Sharp's policy had been consistently hostile to the Government. More likely because governments are apt to regard editors of dissenting journals as dispensable.

Despite Sharp's absence during the next two years, it was Sharpian Fabianism, a sort of political existentialism *avant la* Sartrian *lettre*, which ballasted the paper in the rising tide of world Socialism; freedom from Party ties meant complete freedom of opinion and in the face of Bolshevism the *New Statesman* remained, as it were, as cold-eyed as it was, for example, in its examination of the German *mystique* in a remarkable series of essays, '*Wie Steht's Mit Der Deutschen Kultur*' by Karl Pearson. In these studies the author put his finger on the real nature of the German danger, exposing that '. . . frame of mind which we find in a Kaiser who can found institutes for scientific research *and* appeal on the field of battle to his tribal gods'. Hitlerism is forecast by implication. Socialism at home is looked at just as coolly as Bolshevism and embryo-Fascism abroad: when in 1917 Philip Snowden spoke angrily in the House against the Government's supposed annexationist and imperialist war aims, he was treated in 'Comment' with contempt, and Lord Robert Cecil's demolition of his arguments was applauded; the paragraph of Fabian imperialism in question was written by Squire, but might as well have been written by Sharp or by Mostyn Lloyd, of whom more anon. For the paper was, as it were, now 'writing itself'. And its whatness was naturally hostile to woolly-mindedness: it attacked Ramsay MacDonald for the ridiculous inconsistency between his support in the House for the principle of nationality and his pacifism which would if triumphant make it impossible to enforce. The paper's motto might have been *Surtout, pas de zèle*, and it was not until many years later, under Kingsley Martin, that a way was found to give expression to both sides of the British Socialist spirit, to the warm heart as well as the cool mind.

The first Russian revolution received cordial support

which, however, was cautious. There could be no doubt that democratic collectivism under educated leadership was much better than Tsarism. Thereafter, every move made in Russia, in so far as they were known abroad at all, was commented on, and whether the comment was short or long, whether made by Ensor, Squire, Lloyd or Lewis Namier, it had the same sound. Liberty by all means, but no excesses, please. The fall of Riga led to a long article by Ensor on the effects of Leninism [*sic*] on the armies; the important thing was that Russia should continue fighting as our ally; but with her armies demoralized and her workers making unrealistic demands, she would probably be of little use to us now; however, we could get on very well without her. Using the Sartrian terminology, there is no doubt at all that all *New Statesman* writers were, in their attitude to Bolshevism, *salauds*. The fact is that Fabian Socialism was completely ignorant of and unable to understand the feelings and ideas of revolutionary Socialism. Here, for example, is an entry in Beatrice Webb's Diary for 5 October 1917:

Meanwhile revolutionary ideas, more especially of the syndicalist type, are being discredited by the collapse of Russia. The folly of the I.L.P. in acclaiming the Russian Soviet Government of 'Workmen and Soldiers' represent- atives as the 'new model' is becoming every day more obvious. The success of the Labour Party depends largely on how far its leaders can free themselves of the old assumptions of the capitalist State whilst keeping themselves free from the cant of anarchic rebellion against any form of deliberately ordered social action.

But the paper had, of course, nothing but contempt for the excited abuse which the daily Press was pouring out on the Russian revolutionaries, and steadily pointed out that what- ever form the new Russian régime might take, the destruction of Tsarist autocracy, 'one of the most corrupt, degraded and degrading governments that have ever disgraced European civilization', was a positive gain.

A contributor who, despite the like-mindedness with Sharp which Beatrice Webb had remarked on with what looked a little like contempt, did not succeed in striking a new statesmanly note, was Arnold Bennett. His column, headed 'Observations' and signed 'Sardonyx', sticks out like a sore thumb. It consisted of a series of paragraphs of wide-ranging war commentary; it reads like a gossip-column. Beginning as a whole page, it shrank rather quickly and that this was not owing to want of space but rather to want of anything to say is clear from the fact that within months Ensor and Squire were having to fill out the column which Bennett was unable or unwilling to complete.

5

Management

A NEWSPAPER, being a business, requires business management and a non-editorial office staff. Books have to be kept, materials such as paper and ink bought, contracts made with printers, advertisements solicited and invoiced and attempts made to promote the sale of the paper. In the case of a new and small undertaking the editor or one of his assistants may double some of the business roles. The editorial people of the *New Statesman* were singularly ill-equipped to do so and had little taste for commerce. As a journal grows, the business side becomes more onerous and the doubling of roles more difficult. Moreover, in 1913 there was, among persons of intellect, a greater distaste for dabbling in commerce than is now the case. The influence of American manners has led to an increased respect for business as an occupation for men with brains and education, and this change is welcomed as a victory over an absurd form of snobbishness, and as a socially progressive step. It is, perhaps, not quite clear that this attitude is perfectly sound.

The original business side of the *New Statesman* seems to have been somewhat makeshift. A mysterious character who haunts the memories of the oldest contributors as a figure of masculine appearance but feminine gender who hung about the Great Queen Street office wearing velvet trousers and smoking pungent cigars, was the firm's book-keeper and Clifford Sharp's sister. She was, or wished to be considered, manly. Whence she came and when, when and why departed, I have no idea. Another female member of the staff who seems to have been in the office from almost the first days was of very different stuff: Mrs. Vincent was in theory Sharp's secretary, in fact everybody's. Will it ever be known how many business and professional undertakings large and small depended in the great era of commercial expansion which coincides with the first half of the twentieth century on such women as Mrs. Vincent? I have a theory that many and perhaps most businesses are in fact really run by them, for obviously women are better equipped for such work than men; and that half the captains of industry and commerce are no more than decorative, or often not even decorative, figureheads. Of the *New Statesman*'s *maîtresse femme* MacCarthy was to write in a reminiscence of those early years:

> Mrs. Vincent was not only equably and promptly practical, but as far as I was concerned she developed an extraordinary instinct for distinguishing before-hand between the kind of engagements I would and those I would not ultimately keep, thus saving others from inconvenience and me from shame. 'Oh, no', she would say gaily over the telephone in answer to some reasonable or even to some delightful suggestion, 'he won't do *that*', long before I had any notion that I wouldn't myself. Those awful Literary Supplement and Library List rushes—I remember them well! How she would stay with me until after eleven at night, doing my work with me, seeing that Edmund Gosse did not figure as Edmund Goose, and that other hardly less disastrous errors were avoided. . . .

It was good sense to put the physical publishing of the *New Statesman* into the hands of an experienced publisher who would manage the paper as a part-time job: only so could it be done economically. The man chosen for this task was a friend, or at least a business acquaintance, of J. C. Squire, R. B. Byles. Mr. Byles was managing director of a publishing firm, Alston Rivers, and he was known not only to Squire but to other members of the *New Statesman* staff. It is clear that the Webbs, and even Sharp himself, did not regard the question of who was to business-manage the paper as one of importance, or one requiring more than the briefest discussion. They were incapable of seeing the business-management of the *New Statesman* as anything but an elementary mechanical task well within the powers of some simple, honest toiler. Such work might require a sort of intelligence, something perhaps more than animal sagacity, but it certainly did not require brains in their sense of the word. Probably someone—Squire, no doubt, since he had been associated with Byles in launching the publishing house of Howard Latimer—mentioned the publisher's name when the matter of who was to look after the office came up, and since this candidate was known to be competent the matter would not need discussion. The generally rather frosty or at best condescending attitude of early new statesmanship to men of commerce must have been very discouraging for the latter; a little more warmth and interest in their side of things might have cut those losses which, by 1916, were putting the paper's life in peril.

Late in 1904 Alston Rivers had engaged, as office-boy, a promising and industrious youth named John Roberts. He was the son, one of eleven children, of a Bermondsey tinker. He knew himself clever and he was certainly ambitious, and he came to Alston Rivers, to better himself, from the publishing firm of Eyre & Spottiswoode which he had entered at the age of thirteen. Nothing is more difficult than for an office-boy to show outstanding ability: the tasks commonly assigned to him are not such as attract attention unless he steals the stamps. But somehow Roberts contrived to demonstrate that he had ability, and Byles soon conceived a very good opinion of the lad. Byles had no distrust of youth and by rapidly promoting Roberts he probably saved money, since he would not have to pay a boy as much as a man though the boy did a man's work. By the time Roberts was seventeen he was virtually managing Alston Rivers's business office. But this meant that he could get no higher with that firm, and his ambition was far from satisfied. He took the first real opportunity to move upward by leaving Alston Rivers, to undertake the reorganization of the business side of a suburban newspaper publishing firm. From there he went to Messrs. W. H. Smith & Son; they were planning to start in book publishing on their own account and John Roberts had a hand in the new department. This did not, apparently, impress that shrewd young man as likely to come to much, and in due course he left Smiths to join *The Athenaeum* as deputy to the manager, J. E. Francis. His principal task at *The Athenaeum* was to build up the sagging advertising revenue.

Roberts had been with *The Athenaeum* for a year when Byles approached him again. The weekly *Public Opinion* needed a business manager. Roberts took the job and worked at it for fifteen months. Meanwhile, Byles had become tired of the *New Statesman* work and again applied to Roberts, suggesting that he should work under him until he was competent to take over the responsibility entirely. Roberts agreed, and joined the *New Statesman* with a contract early in 1914 before the paper was a year old; his salary was £200 a year*; he was then twenty-three. His first task was to build up advertising revenue if he could do so: as already explained, this work was in the hands of a man called George Radford, an advertising agent who, however, had some claim to notice by the Fabians because of his liberal theories of land-tenure reform, which he had published. Radford had looked almost solely to publishers for *New Statesman* advertising revenue.

Before Roberts was able to make much impression on the advertising revenue, he was called up. Although he had only been with the paper for seven months he was given a retainer of £1 a week while in the Army. Only Beatrice Webb, among the directors, had opposed the arrangement: the John Robertses of this world if they lost one job could get another, and the paper had enough of a financial burden to carry already. However, she was over-ruled. Roberts got his £1 and kept it until a year later, when he gave it up as a condition of cancelling his contract with the *New Statesman*, whose survival after the war seemed improbable. Byles and Radford carried on meanwhile, but the difficulties of maintaining, let alone improving, advertising revenue were too much for them. While the paper's circulation kept rising— by the end of 1916 it had reached 6,000—advertising revenue fell. In the year 1914-15 it was £723, in the following year £467 and in 1916-17 it fell to £417. Thus the loss on publication of the *New Statesman* was rising in a way to threaten its survival again. And although in the last year of the war the advertising revenue rose again, reaching £950, the circulation, and therefore the costs, had also risen even

* Say £1,000 of our money.

more, so that there was no net gain of money and probably an increased loss.

But the question of the paper's continuance in being had been raised before this: the losses incurred by the end of 1914 and the rising costs of materials made it seem improbable, as Beatrice Webb noted in her Diary, that the *New Statesman* could carry on, and on 22 January 1915 a meeting was called to discuss this, attended by the Webbs, Bernard Shaw, Sharp and Ernest Simon. Sharp produced an estimate showing that the loss in the next year would be about £1,800. After discussion it was agreed to carry on for a year. Shaw put up another £500, Simon £600 and the Webbs £200. Sharp still had to find £600. For this he wrote to Edward Whitley, the other principal 'angel', and to the fourteen people who were smaller shareholders in the Statesman Publishing Company. The whole sum required was forthcoming, and when the accounts were made up in November 1915 the loss was found to be £800 for the half-year, and must, therefore, have been running at an annual rate rather lower than Sharp's estimate. This conservatism in Sharp's business estimates inspired confidence; he was invariably honest with the *New Statesman*'s angels. When, for example, he wrote after the meeting to Whitley for more money, he candidly told him that the paper's advertisement business was 'hopeless': 'Roberts', Sharp said, 'appears to be dealing with it, but he has enlisted, and there would be no point in replacing him since, conditions being what they are, a space salesman would not make his salary.' There is, in this same letter, an interesting reference to Bernard Shaw's influence on the paper's circulation: Sharp tells Whitley that, in the four weeks following publication of 'Common Sense About the War', the sale of copies rose by 600, 1,400, 700 and 900 respectively above the average. But, Sharp adds, he expects to keep no more than 200 as a net gain.*

For the first seventeen or eighteen years of its life the *New*

* Money values: as a means of estimating the then value of the sums the *N.S.* backers were finding: in Feb./March 1915 a party of *New Statesman* contributors and backers spent a sort of conference week-end together at the Royal Crescent Hotel, Brighton. The *inclusive* charge from 27 Feb. to 1 March was 22s. 6d. per head.

Statesman continued in being by virtue of the loans made by its directors; and if, like Bernard Shaw and Arnold Bennett, they were writing directors, their copy and services went unpaid. In August 1917 Arnold Bennett wrote to Sidney Webb about this:

> The paper is undoubtedly increasing in importance and esteem. If it makes a profit* my shareholding interest in it is so trifling that I should derive practically no benefit. I certainly did not come in for the sake of ultimate gain. But it seems to me that the arrangements should be such that when a profit is made those who have devoted time and money to the paper in the unprofitable days have a right to benefit to the largest possible extent, in proportion to the time and money they have devoted.

But it was three years before anything was done about this.

Demobilized in January 1919, Roberts decided that he would, after all, return to the *New Statesman*, since it was still very much alive. Its journalistic and solid success was a promise and its financial losses a challenge; he did not like its politics but, except in so far as they constituted an obstacle in business circles, they did not concern him much. He was again appointed as Byles's deputy; he was styled Advertisement Manager and this time his salary was £400, plus commission on a generous rising scale on the advertisement revenues. Radford would fade out and Roberts was to handle the advertisement side. In June 1920 Byles died of pernicious anaemia and Roberts was promoted and officially appointed business manager. Neither he nor the editor had a seat on the Board.

Roberts's task was a difficult one; in a reminiscence of those days Desmond MacCarthy refers to 'Roberts and his (sometimes) gloomy men'. It is no wonder if they were sometimes gloomy. The revenue from the only industry which was more or less sure to advertise in the *New Statesman* was limited; publishers are as a rule reluctant advertisers, convinced that their advertising procures no advantage, sells no books; if their books are not reviewed in the paper, they become fractious and if the advertisement manager of the paper appeals

* He had applied for and been allotted some shares in April 1915.

to the editor for help in the form of more reviews for some complaining publisher, he is apt to be firmly put in his place. However, they have generally recognized that the *New Statesman* is read by people some of whom buy books and all of whom read them. General advertisers were not drawn to the *New Statesman*. Most of them are naturally concerned simply to get as many readers per £ of their money as possible; although advertisement rates are roughly related to circulation, the rate per thousand readers in the case of papers with very large net sales is lower than in the case of papers with small sales. It is true that the 'quality' of the readership may be taken into account, but it does not interest the majority of big advertisers, whose appeal must be to the masses not the classes. The *New Statesman* circulation in the early Twenties was between 6,000 and 8,000 a week; space in its advertising columns was not a good buy. A great deal of advertisers' money is in the hands of advertising agents; these agents receive for their services between 10 per cent. and 15 per cent. of what they spend for their clients. There is less work for them, and smaller overheads, in placing most of the money out in large lumps, and, other things being equal, they therefore favour the mass-circulation Press. This favour has resulted in the death of hundreds of newspapers, weekly journals, monthly and quarterly reviews, in the past fifty years. The advertising agent cannot really be blamed for this: his client's interests and those of the small periodical publisher rarely coincide, but it is true to say that in an important sense the advertising agent has, during the lifetime of the *New Statesman*, unwittingly been a worse enemy of a free Press than any censorship, not indeed by exercising undue influence on policy (although that is not unknown), but simply by killing half of it and greatly assisting that movement towards fewer periodicals and larger circulations, which has had such lamentable consequences.

In at least one respect the *New Statesman* has long been and is recognized to be an outstandingly good advertising medium: its readers' response to 'causes' is invariably generous and at times startlingly so. The advertiser who has a charitable appeal to make, who is crying for help for oppressed persons in Africa or Asia, for refugees, for the victims of mankind or the gods, cannot do better than put his 'appropriation' into the *New Statesman*. Moreover, in the Fifties and Sixties the problem of advertising revenue for the 'quality' papers, and it should be emphasized that their survival depends on it, has been solved by the growth of what is called prestige advertising under the influence of new public-relations techniques: such advertising does not aim at direct sales of goods but at the creation of an 'image' of a great firm or institution in the minds of the nation's managing class, the minds of what *The Times*, which is not above using gross flattery, calls 'top people'. It should be added that this kind of advertising is very largely a by-product of high income tax; for as money spent on advertising is allowed by the Inland Revenue inspectors as a business expense, prosperous firms are in this position: that of, say, £50,000 spent on prestige advertising, £20,000 would in any case be taken from them as tax if not so spent, and probably more if we take profits tax into account. Thus they can buy advertising space at an artificially reduced rate. The tax allowance for advertising has therefore been responsible for the rising prosperity of, for example, *The Observer*, *The Times*, the *Sunday Times*, and, of late and to a much lesser extent, the *New Statesman*. Thus, what some strict Socialists might consider an abuse of the fiscal system has, with a pleasing irony, had the admirable result of subsidizing the prosperity of the intelligent periodical Press, including that of the Left.

But in the Twenties advertising was still designed to procure direct and traceable sales of goods, and the *New Statesman* was at a great disadvantage. Moreover, such advertisers or their agents as Roberts did succeed in persuading to support the paper, were very apt to cancel their contracts in a rage upon reading, in the very next number, some outrageously collectivist and wickedly anti-capitalist article convincing them that if the *New Statesman* policy prevailed, *they*, who were helping it to propagate its scandalous ideas, would be ruined.

In 1920, and probably as a result of Arnold Bennett's representations, all loans made to the company were converted into ordinary shares. By this transaction Edward

Whitley and Ernest Simon became the largest shareholders, each with 2,400; Arnold Bennett had over 2,000. Bernard Shaw had 861 shares; his support of the company had not been quite as generous as that provided by the other three. The Webbs, of course, had a few hundred each.

But, for long after this transaction, loans were still required and were forthcoming, with periodical conversion into shareholdings for the creditors. For though revenue was rising, so was expense. Like Roberts, Sharp, who returned in May 1919, was costing the paper more. His pre-war £500 became £750 a year, and in 1920 it was raised to £1,000. Staff salaries were raised from time to time to keep up with the inflationary spiral, until that collapsed into a deflationary slough. The record of these transactions in the small copper-plate handwriting of the Company's Secretary, Mr. Hewson —who served the *New Statesman* longer than any other of its servants except John Roberts—reflects a rising prosperity, to be sure; but also a cost of living rising more steeply.

Another of Roberts's difficulties was Sharp's attitude to the business side of the paper, which he seems to have found thoroughly distasteful. It is an interesting fact that to every one with whom he had to do, Sharp presented a different face: we have seen that to Beatrice Webb he was a hard-minded conservative collectivist; to Shaw, an unimaginative and unfeeling intellectual. To his editorial colleagues he was an editor of genius; to his casual or periodical contributors, a slave driver with a sharp temper, critical of all they wrote, very sparing of praise, and all too apt to pour icy water over their most cherished suggestions. To Roberts, Sharp was an unfriendly intellectual snob, contemptuous of the business side and unwilling to co-operate with the manager even to the extent of running a special Christmas number which might earn a little money for the company. When, in 1934, Sharp was writing an account of his association with the *New Statesman*, he used a curiously grudging form of words in paying tribute to Roberts's work for the paper: 'The present Manager, Mr. J. H. Roberts . . . was appointed to take Byles's place. I should be very much understating my self-satisfaction if I said that I never afterwards regretted my part in that appointment.'

Despite these difficulties, Roberts was remarkably successful. From the financial as distinct from the social and journalistic point of view, what was needed was to raise the advertising revenue without any considerable rise in circulation. If a periodical publisher's receipts from the sale of copies of his paper meet the cost of producing that paper, then he can keep forcing up the circulation with no financial loss and, since a higher circulation enables him to raise advertisement rates, with some financial gain. But in very few cases is the 3*d.*, 9*d.*, 1*s.* which we pay for a daily or weekly journal enough to meet the cost of writing and making our copy; our reading is being subsidized for us either by advertisers or by a publishing company willing and able to lose money. The cost of writing a paper, editing it, setting it in type and preparing it for the press, is a fixed one, however few or many copies are thereafter run off; in theory, therefore the more copies printed the lower the cost per copy. This is true in practice also, but if the cost of paper be so high that the cost per copy exceeds the net receipt from sales, then the more you print the more you lose. The cost of newsprint and other paper now, for example, at the time of writing, is exorbitant, so that no publication of any kind can solve its financial problems by increasing its sales unless it can attract advertising at very high rates. In the early Twenties, too, the great obstacle to making the *New Statesman* pay its way was the exorbitant cost of paper, a cost which had, and has now, very little to do with the real cost of manufacture and a great deal to do with the paper industry's determination to make a great deal more money than is really justifiable, from a social point of view, even if it means a serious check to the free expression of opinion, which it does. It is true that in the case of a journal of the *New Statesman*'s quality, it is possible to stabilize circulation and revenue at some profitable point of balance; but this entails sacrifice of growth and in any case the paper had not reached that point. Thus, although Roberts might succeed in raising the *New Statesman*'s advertising revenue, which he did, since the advertisements to be printed meant enlarging the paper, the gain would be less than might appear. At no time between 1919 and 1925 did the *New Statesman*'s net sales reach 10,000, and the average was nearer to 7,000. In that time Roberts raised the revenue from £1,479 per annum in 1918-19 to over £7,000 in 1925. In the year 1925-26 it was £8,572, which represents an astonishing advance in five years, but they were five years of post-war boom.

That a gain of this order was both necessary and not enough to make the *New Statesman* pay its way, is clear from the figures. Sharp returned to take up his editorship again in 1919. The size of the annual loss was, he says, 'an almost terrifying figure'. In 1919-20 it was £4,000 and in the following year it rose to £6,500. As the paper's backers had to find this substantial sum or at least guarantee it—something like £12,000 a year in our own debased money—it was not very likely that they would allow things to continue in that train. Roberts and Sharp, the latter driven to be co-operative by the threat to his paper though not to his livelihood, for he could by then have had his pick of Fleet Street plums, were faced with the task of persuading the Board of *New Statesman* angels that despite the weekly loss of £120 they were in the darkest hour before the dawn. The editor and the manager had one very powerful argument: they knew that the price of paper would shortly fall heavily. They worked out estimates for the next few years 'of varying degrees of optimism'. Sharp was later to confess that Roberts had more faith in these than he had. In the event the falling price of paper and Roberts's success with advertisers resulted in the most optimistic of these estimates being surpassed. Roberts's faith and Sharp's persuasiveness prevented the Board from cutting their losses by killing the paper, which they were in any case very reluctant to do.

The Board, however, did not take the word of editor and manager unsupported. Sir Hedley Le Bas, a specialist in making unprofitable journals pay, was asked to look into the company's position. He did so, made a favourable report and some suggestions for economies, for example in paper and by publishing lesser journals for a fee, and for a short while he served on the Board. One interesting fault which he found with the management was that of failing to publish circulation figures: making enquiries he discovered that the weekly sale of the *New Statesman* was generally, and even by the best informed Fleet-streeters, believed to be 3,000 copies. In fact it was between 8,000 and 9,000. It is curious that so shrewd and able a businessman as John Roberts should not have been making the best of the position. Le Bas claimed that publication of this figure would create a 'sensation', for it meant that the paper's weekly sales were larger than any but those of *The Spectator* and *Punch*. Le Bas also recommended raising the advertisement rate from 12 to 16 guineas a page. Roberts objected that this was too high and they compromised on 14 guineas. Roberts and Sharp together opposed, successfully, a suggestion to put an advertisement on the front page. Le Bas reported that the 'property' was a very valuable one and that he expected the circulation to reach 20,000 in a few years. But he thought the *New Statesman* insufficiently publicized. *'People'*, he wrote, *'do not know the* New Statesman.'

By April 1923 Sharp was able to show that the loss for the next twelve months would not exceed £1,000. It may occur to those whose business experience has not been in the field of periodical publishing that to offer a Board of Directors the prospect of an annual loss, albeit only £1,000, by way of encouragement, is a curious operation. But until recently the primary purpose of periodical publishers was not to make money but to propagate ideas. Now, of course, that the American belief in profits as evidence of virtue, a kind of commercial antinomianism of English Puritan origin, has triumphed all over the world, a journal which loses money must be looked at askance; surely its losses are a sort of divine punishment for perversity of opinion? A generation ago there was perhaps a tendency to consider that the propagation of good sense and better sentiments ought to cost money, not make it. That is no doubt an exaggeration; the *New Statesman* Board probably thought it would be very nice if the paper could pay its way or run at a profit; but its members were quite willing to go on facing an annual loss provided it was not such as to put them personally in actual financial straits, and they would have dismissed with contempt any suggestion to compromise or to allow commercial considerations to affect *New Statesman* policy in any way.

In short, in the 1920s commercial standards had not yet ousted the older ones and it is typical of the similarity between the *New Statesman* state of mind and that of the old socially responsible gentry admired by Taine, that contributors were better paid out of the backers' pockets than those of any other comparable paper. Yet I must not give the impression that the *New Statesman* backers were the only angels. For it is a fact that, apart from the very long established *Spectator*, and *Punch*, no sixpenny weekly review had ever come within £1,000 a year of paying its way, unless, perhaps, *The Athenaeum* during a part of its career; there were, then, other and un-newstatesmanly men willing to spend money on propagating their ideas but who, to some extent, did so at the contributors' expense by underpaying them. Orage, it is said, did not pay contributors to the *New Age* at all! But these men, Belloc and Chesterton for example, insisted on controlling the papers they backed, and usually wrote half of the articles themselves; as we shall see, this was not the *New Statesman* case. Five years after Roberts and Sharp had had to face their Board with the prospect of that £6,500 loss, they were able to show them a paper profit of 90s.; in 1928, that is to say, the paper was almost paying, precariously, its own way; and this was regarded as little short of a miracle.

It was Clifford Sharp's fault that the paper was not, at this time, able to show a fairly respectable profit. Sharp was, among much else, a man who believed that common sense would solve every problem, including legal ones; he had difficulty in believing that there were no special rules and special cases which would not give way to it. Moreover, in the 'Comment' quoted below, he may have been influenced by the fact that one of the men who had suffered gravely as a result of police interference with amorous liberty in Hyde Park was Leo Chiozza Money, an old friend of and contributor to the *New Statesman*. Here, at all events, is what he wrote about police behaviour:

> At the first meeting of the Royal Commission on Police Powers and Procedure, its Chairman, Lord Lee of Fareham, made a long opening statement, in the course of which he said that the main effort of the Commission 'must be to find means

of restoring mutual confidence between the police and the public', that he had no intention of using whitewash, but they must 'remember always that law-abiding citizens did not wish to see the police discredited'. He added that it was no business of theirs to go into questions relating to the supervision of Hyde Park. This is surely an ill-omened beginning. For certainly if Lord Lee is not prepared to go into the question of the supervision of Hyde Park, with all the blackmail and sensation which it involves, he will find it quite impossible to restore the confidence of the public in the police. Moreover, the whole substance of his opening speech suggested a very strong faith in the virtues of whitewash, and the long leading questions which he put to the first Home Office witness implied even more obviously that Lord Lee's conception of his duty in connection with this Commission is that at all costs it must find the police blameless. If the inquiry is really to be carried out on these lines, we can only say that it seems to us a great waste of public money. Such an inquiry might be of great value if it put an end to the Horwood-Childs-Bodkin methods—an end, that is to say, to the 'Hyde Park scandals', to the creation of crime where there is no crime, and to the attempted enforcement by the police of moral standards which have nothing whatever to do with the preservation of public order. But we do not see the use of any inquiry at all if its main purpose, as Lord Lee suggests, is to prevent the police being discredited.

This paragraph appeared on 13 October 1928. As a result of it writs were served on the company by Sir William Horwood, Commissioner of the Metropolitan Police, and by Sir Borlase Wyndham Childs, the Assistant Commissioner, claiming damages for libel. They were represented by Norman Birkett, and the defendants, including Speaights, the printers, who published an apology on their own account, by Patrick Hastings. If Hastings had any hope of a favourable verdict it vanished when Sharp recognized, in court and in plain clothes, two policemen who, many years before, had arrested him in Tottenham Court Road, outside H. W. Nevinson's house where he had been calling, and charged him with being drunk and disorderly. He had not been either, and the police had behaved disgracefully, for he was not even allowed to see a doctor who might certify that he was sober. Sharp had pleaded guilty and paid a fine because the friends with whom he had spent the evening, mostly people of consequence, had been reluctant to appear as witnesses on his behalf. He might be supposed, however, to bear malice against the police for the way they had treated him, and Hastings was at once convinced, when these two policemen appeared in court, that Birkett would try to prove malice; he realized that if Birkett got Sharp in the witness-box he would very easily do so, in view of Sharp's temper. He therefore persuaded his client not to go into the witness-box, thereby throwing away the case, but in order to save the Company and Sharp from a much worse verdict than the plaintiffs obtained: they were each awarded £100 damages, but the costs of the case were heavy: £3,126.

Now, as will appear in Chapter 6, the paper had, earlier in this same year, incurred costs of an action brought against Sharp by the Public Prosecutor for contempt of court. In that case the Company got off more lightly, but the whole cost of both cases cannot, one way and another, have been much less than £1,000. In 1928 to 1930 inclusive, the *New Statesman* Company's losses totalled £3,618. It seems clear that all of this is accounted for by the two legal cases. The losses were covered by loans to the Company made by Edward Whitley, Glynne Williams and Arnold Bennett. The long-suffering Board found it necessary to reproach Sharp, though quite gently, for his failure to realize that when dealing with the Law, common sense is usually out of place and invariably dangerous: a minute of the Board meeting on 30 October 1928 reads:

> Mr. Sharp attended in order to discuss with the Board the question of the tone of editorial comments and leading articles. The Board expressed the view that these comments and articles were sometimes characterized by violence of phrasing and desired that such violence be avoided in future.

If the *New Statesman*'s backers, all of whom were on the Board, were willing to stand heavy losses, it is natural to suppose that they insisted, at least, on directing policy as some return for their money. Nothing of the kind; it is as if the existence of the paper just as Sharp and Squire had made it was enough in itself to satisfy their social consciences. Sharp is quite clear about this:

> I have always thought it a little strange how many people there are who like to have a more or less expensive finger in some journalistic pie or other, without in the least wishing to dictate to the cook or even ask to see the menu in advance. The interest of the original Board of the Statesman Publishing Company in the conduct of the paper was, however, by no means that of the well-to-do dilettante, and the complete freedom which they always gave me was therefore the more remarkable. Apart from the general denunciations which G.B.S. occasionally felt moved to address to all his fellow directors, policy was scarcely even mentioned at the quarterly Board-meetings. I do not suppose that any young editor who was not also effective proprietor—as Scott of the *Manchester Guardian* and Strachey of the *Spectator*—had ever had so free a hand as I enjoyed. . . .

During the war it had become the practice for Squire to lunch with the Webbs in Grosvenor Road every Tuesday, and when MacCarthy was available he went too. These luncheons continued in the Twenties; Sharp was only occasionally one of the guests, which is curious and which I cannot explain. Sharp says that during these luncheons Webb, albeit Chairman of the Company and a regular contributor of unsigned articles and paragraphs to the paper every week for the first seven years of its life, 'was always careful to avoid even the appearance of seeking to direct general policy'. Webb no more tried to influence Sharp about politics than Squire and MacCarthy about the literary end of the paper. This deliberate and conscious non-interference was, indeed, carried so far that one cannot help suspecting that Sharp owed a good deal of his freedom to the forecasts of the experts who had said that the Webbs would do nothing *but* interfere. These cries had doubtless made the Webbs self-conscious, and I have already pointed out that they, especially Sidney, were of that very rare category of human beings who can correct their own faults by applying their intelligence to doing so.

Sharp's and the Webbs's care to ensure the paper's

independent 'image' went very far. When the first Labour Government was formed in 1924 Webb, who had become an M.P., was of course made a member of it. The connection between the Webbs and the paper was widely known, and inevitably the public assumed that the *New Statesman* was a Labour Party organ. It was not, it had never been, and it was not to be, except in so far as Fabians generally were turning towards the possibility of making the Labour Party their principal political instrument. But editorial disclaimers were ignored and criticism of the Labour Government in the *New Statesman* was apt to be denounced as disloyalty. Webb did his best to put an end to this nonsense by resigning first his Chairmanship and later his seat on the Board.

A major crisis of management arose in 1926 at the time of the General Strike. Policy, discussed later, having laid it down that the *New Statesman* should continue publication if it could, it remained to find a way of publishing, or rather of printing, it. John Roberts did so, thereby achieving a triumph which boosted the circulation—an advantage now that paper was cheaper—to a peak from which it fell, indeed, but never again to the old low level. Only two weekly journals appeared as usual during the strike, one being the *New Statesman;* the other was the *Feathered World*.

The *New Statesman* was normally printed by Speaights, a Union house, of course. In the event of a strike they would not be able to print the paper. The *New Statesman* bought its own newsprint, as is customary, and it had two weeks' supply in hand at the printer's. Before it was certain that there would be a strike Roberts was out scouring London in search of a small, non-union firm capable of printing something like the normal issue. He found what he was seeking in the house of Parsons & Baverstock whose works were in Wandsworth. Sharp, rather ungratefully, described it as a 'one-horse kind of establishment'. Roberts carried the supply of newsprint from Speaights in his car, running a gauntlet of pickets. If the Parsons & Baverstock imprint had been used their shop would have been picketed after the first 'blackleg' number of the paper had appeared; an agent's imprint was used to avoid this. The *New Statesman* which appeared in a printless week was smaller than usual and had fewer pages, but all its features were there, for a smaller size of typeface was used. Twelve thousand copies were printed and sold, the distribution being managed by hiring street vendors and by sending the paper to the suburbs and provinces in volunteers' cars. It should be added that the paper came out in uncompromising support of the strikers, while it condemned the instrument of the General Strike as such. Roberts was faced with the exasperating situation of a huge demand which he could not supply; 20,000 or 30,000 copies of the paper could have been sold quite easily, but Parsons & Baverstock could not have printed them in time even if the supply of paper could have been found. A second strike number was in train with Parsons & Baverstock when it was learned that the men would return to work on the coming Friday. Roberts thereupon moved the whole job back to Speaights, where the rest of the type-setting was done by apprentices—apprentices are not obliged to strike—and the paper was printed by the *Law Times*.

The General Strike left the *New Statesman* in a stronger position, not simply because the paper had appeared during the strike, but because the strike was a shock to opinion which had some effect on the small minority of people willing to admit that anything was wrong with the State and the people. The years of Baldwinian government were flat, stale and unprofitable. From the mid-Twenties until the mid-Thirties England was really dominated by the mean and chronically terrified spirit of the small businessman running an unviable shop on the border-line of bankruptcy, and pretending, with the encouragement of the *Daily Mail* (the, as it were, *Daily Express* of those days) that this was good and brave because it was private enterprise. Such enterprise is necessarily unenterprising, obsessively conservative, almost miserly; it has not the means to be anything else. In the context of twentieth-century technology and the needs of the huge populations of twentieth-century cities and industrial conurbations, only two kinds of undertaking have the means to be enterprising: the State, and the colossal industrial cartel with the resources of a small State. But in England the latter, dominated by men who ought to have been keeping suburban tobacconist shops, were precisely as unenterprising as the small men. It is from their inertia then, their complete failure to grow up into their century, that we suffer even now; it is because of what they were that we are being forced, now that we are short of means, to retool our industries, remake our railways and roads, and rehouse our population. True, there was a post-war boom in the Twenties; but it was, to a large extent, a boom in gambling; speculative builders began that hideous desecration of the countryside, unplanned, shoddy, mean and wasteful, which is an affliction to us now; in the United States, and to a lesser extent here and even in Europe, the money which the middle class had to spend was made less out of rising productivity than out of gambling, the great gambling mania which brought about the crash of 1929.

The key figure of this period is Ivar Kreuger of Swedish Match and Kreuger & Toll, who created literally hundreds of millions in paper credits by a long-sustained confidence trick playing upon the greed of individuals anxious to get rich quick without working, and on the desperate need of bankrupt governments. The hundreds of millions of dollars with which Kreuger juggled stood for nothing substantial: they were not wealth, they were simply paper. Yet because the need of the times was to render American wealth liquid so that it could be used to irrigate the money thirsty soil of Europe and so realize Europe's growth-potential; and because the bankers refused to do this, Kreuger was respected and admired even by such men as Maynard Keynes who, of course, had no idea that the Swede had over-reached himself catastrophically and was not merely a gambler but also a liar and a forger.

As the boom died out, millions in Britain began that long and seemingly hopeless period of bread-and-scrape starvation which was to leave them sullen, despairing, apathetic. This great body of workers, a standing reproach to the middle class, an almost inarticulate suffering mass, roused in that middle class the defence reaction of hatred, so that men who would have given their souls for work were abused as idlers, won't-works, dole-consumers existing parasitically on the decent hard-working middle class.

It is painful and humiliating even now to recall that

period of Baldwinism. On top of the pyramid of fear and hatred partly disguised by a wildness in the monied class which could be mistaken for gaiety, sat Baldwin with his pipe, his indolence, his cunning and his complacency. Biographers have been found to defend and even to praise him. I think it fair to say that he presided over and represents the one period in our history when the English, all their worst qualities to the fore and their best suppressed, were the reverse of admirable.

At such a time those who were concerned to see social changes, to alter all this, to sweep away the sheer nastiness necessarily engendered by small capitalism, and small-minded big capitalism, could not but feel that they were expending their spirit in a waste of shame. Why read the *New Statesman*? Why read anything but Edgar Wallace? The inertia of the middle class, the very class in which the men who hated what they saw around them were found, seemed eternal and immovable. Not until the excesses of the Bolshevik revolution had been in part forgotten was it possible to turn to Communism, which was what happened in the Thirties. But the General Strike, colossal blunder though it may have been, was also a strong stimulant force; it managed to wake up a few people who added themselves to the small minority of men who were aware that changes were overdue and who had studied the means of making them. For a few weeks 1926 had, as it were, a foretaste of the Thirties; as I hope to show, the *New Statesman* can be seen as the very symbol of the Thirties. Thus, with more people reading it than ever before and, even, more advertisers supporting it, we might almost say that the General Strike set Clifford Sharp's weekly firmly on its feet.

6

Policy in the Twenties

D URING the latter part of the war, political economy in
the *New Statesman* was almost entirely in the hands of
Sidney Webb, while foreign politics and international
affairs were dealt with by Ratcliffe, Ensor and Lewis
Namier. But at the end of and just after the war a new
influence began to work upon the character of the paper,
that of G. D. H. Cole. At the same time Sharp began to
make more use of a Fabian writer who was sound rather
than brilliant and who had worked with Beatrice Webb and
Sharp himself during the Minority Report campaign:
Mostyn Lloyd. It was as well that he did so, and almost as if
he foresaw his own decadence and was preparing someone
else to take control of the paper when drink had made him
incapable of exercising it. I do not suggest that this was
actually the case, there is no evidence that Sharp's alcoholism
began as early as this, although in fact nobody seems to know
when it did begin.

Both Cole and Lloyd played themselves in carefully,
contributing little and occasionally at first, and then, as they
learnt to accommodate themselves to new statesmanship and
to modify it in doing so, they were given more space by the
editor. Lloyd, however, was neither obliged to do much in the
way of accommodation nor did he cause the paper to grow;
for he might have been made-to-measure for what the *New
Statesman* had by 1919 become. He was a Fabian technician,
sound, extremely able and perhaps a little dull, although
some of his articles are lively enough. But Cole was one of the
half-dozen men who altered the paper, and caused it to grow.

A paper with as strong a character as the *New Statesman* is
resistant to change; but the kind of change, the kind of

growth of which it is capable is potential in it. That is to say, it cannot be brutally imposed from outside, say by a new editor, without serious damage to its character. Consequently, growth depends on finding the man who can realize its potential; the process is analogous to that whereby a good teacher brings out the qualities of a pupil, rather than that whereby a mechanic modifies an engine.

Mostyn Lloyd was a first-class leader-writer, clear, sharp and well informed. He was a Labour Party stalwart whose loyalty persisted despite his disillusionment. In conversation his tone on the subject of politics was ironical and his outlook pessimistic. He once—probably at the time of the infamous Nazi-Soviet Pact—remarked that 'anything is possible; nothing is likely'. He was completely disinterested and never asked for any kind of recognition. He kept the paper at a high standard when, during Sharp's bad times and later during Sharp's year of absence (see below), he was wholly responsible for it, maintaining its reputation as a model of integrity and clear thinking. He did this, moreover, without ever being recognized as Editor, on half-pay and as a part-time job. When, in due course, he was passed over and a young editor appointed to replace Sharp, Lloyd showed no jealousy and helped the new man more than anyone else could have done. In 1931 Lloyd was to go to Russia and return full of enthusiasm for the Revolution and with a vision of what our own Soviet State might be. 'I have seen the future, and it works!' He kept that faith until the massacre of the kulaks and the resultant famine in the U.S.S.R. Lloyd had, in fact, everything except enthusiasm, and it was enthusiasm that the paper now needed. If, as Mrs. Cole says in her *History of Fabian Socialism*, Lloyd was on the *New Statesman* staff from the beginning, I cannot find that he did much writing for it until just after the war, that is in 1919. Primarily a political economist he subsequently became head of the Ratan Tata Department of Social Science at the London School of Economics. He was, with the Coles, H. L. Beales, and G. R. Mitchison (later M.P.) a founder of ZIP, the Society, for Socialist Enquiry and Propaganda which, albeit very short-lived, had an important effect in revivifying the Fabian Society.

G. D. H. Cole was born in 1889, educated at St. Paul's and Balliol, and was a Fellow of Magdalen College, Oxford, from 1912 to 1919. His writings (excluding those admirable detective stories which he and Margaret Cole wrote together), from *The World of Labour* (1913) to the work he was doing at the time of his death and including his work for the *Manchester Guardian*, constitute, almost on their own, an encyclopaedia and dictionary of the Labour movement as well as a special socialist philosophy. As a journalist his first paper was *The Nation*, and he was writing for it at the beginning of the war. He continued to do so, but with increasing uneasiness. At the outbreak of the war he was in favour of fighting. But, like Robert Dell, the spectacle of war changed his mind; he began to feel that nothing could justify it and became a pacifist. In 1918 it seemed to him that *The Nation* was no longer his kind of paper. He ceased writing for it and transferred his allegiance to the *New Statesman*. He told me, shortly before his death, that he had done this because the *New Statesman* was more appropriate to his pacifism and socialism. This must certainly have been the case as to his socialism; but there is no sign that the *New Statesman* was any more pacifist in 1918 than it had been in 1914. Whatever some of its contributors may have believed, Sharp was too much of a tough-minded imperialist to believe that the war had ended war. He was, for example, perfectly ready to face resumption of the blockade if Germany went on prevaricating about signing the peace treaty.

The *New Statesman*'s policy of non-attachment to party not only made it more useful for Cole's purpose, it made him more valuable to the paper. He could have been an embarrassment to any editor with a definite party political attachment. And although by the end of the war the paper was moving towards a new policy, that of support for and if possible intellectual 'direction' of the Labour Party, it was still like the Fabians, behaving as if it might be possible to impose scientific economics on the old parties. Not until the early Twenties was it fully accepted that the likeliest political instrument of new statesmanship was the Labour Party. That this judgment was perfectly sound is self-evident now: the programme of legislation carried through by the Attlee administration in 1945-50 bears witness to that. In time this loose but definite alliance was to entail compromises; but immediately following the war an idealist like Cole could see the possibility without too much regard for the fact, in any case always accepted by Fabians, that politics is the art of the possible.

Cole was not a Marxist. His advocacy of Guild Socialism and his connection with Orage's 'syndicalism' have been described. His political master was Bakunin. And this fact, as well as his manner of giving expression to Bakunist ideas, was bound to be of enormous value to the *New Statesman*. For what Cole wanted and spent a great deal of his working life trying to get, was a policy which would reconcile the intellectual and emotional, the scientific and aesthetic, sides of British Socialism, the British Left in general. Such a policy might resolve the problem of that sometimes paralysing ambivalence—Socialist, yes; but *étatiste*, never!—which is apparent throughout the history of the *New Statesman*, as throughout the whole history of the Left in Britain.

A revolutionary movement revolts from tyranny towards freedom. But because Marxist discipline, entailed in breaking the economic tyranny of capital, is itself a social tyranny, Cole wanted nothing to do with it. There must be a way of getting the economic benefits, and the social benefits, of Socialism *without* conceding such power to the State as must impair the freedom of the individual. He detested the social consequences of large-scale industrialism and it really did not seem to him to make enough difference whether the master of that industry was the State or the capitalist. The history of the past fifty years has shown that he was quite right. But the point here is that his strong feelings about this appealed to the *New Statesman* reader, and to the much greater body of potential *New Statesman* readers who would have been prevented from becoming such by doctrinaire Marxism.*

* In a talk I had with Cole not long before he died he showed great interest in and asked a lot of questions about developments of small, light, cheap machine-tools for agriculture and horticulture, and their equivalents in industry. He saw in them a possible means of freeing the individual from excessively heavy physical toil *without* condemning him to the degrading influence of mass-production factory work. His ideal was, in fact, the small workshop of the Guild Socialist raised to a higher power of efficiency by machines not beyond the individual's means to buy and to operate.

In Cole, therefore, Sharp had found a man who could
stimulate into active growth one of the, as it were, dormant
buds on the body of new statesmanship. They could work
together because although Cole did not particularly like
Sharp, he admired him as an editor and above all as an
editorial strategist in his political purpose. He approved of
the way in which, during periods of social and political
calm, it was Sharp's deliberate practice to keep the paper
'moderate', at which times Mostyn Lloyd was his most
valuable assistant, so that, at every social or political crisis,
he could turn briskly Left, taking with him many of the
readers gathered in by his moderation. In these crises, the
Liberal contributors could be played down, the Socialists
given their heads. The result was very much what Sharp,
and behind him the Webbs, were aiming at: a growing body
of readers who, won over by a simple but nourishing diet of
sound common sense in politics and a somewhat richer
dessert of music, art and letters, were on hand to be fed a
redder meat when it became important that they hold Left-
wing opinions. With regard to the music, art and letters, it
was Cole's opinion that Sharp took a greater interest in that
section of the paper than his successor was to do, and that
Sharp was right. Mr. Leonard Woolf tells me that this was
not so, that Sharp took no interest at all in the literary end
of the *New Statesman*, leaving it entirely to MacCarthy. And
even Cole agreed that Sharp's interest was not what it
should have been, for in his opinion the literary editor ought
to have been 'a sincere and committed Socialist', which
MacCarthy never was. But from the point of view Sharp was
bound to take, that of an editor who wished to increase his
paper's influence, he was surely right. For there was a body
of readers who turned first to the back, not the front, of the
paper, who read MacCarthy, Squire and Gerald Gould,
above all Robert Lynd, whose unbroken series of essays were
not yet being signed 'Y.Y.', who admired Turner's music
criticism—W. J. Turner, who wrote on music for many
years in the paper—and who only thereafter glanced at the
politics in front; people who wanted to read Roger Fry on
painting, who enjoyed, as well they might, Belloc's series of
'Miscellanies' in the early Twenties, and the first of S. L.

Bensusan's articles on farming and the countryside which were to continue, at first irregularly and later as a regular feature, into the Thirties and which were, I think, the best thing of their kind until Lawrence Easterbrook's work in this field. Other readers were gained and held by the very great improvement in novel reviewing introduced with Rebecca West, who could be very entertaining ('. . . D'Annunzio . . . passed out of the world of letters into an adventure as large and spurious as his work') and who was always enthusiastic whether *pro* or *con*. Her review, for example, of Lawrence's *Women in Love*, when it appeared, is not mere reviewing, it is criticism at a high level. Philip Guedalla, too, had a following, and the frequent trials given to young poets and journalists made the paper stimulating in the first half of this decade. It is quite certain that the *New Statesman* would never have had this following had the Editor appointed his critical writers for their Socialism. Socialist critics of the arts are apt to find themselves preaching only to the converted, and those who can attract the uncommitted—a John Berger or a Kenneth Tynan—are very rare birds indeed.

From the first months of its life the *New Statesman* had been able to rely on a page or two, sometimes more, being written by its readers. The challenge of its editorial pages and the quality of its readership attracted letters which were very often as distinguished as, and less temperate than, the writing which had provoked them. All newspapers and weeklies attract readers' letters: but only in the case of two or three are these letters anything more than a sort of safety valve for the feelings of such readers as feel strongly about something or other. The *New Statesman* became very quickly one of the few papers whose Correspondence columns are almost as important as any other part of the paper. These columns were particularly valuable because, new statesmanship in all its fields being provocative, letters were apt to be from readers who had as high a standing, on the other side of the question, as the writer they challenged.

Under Sharp, moreover, an unwritten rule which tends to exclude a paper's contributors from its correspondence columns except when they are required to answer a criticism, was disregarded, so that these columns became to some extent the part of the paper where its own writers conducted debates, and even serious rows, in public, which were frequently entertaining and rarely unedifying. An excellent example of this was the epistolary row between Bernard Shaw and Desmond MacCarthy after the latter had described Shaw's delineation of Christ's character in one of his Prefaces as a blasphemous disgrace. MacCarthy accused Shaw of modelling Christ on himself. Shaw did not altogether deny it; he seemed to think that there wasn't much difference.

Letters from readers were not only in response to the new statesmanship of contributors: they also broadened and deepened the field of that quality by bringing a new topic within its influence. New statesmanship became less and less confined to the, as it were, professional new statesmen and spread to include a body of several thousand people, readers of the paper who shared a common spirit, a common approach to the day's problems and movements. It was this process which brought into existence a sort of entity composed of the *New Statesman* and its readers and which, in the following decade, Kingsley Martin was to transform into the social and political expression-symbol for a generation. Neither Sharp, nor Lloyd, nor even Cole could have wrought that transformation; but they prepared it.

There is, of course, a danger in this kind of cosy get-together between a paper and its readers. A certain smugness may be generated. On the whole Sharp avoided this; he was never complacent, and, unlike H. W. Massingham, he never, in his approach to his readers, implied that famous toast, *Here's to us, there's none like us*. Yet it might almost have been justified: a few hours spent reading the *New Statesman* correspondence columns for the Twenties leaves one with the impression that *New Statesman* readers foresaw every political and social problem which would be important in the next decade and sketched solutions for most of them.

Robert Lynd's achievement in the *New Statesman* must be unequalled. During the war and for some years thereafter his brilliant and entertaining essays remained unsigned; for a short while they were signed with two X's, like beer. Thereafter and until his death they appeared above the signature

'Y.Y.' Quite apart from its intrinsic value as literature Lynd's writing contributed to enlarge that imaginary envelope I call new statesmanship and thus to make room within it for people who were not seducible by direct political or economic arguments. His many hundreds of essays on every conceivable subject, while they were entertainment of a very high order were also and incidentally and because of the essayist's character and attitude to life, a course of treatment in intelligent goodwill. If you turned to Lynd every week and enjoyed what he wrote, you were apt to be persuaded into a state of mind and spirit such that you would accept the practical means advocated by Lynd's colleagues for realizing the kind of world his writing implied as desirable. There was, of course, no deliberate policy in this: it was a more or less fortuitous by-product of Sharp's and Lloyd's editorial 'instinct'. In one minor respect Lynd was a not untroublesome contributor; his essays were received in manuscript, not typescript, and as time went on his writing became so bad that the printers were obliged to detail a particular compositor to read it and set it in type; and to charge 1s. 6d. a folio extra for their trouble.

I have already dealt with the way in which John Roberts handled the difficulties entailed by the General Strike. Sharp had no hesitation whatever in bringing out the paper when Roberts made it possible to do so, for nothing could justify the silencing of opinion, and especially of opinion favourable to the strikers.

> Some of our readers seemed inclined to mumble the words 'scab labour' when they first set eyes on that issue, but when they had read it we obtained forgiveness. For we had no hesitation in supporting the strikers without reserve. We had always, of course, condemned the weapon of the General Strike on the ground that it was certain to break in the hands of anybody who attempted to use it in the furtherance of an industrial dispute.* But if the Union leaders had been unwise the conduct of the Government had in our opinion been criminally foolish, negligent and provocative. The

* Not quite true. Twenty years before this was written Shaw and Webb had conducted a debate in the *New Statesman* in which, while Shaw held that the General Strike was not a possible weapon, Webb argued that in certain conditions it could be effective.

section of the Cabinet which, under the leadership of Mr.
Churchill, wanted the strike, in order to crush it and
hamstring the Unions as effectively as possible in the reaction
they foresaw, proved too strong for the more moderate group,
and so the conflict was quite unnecessarily precipitated.

On that ground alone our sympathies if not our judgment
were wholly with the strikers, but our attitude had older and
deeper foundations than that. For although in the political
sphere we had never found it possible to place great confidence in the wisdom or breadth of view of the Labour caucus,
we yet held that in the case of a strike or lockout in the
industrial field on any really large scale the men are always
found upon investigation to be at least morally in the right,
by any acceptable code of social ethics. It was might, however, not right that ruled in such matters when Baldwin
ruled.

In the weeks before the strike Sharp and Cole in
'Comments', and Mostyn Lloyd in his two-part 'Economic
Consequences of Mr. Churchill' were foreseeing what was
going to happen, and rather hopelessly urging the only
policy which could prevent the disaster. It was in 1926 that
the paper carried every week for some months Low's brilliant
pencil drawings beautifully reproduced on special paper of
men at the top. The issue of 1 May carried his Winston
Churchill; it was not reassuring to those who hoped for a
peaceful settlement of the dispute. The following number,
8 May, was the famous strike issue. It has the usual format
and apart from faulty inking is not ill printed. The leader,
'This Unnecessary Strike', puts the blame for the strike on
Baldwin and his Government but, new statesmanly as ever,
condemns those men in the *Daily Mail* composing room who,
by refusing to print a leader which Sharp described as 'a very
harmless, commonplace sort of article', gave the anti-
working-class militants in the Government the excuse they
were seeking to provoke the strike. Sharp's leader contains
one splendid example of new statesmanship:

> On the general merits of the coal dispute we certainly think
> that the mineowners are in the wrong. They have shown
> themselves a very stubborn and stupid set of men. But they
> have only acted after all as most owners act in trade disputes.

That is to say they stood out for impossible terms, knowing them to be impossible, but unwilling to make concessions until the real bargaining should begin.

It was this sort of recognition of facts, this cold appraisal of motives, which was, and is, foreign to the rest of our Press, which does not resist the temptation to introduce emotion and to attribute moral qualities to purely economic acts. It was this kind of thing which, while it ensured the loyalty of an élite body of readers, almost certainly checked the paper's growth beyond a certain point. For the English are a subtle, devious and fact-evading people.

'Comment' that week was in the same spirit. The T.U.C. was curtly rebuked for the idiotic short-sightedness of suppressing the newspapers (Sharp). The fact that the whole working class was genuinely loyal to the miners in their predicament was made clear (Lloyd). The nature of that predicament was set out clearly in figures: the miners were to lose from one-third to a half of their already inadequate wage; they were, in short, to starve, slowly if at work, quickly if on strike (Lloyd). The fact that the stoppage in the mines was not a strike but a lockout was established (Sharp). Robert Lynd's essay made fun of the B.B.C. contribution to the emergency, a talk on Ants and Grasshoppers. Only one article in the front half of the paper had nothing to do with the strike, and that was the Rome correspondent's long and amusing exposure of the hollowness of Fascist 'prosperity' and his witty mockery of the Duce's bombastic goings on. The 'Miscellany' was by Belloc, MacCarthy reviewed Komisarjevsky's production of Gogol's *The Government Inspector* at the Barnes Theatre. 'Books in General', now being written by MacCarthy as 'Affable Hawk', appeared as usual. In fact nothing was missing from the paper except the Low drawing for that week.

Two weeks later the strike was, of course, still the principal topic. Under the somewhat startling headline 'Should We hang Mr. Churchill?' the paper revealed that while Baldwin, Birkenhead and Steel-Maitland worked hard to avert the strike, Churchill and Neville Chamberlain, sabotaging these peace efforts, had done all in their power to provoke it.

In 1926 began that process which was to bring the *New Statesman* into the doldrums of a tedious calm which endured for several years: this was the withdrawal of Sharp's interest in the paper and its replacement by that of Mostyn Lloyd, who became *de facto* though never official Editor. This began, of course, slowly; there was no sharp break. It was first noticeable in the fact that much which Sharp would formerly have written himself was now written by Lloyd or by Cole or by S. K. Ratcliffe. The reason for this was, in one word, drink. But one word is not enough. It took several years for drink to reduce Sharp to a state of uselessness, and his drinking was so discreet and gentlemanly that nobody realized what was happening until Sharp was a wreck. The reason probably is that Sharp was not soaking in secret like a real alcoholic; he was moving in with a set of people whose manners were such that his drinking was covered by theirs— the Asquith set. Asquith himself was not a strictly sober man, but he drank in style. The story of his reply to a heckler at a public meeting who apologized for an interruption by saying that he was drunk, is well known: 'It's all right, my friend, so am I.' There is all the difference in the world between what one may call frivolous drinking, and serious drinking. Sharp did not have the gift of being frivolous, but he found Margot Asquith amusing and he seems to have been seduced by the easy frivolousness of her set. At all events his drinking did not strike anyone as excessive, and had you suggested to any man of his acquaintance that drink was his trouble, he would have replied that you were wrong and that Sharp's trouble was women.

A curious by-product of Sharp's involvement with the Asquith set was that it contributed to a temporary reversal of political roles for the *New Statesman* on the one hand and, on the other, *The Nation*. Massingham, disgusted with Lloyd George, was conducting a persistent campaign against him, invariably referring to that statesman as 'Mr. George'; and as he was employing, at the same time, Leonard Woolf, Hobson, and Harold Laski among his contributors, the whole tone of *The Nation* had become more or less Socialist. Meanwhile, Sharp, under Asquithian influence, was giving the *New Statesman* a distinctly Liberal tone.

It may perhaps have been Sharp's growing carelessness which led to his writing, in the *New Statesman* of 28 January 1928, a phrase which involved the paper in its first serious legal trouble and a major financial crisis, for very few luxuries in Britain are as ruinously dear as justice. The facts are as follows: Dr. Marie Stopes had been advertising her birth-control service in the *Morning Post*, although one would have supposed its aristocratic readers less in need of such advice and devices than those of humbler newspapers. Her advertising was suddenly cancelled by the paper. It is not clear who was responsible for this, for the editor does not seem to have known anything much about it. Dr. Stopes—readers may need reminding that her doctorate was for chemistry and that it was as a feminist that she became the evangelist of birth-control—then did something which Sharp later condemned as silly: she wrote to the Duke of Northumberland, who was proprietor of the *Morning Post*, to complain of the cancellation of her advertising and to suggest that Roman Catholic influence had been at work. The Duke forwarded her letter to the editor of the newspaper. This gentleman, H. A. Gwynne, of a distinguished journalistic family, must have been excessively touchy, for he immediately started legal proceedings against her for libel on the ground that his integrity as an editor had been impugned. The case was tried by Mr. Justice Avory and the editor was awarded a verdict and £200 damages. Dr. Stopes considered that justice had miscarried and brought her complaint to Clifford Sharp. He agreed with her and wrote this in 'Comment':

> We cannot help regarding the verdict given this week in the libel action brought by the Editor of the *Morning Post* against Dr. Marie Stopes as a substantial miscarriage of justice. We are not at all in sympathy with Dr. Stopes' work or aims, but prejudice against those aims ought not to be allowed to influence a court of justice in the manner in which they appeared to influence Mr. Justice Avory in his summing-up.

Sharp then gave the facts of the case and went on as follows:

> We do not think this action ought to have been brought. Dr. Stopes' letter was foolish, partly because it is always foolish to write to a proprietor behind a trusted editor's back

and partly because it is always foolish to talk of 'Catholic plots'—or of 'Bolshevik plots' for that matter. But Dr. Stopes obviously intended no reflection upon the Editor personally—did not even know who he was. And from what we ourselves know of newspaper practice there could be no injurious reflection upon him, first because he may never have heard of the censoring of the advertisement, and second because the suggestion that a man is influenced by Catholic ideas of right and wrong is surely not an 'injurious reflection'. That certain advertisers threaten to boycott any paper which accepts Dr. Stopes' advertisements is a fact for which we can vouch. Their exclusion may, therefore, be no more than a matter of commercial policy, implying no reflection at all upon an editor—since he may not even know what has happened. The serious point in this case, however, is that an individual owning to such views as those of Dr. Stopes cannot apparently hope for a fair hearing in a court presided over by Mr. Justice Avory—and there are so many Avorys.

In Britain a newspaper is free to criticize the administration of justice and therefore the verdicts of the courts. But it was held that Sharp had not merely done this, he had accused Avory of colouring his summing-up with a personal prejudice against birth-control and the defendant's activities. To anyone reading the summing-up today this imputation is understandable. But it constituted, unless it could be effectively denied, a contempt of court of the worst possible kind, and on 6 February the Lord Chief Justice—'on the application of the Attorney-General granted a Rule against Mr Clifford Dyce Sharp calling upon him to show cause in respect of an article, etc., etc. . . .' Sharp was tried by the L.C.J., Hewart, and Justices Shearman and Branson. The Attorney-General appeared for the prosecution, and Sharp was defended by W. A. Jowitt, K.C. Jowitt took the only line open to him: he admitted that there had been criticism of the verdict in *Gwynne* v. *Stopes* but argued that this was well within the rights of the Press; there was no intentional imputation against Avory's integrity; if it was felt that there was such an imputation, it had been quite accidental, a matter of careless language, no more. He apologized, in Sharp's name, very amply, and read an affidavit of apology signed by Sharp, for this 'accident'.

Jowitt: If your Lordship thinks that the language is so un-happy as to make it possible to read that imputation into it, then I desire to say in the fullest, frankest and most extreme manner that I can, that I on behalf of my client express my deep regret to the Court and to Mr. Justice Avory.

L.C.J. How if we should think, Mr. Jowitt, that the only reasonable meaning is the meaning which you repudiate?

Jowitt: Still more do I desire then to make my apology in that respect quite independent of the question whether this is or is not within the rule as to contempt of Court. If your Lordships think that people might take that view, *a fortiori* if your Lordships think that people ought to take that view, the apology holds good. The point I make is this: that however infelicitous that language it was not the intention of the writer of the article to convey any such meaning.

Jowitt's authorities were selected to show that when a case is over judge and jury are given over to criticism. And that that criticism is still such 'even though it is harsh criticism, even though it is infelicitous criticism, even though it is unfair criticism'. The Attorney-General argued that all his learned friend's authorities were beside the point, nobody was denying an editor the right to criticize a verdict, but Sharp had called the judge's integrity in question.

A.-G. . . .To suggest that a learned judge was so steeped in prejudice and bias that he was unable fairly to try the case would be just as much an attack on his authority and an undermining of his influence as to say that he had deliberately allowed his mind to be affected.

L.C.J. One could imagine that it might be said that it was even more so.

A.-G. Exactly.

L.C.J.: Did not somebody define a gentleman as a person who was never rude unless he intended to be so?

A.-G.: Yes, that is quite true. Looking at the article in the light of that distinction there are only two paragraphs which I think I need trouble about. I agree that the whole centre part of the article is criticism and legitimate criticism; but the second sentence and the last sentence . . . in my respectful submission it is saying in terms: 'If you come before this judge and hold the kind of views which Dr. Stopes holds you cannot have your case fairly heard. The Judge, whether

deliberately or unconsciously, has a mind so steeped in prejudice and bias on this kind of topic, that he cannot and
will not give a fair hearing to a case which is brought by an
individual holding these views.'

Hewart, in his judgment, which was not deferred and
which the *New Statesman* subsequently described as a 'brilliantly elusive extempore judgment', held that Sharp's
words had been free from ambiguity: 'The words mean what
they say and say very plainly, that persons who hold certain
views cannot hope for a fair hearing in a Court presided over
by the learned Judge who is named.' Had Sharp's apology
not been unconditional, 'it would have been necessary to
take a very serious view of the case'. He then quoted Russell's
judgment in *The Queen* v. *Gray* as the principle applicable in
such cases, 'fortunately very rare', and concluded that, 'We
have no doubt that this paragraph does constitute a contempt
of Court':

> The gravamen of that matter is not in the smallest degree
> that it is a reflection upon the individual judge, but that by
> tending to lower his authority it does tend to interfere with
> the due administration of justice; and if we come to the
> conclusion that that attack, that contempt, going as it does
> clearly beyond the limits of any criticism which could be
> called legitimate, was deliberately intended by the writer
> who happens to be also the editor of this periodical, it is
> quite clear to us that the only proper conclusion of the matter
> would be that he would be committed to prison for contempt
> of Court. . . .

The L.C.J. then considered the nature and meaning of
Sharp's apology and gave him the benefit of the doubt:
Sharp's words had meant what they said but perhaps he did
not intend them to have that meaning. 'In these circumstances we order and adjudge that Mr. Clifford Dyce Sharp
is guilty of the contempt referred to, and feeling as we do
that if the true analysis of this case were such as to exhibit its
graver aspect, the only proper course would have been
committal to prison, we refrain from imposing a fine and
we order Mr. Sharp to pay all the costs of these proceedings.'

The Lord Chief Justice perhaps had in mind that those
costs would be sufficient punishment. However, in the

event, Sharp's carelessness or recklessness cost the paper only a few hundred pounds. It was his other major blunder against the sensitive shins of the law dealt with in Chapter 5 that might have ruined it.

That loss of high spirits, that settling down into a routine of sound but unexciting journalism which I have referred to, became more marked towards the end of the decade. It was not owing solely to Clifford Sharp's absorption into the social round of the Asquith set and his increasingly heavy drinking. It was also a product of the Labour Party's rise to power. True, the *New Statesman* was not tied to the Labour Party, it did not yet openly accept that Party as the chosen instrument for the realization of Socialism. But it was increasingly difficult to avoid such acceptance. While the Party was small and confined by its smallness to opposition in Parliament, it could be an ally in dissent when its policy agreed with the *New Statesman*'s, and ignored when it did not. Even so, its very existence entailed on the paper a measure of restraint, of compromise. I will try to make this clear.

In one of a collection of essays published as *The Yogi and the Commissar*, Arthur Koestler contrasts the situation of the Left-wing intellectuals in nineteenth-century Russia, treading virgin soil as they preached Socialism to the peasants and were martyred, for their faith, and that of the western intelligentsia who

> ... found no virgin fields to plough, no natural allies to realize their aspirations. According to Marxist theory the intelligentsia was to join the ranks of the working class and to become their strategists and tacticians. . . . But from the middle of the 19th century onwards, the workers of central and western Europe had rapidly developed their own organizations, parties, trade unions, produced their own leaders, above all their own bureaucracy—men with iron wills and wooden heads. In an age of accelerated development the Fourth Estate had become stagnant much quicker than the Third in its time, and without even ascending to power.

Well, by 1929 the Labour Party had twice ascended to power, albeit very partially and precariously. The *New Statesman* was at once bound to support it and obliged to criticize it for those stupid blunders and that craven falling short of Socialist solutions which were owing to the wooden-headedness that Beatrice Webb had discovered even before Mr. Koestler. But in this criticism the paper had to pull its punches, for, after all, the Labour Party was the best hope for the future of scientific government. A new kind of crippling ambivalence was apparent in the paper's attitude; it was beginning to hedge a little. Koestler, in the same book, sneers at the *New Statesman* of the Thirties for being the apologist of that Stalinism which he foreran Khrushchev in condemning. But this was a consequence of the necessary struggle against the fostering, by the Right, of that working-class stagnation which Koestler regrets, and in which the Right was quick to see the best hope for its own retention of power. That, however, belongs to a later chapter.

The closer involvement in the compromises of practical politics entailed by support, however 'unofficial', for the Labour Party also increased the difficulties of keeping the fore- and hind-quarters of the *New Statesman* in step. There are moments in the paper's career when it looks all too like a pantomime horse, not one integrated creature but two covered by an unconvincing skin which absurdly fails to conceal the struggles of the fore- and hind-quarters to get away from each other and dash off in opposite directions. In the early years of the paper's life, the politicians of the front half could be exactly the same kind of high-minded and high-browed people as the critics of the rear half. All were writing from the same point of view and from the same humanist education. But when the Labour Party became the instrument of Socialist ideas, an expedient common touch had to be used. It was better to eschew judgments so sharp and clear that they would bounce off wooden heads, to be less uncompromisingly scientific and a shade more rhetorically woolly. To use Koestler's analysis, in the front of the paper the working-class bureaucrats had to be given a sop; in the back half the intelligentsia could still be its uncompromising self.

Sharp was not, never had been, the man to cope with this dichotomy. Nor was Mostyn Lloyd. Had G. D. H. Cole become Editor of the paper at this point, as might easily have happened, the *New Statesman* would certainly have become an integrated being again, with fore- and hind-quarters united in one spirit. But it would never, in that case, have become what it did, the voice and symbol for a whole generation of 'intellectuals', using the word in a very wide sense and not to designate an élite. Cole's readers would have been an élite all right, but a politically as well as artistically 'exclusive' one, because Cole was no compromiser, no politician. The curious fact is that the astonishing *essor* of the *New Statesman* which was to follow the period of stagnation was to be in some measure a consequence of its new Editor's personal ambivalence, a state of mind and spirit which matched what the paper's had to be if it was to conquer a wider readership.

It was in 1929 that the first move was made by *The Nation* towards that amalgamation with the *New Statesman* which was to coincide with Kingsley Martin's advent and so to give his editorial genius—I use the word advisedly—more raw material to work with. The preliminary advance which *The Nation*, in the person of J. M. Keynes, made to Arnold Bennett* was, however, conditional. A united *New Statesman and Nation* would have to bear the label 'Liberal Party'. To this Sharp would not agree. Sharp, Roberts and the Board considered that to carry any party label would be against the paper's principles; Roberts, moreover, was of opinion that it would be bad for business. The offer to amalgamate was refused.

* Possibly to keep it unofficial, but Bennett negotiated, with the Board's permission.

7

The New Statesman and Nation:
Kingsley Martin

THE period of Clifford Sharp's dominion over the *New
Statesman* ended approximately with the decade of the
Twenties. Thereafter, the paper was to be dominated
by Kingsley Martin; it is convenient to say something of his
antecedents and advent in this place.

Kingsley Martin was born in Hereford in 1897.

His father was a Congregational Minister who later
became a Unitarian and whose book, *An Impossible Parson*,
throws some light on Kingsley Martin's training. Basil
Martin fought his way out of Calvinism, became in effect a
free-thinker whose faith was in the Christian ethic. He
offended the good people of Hereford, where he worked, by
his pacifism during the Boer War and by leading the newly
founded Labour Party in the Hereford 'local Parliament'.
Kingsley Martin grew up expecting to be always in the
minority, the minority of the righteous, and to be always on
the losing side in the battle against the Establishment. In
1913, when the *New Statesman* was being founded, Basil
Martin moved to Finchley, and Kingsley was sent to Mill
Hill School where he at first made an effort to conform, even
in the matter of the Officers' Training Corps, but he could
not keep it up and in his last year at school was a conscientious objector. On those grounds he was given, in 1916,
exemption from military service, but in 1917 he joined the
Friends' Ambulance Unit and for eighteen months he served,
first in a hospital at home, later on a hospital train in France.
His experience of attending to war wounds, especially after

the German offensive in March 1918, strengthened his inherited pacifism.

In 1919 Martin took up a scholarship he had won to Magdalene College, Cambridge, where he arrived at the same time as many other relatively elderly undergraduates, among them P. M. S. Blackett, men who got more out of Cambridge than was usual, because they were older and had some experience of war; several of them were to become distinguished in various fields. He became a member of a group which supported the Union for Democratic Control (U.D.C.), read hard, was befriended by Lowes Dickinson, got to know J. M. Keynes and other well-known King's men. He did spectacularly well in Honours History finals, which he always holds to be no more, at Cambridge, than a preparation for the higher journalism. The next years were spent as a Bye-Fellow of Magdalene, doing Workers' Educational Association lecturing, tutoring, and following a line of research. The year 1922-23 was spent at Princeton where Kingsley Martin wrote his first book, *The Triumph of Lord Palmerston*; it was a significant book, for it is a study of the way in which public opinion, influenced by a false image of the situation presented by the Press and by the opinion of a popular minister, can be turned against common sense to favour war. With this book he had a *succès d'estime*, but it did not make his fortune. It was presented as a thesis for a Fellowship at King's, Cambridge; it did not win him the Fellowship, which went to Blackett, but Keynes had had to read the thesis, was impressed by it, and having just bought —in association with a group of Summer School Liberals— *The Nation*, he asked Martin to review books for that journal.

Meanwhile, Kingsley Martin had made friends with Harold Laski; it was a friendship which was to be a very close one, continuing until Laski's death and rounded off by Kingsley Martin's biography, *Harold Laski*. This friendship introduced Kingsley Martin into the London School of Economics where, in 1924, while still doing some teaching at Cambridge, he became first part-time and then assistant lecturer to Laski in the Political Science department. He remained at the L.S.E. until 1928.

In the vacation following the General Strike in 1926
Martin wrote a small book on the subject of the strike (*The
General Strike*). Among those who read it was C. P. Scott who,
on the strength of it, invited the author to come to Manchester and work on the *Manchester Guardian* as a leader writer.
The salary offered was £1,000 a year and Kingsley Martin
might have been excused for saying *il n'y a pas de refus*. In
point of fact he might have hesitated, but he was not very
comfortable under Beveridge's directorship of the L.S.E. In
his book on the General Strike he had denigrated the Coal
Commission of which Beveridge was a member, and Beveridge had not been pleased. Moreover, the book had led
Beveridge to feel that Kingsley Martin was more likely to
make a good journalist than a dedicated teacher. The parting
was, therefore, an easy one. There is, however, no doubt that
the man who recreated and became identified with the *New
Statesman* might have had an academic career; the Chair now
graced by Professor D. W. Brogan at Cambridge might have
been Kingsley Martin's; and at a later date he was approached
by Evans of Aberystwyth University with the suggestion
that he might accept the Chair of International Affairs
subsequently held by E. H. Carr.

Thus, in 1928, Kingsley Martin found himself living in
Manchester, earning £800 a year—he had preferred to
sacrifice £200 on condition of being allowed to spend two
months of every year out of Manchester. He very soon
discovered that although Scott had drawn him into the
Manchester Guardian fold, he distrusted his new leader
writer's politics. Nor was that the worst; Kingsley Martin
discovered that he had neither the knowledge nor the skill
which Scott had supposed him to have. *Manchester Guardian*
leader writers were omniscient and godlike men, needing
no contract with mortals to know all about their affairs;
they lived in the suburbs of Manchester, they read all
the daily papers, they came to the office late in the after-
noon, wrote their leaders out of their heads, and having
thus provided the world with a blue-print for tomorrow,
went home again. During a few probationary weeks before
being officially ordained, as it were, the acolyte had managed this ritual very well. But it had been by sheer fortunate

accident that, in those weeks, he had happened to find subjects he could deal with, and on the strength of his success he was received into the hierarchy with a three-year contract. Only then did he discover his own want of the necessary experience and the relative uselessness of the academic stuff with which his mind was stored and perhaps overcrowded. And only then did Scott seem to realize that he had laid his hands on a heretic; in short, that Kingsley Martin was a Socialist, though rather of the sentimental than the doctrinaire variety.

The reason for Scott's misunderstanding must be sought, I think, in the nature of the Socialism to which Kingsley Martin had been drawn at the university; it had given his writings an anti-State colour quite congenial to Scott's liberal eye. Upon his arrival at Cambridge, Kingsley Martin had at first been happier than he had ever been in his life; like thousands of other young men he relished the joy of sporting his oak as a symbol of independence; he told himself that he was now his own master and could do just as he liked for three years. This feeling, combined with the intellectual excitement generated by Cambridge in the early Twenties and the relief of being civilized after years in uniform, went to his head. He did not know what he was about; he was like a dog in a fair, friendly, bustling, dashing into everything, his state of mind a mixture of timidity and excessive assurance. He did not immediately recognize antipathy among the people he frequented, and he was hurt when he did discover himself unwelcome. Perhaps because of his poverty (he saved the train fare to Cambridge and did his travelling on a bicycle), he needed to believe that everyone liked and wanted him. He did believe it; and the smallest rebuff toppled him into the depths of despair. Again and again his own candour, not to say simple-mindedness, betrayed him into the company of men who did not like him and who were not really congenial to him.

But all this changed when he discovered a set of people who felt and thought as he did and who liked and accepted him. The ideas of these people were soon influencing his own. But the Socialism of his chosen set was dominated by the ideas of Eric Gill and G. D. H. Cole: they were by no means orthodox, not such as were propagated by Sidney Webb and by the Fabians generally. Cole and his friends distrusted the State as much as any Liberal could do, and they were busy trying to devise means, social, political and economic, which could be used to install Socialism without elevating the State to omnipotence. Either such ideas were congenial to Kingsley Martin or the pleasure and relief of finding himself accepted into a set of men including some of outstanding brilliance made them so. Nor was it only in Cole's version of trade union Socialism or Gill's version of craft Socialism that he encountered this modified Marxism; Harold Laski was taking a similar line and developing an appropriate legalistic theory. Thus there was, in Kingsley Martin's own writing, none of that Marxist State-worship which was and is anathema to Liberals and which would have been repulsive to C. P. Scott.

On the *Manchester Guardian* Kingsley Martin worked with Malcolm Muggeridge and with F. A. Voigt in a period made difficult for all the leader writers and for Ted Scott, heir to the editorship, by the fact that C. P. Scott was too old for his work; he refused to give up the power he had for so long enjoyed, but his exercise of it had been made whimsical by old age. But although Kingsley Martin never felt at home on the *Manchester Guardian* and had an uneasy feeling that he was not earning his pay, his three years were valuable. When he came to Manchester he had been full of admirable sentiments, but he had no thought-out position. Three years of leader-writing taught him to convert feelings into ideas and to embody ideas in policies.

While these things were happening to Kingsley Martin the *New Statesman* was saved from drifting, the condition in which Clifford Sharp's increasing alcoholism must have left it, by Mostyn Lloyd who set it on a course and steadily kept it there, and who had neither the time, the nature nor the inclination to indulge in journalistic adventures. In the Twenties Kingsley Martin had some acquaintance with several new statesmen but none with their journal, except as a reader: he had worked under Lloyd at the L.S.E. and had been introduced to Sharp at a Bloomsbury party given to celebrate Thomas Earp's appointment as *New Statesman* art critic.

Had Mostyn Lloyd not been the kind of man he was, he could not have been head of an L.S.E. department and also editor of the *New Statesman*. He accomplished this feat by running the paper on tramlines. Monday afternoons were spent planning the week's paper and arranging for it to be written. The routine arrangement included a telephone call to G. D. H. Cole to discuss Cole's economic or political contribution for that week. Science articles by Lens, country or farming articles by S. L. Bensusan, and natural history or biology articles by J. Arthur Thomson, were kept in stock ahead of requirement so that there was never any rush or last-minute difficulty about them. A stock of 'Miscellanies' was likewise kept ahead of requirement. Turner's and MacCarthy's articles were apt to be late and there might sometimes be a last-minute scramble about a book review or a play critique. A certain amount of anxiety was entailed by the journalistic eccentricities of Robert Lynd. He was always late with his copy and it was always illegible; but this weekly essay signed Y.Y. was of the utmost importance to the paper; it is certainly the case that a very large body of readers took the *New Statesman* for no other reason than to read Y.Y. Lynd used to arrive at the office in a taxi, either bringing his copy with him or prepared to write his essay on a corner of somebody's desk; he wrote a top line the width of the paper and each subsequent line a little shorter so that the last line on the sheet consisted of one word. As nobody in the office could read what he had written, but only the compositor employed by Speaights the printers, the Editor first saw the essay in galley proof. Lloyd would be at the office for a couple of hours on Tuesdays and Wednesdays, spending the rest of those days at the L.S.E.

It was possible, by these methods, to run a weekly paper of the highest standards and Lloyd did so; there was nothing wrong with the thinking or writing of the *New Statesman* in the later Twenties. But it was monotonous and to me it seems dull. These faults did not damn it, for a reason which I discussed in Chapter 1: there is a body of people in England who are perfectly prepared to be bored at regular intervals if their boredom is in a good cause; in fact it is probable that if what they are reading is not dull it is suspect. Dullness is associated with soundness, it reassures the earnest man of goodwill; and the amusing political journalist, a Shaw for example, or a Muggeridge, although he gives pleasure to his readers is apt to be shrugged off as frivolous. But the body of people in question is a strictly limited one and it is very unlikely that had the *New Statesman* continued long in Lloyd's hands it would ever have sold more than 10,000 copies a week.

After Kingsley Martin had been on the *Manchester Guardian* for two and a half of his three years, C. P. Scott retired and left Ted Scott in charge. He, shortly after becoming editor, wrote Kingsley Martin a letter drawing attention in the most friendly and tactful way to the incompatibility between the paper and its leader writer and suggesting that Kingsley Martin had better keep his eyes open for another job. This letter, although it contained, perhaps, nothing which Kingsley Martin did not know already, upset him badly, for it was written confirmation of his own sense of failure. He no doubt felt a certain irritation with the Scotts; they had seduced him from his academic career, and were now preparing to abandon him when it was no longer possible to resume that career without suffering, all his life, from the loss of three years at a most important time. He went to London with little idea of what sort of job to seek and there he picked up a rumour that Clifford Sharp was relinquishing the editorship of the *New Statesman* and that a new Editor would be appointed. It seemed to him probable that either Mostyn Lloyd or G. D. H. Cole would be offered the job and certain that one of them would take it; but somebody suggested that there was, in fact, a chance for him, and he let J. M. Keynes know that he was free. He knew that Keynes and Leonard Woolf, literary editor of *The Nation*, were his friends and he had worked with them when he was book-reviewing for *The Nation* while he was at the L.S.E. He returned to Manchester and there he found that this was true, for Ted Scott had received a letter from Arnold Bennett, the most active director of the *New Statesman*, asking Scott whether he would be prepared to recommend Kingsley Martin for the job. Kingsley Martin asked Scott if he had done so and Scott replied that he had, that he had 'done his best' to help him.

In the lives of English institutions, as in the lives of Englishmen, provisional arrangements, if they are found to work well, tend to perpetuate themselves. The English are masters of what the old seamen called a jury-rig. While it continued possible to regard Clifford Sharp as Editor of the *New Statesman* and to get the work done by Mostyn Lloyd, G. D. H. Cole and Desmond MacCarthy, it is probable that it would have occurred to nobody to make a change. Everyone would have gone on pretending that Sharp would soon be 'better' and able to take responsibility for the paper again; in fact it was only very reluctantly admitted that he was anything else. It is not, thank God, in the English character to face the fact that a man is a dismal failure and kick him out; some other way has to be found to make room for a better man. In war it is easy to remove a general from the field and make him a field-marshal in the War Office; in politics it is, or used to be, as easy: one simply gave the man a peerage. From time to time a crisis may be so acute that the English do themselves violence, overcome their gentle manners, and sack a man openly. Such was the fate, for example, of Neville Chamberlain, but now biographers and historians are busy calling him 'unlucky' and reinstating him to make some amends for the way he had to be treated. It is ironical that Voltaire should have picked on almost the only instance in our history of a leader being treated harshly by us, and so established the shooting of Admiral Byng as typical of our political behaviour. Only death or total collapse could remove Sharp from office as Editor of a paper he was felt to have created and brought to life. But he had gone too far; the way in which the Board of Directors at last made up their minds to get rid of him was to give him the sack quietly and without fuss and pay for him to have a sabbatical year in America. To send an alcoholic to the United States to recover his sobriety is rather like trying to extinguish a fire with paraffin. It is true that this was in the Prohibition era, and it is just possible that Sharp's well-wishers were under the singular impression that it was harder to get spirits in America than in England. In England Sharp had been a drunkard so discreet that, for example, Leonard Woolf who worked with him and for him did not know of his vice and was taken aback when the facts came out. In America, Sharp went completely to pieces, and he had to be rescued by two old associates, Orage and S. K. Ratcliffe, who were both working in the States. They found Sharp without a penny, he had spent all his money on drink, and it was necessary to provide him with funds. He owned a thousand shilling shares in the *New Statesman* and these were bought from him by members of the *New Statesman* Board and by John Roberts for £200. Ratcliffe and Orage shipped him home and Roberts met the ship when it docked. Sharp was not abandoned by his friends as hopeless: several attempts were made to cure him by sending him to clinics; Roberts, Squire and Robert Lynd did their best to reclaim him. They all failed and although he later had periods of sobriety it at last became impossible to pretend that Clifford Sharp would ever again edit the *New Statesman*.

This, then, was the reason for Arnold Bennett's application to Ted Scott in the matter of Kingsley Martin. At no time does there seem to have been any question of appointing Mostyn Lloyd as Editor and it seems likely that this was because Arnold Bennett and some other members of the Board realized that they must have a man who would make the paper his whole lifework. Lloyd was given to teaching, he could never be whole-heartedly a journalist. Had the appointment of somebody else necessarily meant losing Lloyd's services, the Board would have hesitated; but it did not, for though Lloyd would have taken the job had it been offered him, he did not resent the fact that it was not offered. Cole, on the other hand, did. It seems probable that his appointment was discussed and that Bennett at least was hostile to it, for Cole, like Lloyd, would have regarded the editorship of the *New Statesman* as a job secondary to his work of teaching, writing and practising politics. H. B. Lees-Smith, another member of the *New Statesman* Board, was also against appointing Cole; he thought both Cole and Lloyd 'dull dogs'. Whitley, the Chairman of Directors, does not seem to have had strong views either way.

Kingsley Martin came to London from Manchester in the autumn of 1930. He was chosen as Sharp's successor, but the appointment was not at once made public. Martin's own

account of the decisive meeting with Arnold Bennett is more
entertaining than convincing:

> The others present that day at the Savoy were Bennett's three
> colleagues on the board of the *New Statesman*. It was
> summoned for business reasons. I was still wondering
> whether I should return to my job as a historian from which
> I had been seduced by the blandishments of C. P. Scott
> three years before. My period at the *Manchester Guardian*
> was over. I was being vetted for the post of Editor of the
> *New Statesman*. The lunch I believe was about as good as
> any given that day in Europe, but if I can recall only one
> item of the menu it is because a relaxed mood suitable for
> the appreciation of food is not the right frame of mind in
> which to undergo a cross-examination on one's career,
> abilities and opinions.
> . . . . Bennett suddenly asked me, with a portentous drop
> of the jaw, to define my political opinions. I opened my
> reply cautiously with the remark that 'I should call myself
> a socialist'. 'I should hope so', said Bennett, as if all the
> world knew that no sensible man, least of all Arnold Bennett,
> could possibly be anything else.
> At that moment there was an interruption. The head
> waiter entered with much solemnity and uncovered a
> large fish for Bennett's inspection. 'Ah,' he said, 'that's the
> fish from the Lake of Geneva, isn't it?' 'Really?' said one of
> the guests. 'You must have arranged for that to travel
> during the night so that it would be fresh today.' I had a
> small brainwave. 'I expect it was caught this morning and
> came by air,' I said. 'Of course,' said Bennett, obviously
> pleased. I felt that my cautious championship of socialism
> was forgotten. Anyway, they appointed me.

It can have done Kingsley Martin's candidature for the
editorship of the *New Statesman* no harm that Keynes, who
was known to have a high opinion of him, had expressed the
opinion that this might be a good moment for a merger with
The Nation. Negotiations were started while the new Editor
was playing himself in, writing reviews for *The Nation*, and
for the *New Statesman* his first article, on Liberia—he had
become something of a specialist on Africa and especially on
Kenya while still on the *Manchester Guardian*, learning a great

deal from that eccentric Afrophil, if there is such a word, Jack Driberg.

Keynes and the other proprietors of *The Nation* were ready for a merger with the *New Statesman* because not only was their paper losing a great deal of money, it had become rather a flabby sort of paper. It was, at that time, twenty-three years old. From its birth and while Massingham continued to edit it it had been a good though never a profitable paper. In 1921 it had swallowed the greatest of the Victorian literary weeklies, *The Athenaeum*. That journal was, at the time, in a state which bears out my argument that a paper's success is not made nor is it sustained by distinguished contributors but by the kind of editing which gives it a life of its own, a *whatness*. Consider, for example, these facts: when, in 1920, after a three-year period as a monthly, *The Athenaeum* resumed weekly publishing, its editor was J. Middleton Murry, its typography and general appearance were brought up to date, and its contributors included such stars as Max Beerbohm, Katherine Mansfield, Virginia Woolf, Thomas Hardy, Robert Graves, Edith Sitwell, T. S. Eliot, Edmund Blunden and Julian Huxley. Blunden and H. M. Tomlinson served terms as literary editor. All to no purpose, *The Athenaeum* had lost its *Athenaeumness*, it could not recapture it, and the only way to salvage any of its good-will was by merger with a younger journal.

Massingham had lost *The Nation* because of his persistent attacks on 'Mr. George' and his swing to the Left. His Liberal owners were patient, but at last told him that they were unwilling to continue to subsidize opinions which they were far from holding, and they gave him a chance to buy the paper himself. He failed to raise the money. Keynes, Walter Layton, the Cadburys and the Rowntree Trust bought the paper.

From 1923 until 1930 *The Nation and Athenaeum* was well edited by H. D. Henderson. His loss and replacement by Harold Wright, an amiable man and an entertaining essayist but no editor, forced the owners to realize that the paper was no longer viable, that while its continued independent existence was restraining the growth of the *New Statesman*, the latter was slowly killing their paper.

Keynes was Chairman of *The Nation* Board and negotiations were left in his hands. The *New Statesman* Board appointed John Roberts to negotiate on their behalf; it was a clever move, for Whitley was a gentle, persuadable man, whereas Roberts was tough; time has mellowed him, no doubt, but I would still rather be with him than against him in a deal. Keynes, on his side, having made the condition, by implication, that Kingsley Martin must first be appointed Editor of the *New Statesman*, which was done without publicity, envisaged an amalgamation between equals, with both sides waiving, in a gentlemanly way, the obvious fact that such a deal would be inequitable. This was far, very far, from Roberts's ideas: Roberts was determined that the *New Statesman* should acquire *The Nation and Athenaeum* and be in complete control of the new weekly; that the *New Statesman* staff, not *The Nation* staff, should keep their jobs; and that the new joint paper should be as new statesmanly as ever. He foresaw a very bright future for the paper if he could get his own way, and he was not in the least intimidated by the tremendous standing of his opposite number.

While Keynes and Roberts were negotiating, and Roberts was proving himself equal to the great economist, Kingsley Martin was writing for both papers and finding out from Mostyn Lloyd on the one hand and from Harold Wright on the other how to edit a weekly journal. But although he might need such instruction in technicalities, he did not need it in the spirit of the work; he knew the kind of paper he wanted and he was confident that he would know how to get it. And Keynes's strong support had given him new confidence.

In the course of the merger negotiations John Roberts had certain advantages over Keynes: for one thing the *New Statesman* was now making a small profit,* whereas *The Nation* was losing money. More important than this was Roberts's single-mindedness. Keynes was a very busy man and this business of *The Nation* was not of the first importance to him; his object was to get rid of it, to have the business over and done with as soon as possible. But for Roberts these negotiations were the only thing to work at and think about

* A trading profit: Sharp's court cases had converted this into a loss.

until he had got his own way, and he would sit up half the night or work all through his week-ends thinking round Keynes's points and devising new arguments. He knew exactly what he wanted: the two old publishing companies to continue in being, as shareholders in a new company to publish the joint paper, with the old *New Statesman* company having the controlling interest. Keynes gave way to him under the impression that once the new paper was being published the 'absurd' system of two separate Boards and a joint Board would be quietly dropped, and the Boards would sit together. It did not matter to Roberts what Keynes *thought* would happen, provided he got an arrangement which would, in fact, give him the power.

After a month of horse-trading had made it probable that the two men would eventually come to terms, but with a month still to go before they did so, Kingsley Martin, now Editor of the *New Statesman* but still letting it run on as before for the time being, began to prepare his first number of the *New Statesman and Nation*. He was given all the help he wanted. Harold Wright's amiability does not seem to have been impaired by the prospect of losing his paper, and he declared himself impressed when, at a luncheon he gave Kingsley Martin at *The Nation* offices and during which he asked his guest what essential new thing he would bring to the *New Statesman and Nation*, Kingsley Martin replied, 'high spirits'. To that he might have added, 'hard hitting', for both the *New Statesman* under Lloyd and the *Nation and Athenaeum* under Wright had got too much into the way of rebuking the Government *de haut en bas* and more in sorrow than in anger. Wright, indeed, had deliberately set out to make *The Nation* urbane. Urbanity is an excellent quality, but not very exciting. Anger was what both papers lacked; anger was what, among other things, Kingsley Martin was to inject into the *New Statesman and Nation*.

The negotiations between Keynes and Roberts were completed; a new publishing company was formed, The Statesman & Nation Publishing Co. Ltd., with a capital of £32,000. Its shares were held by the two old companies, which thus became simply holding companies. The old Statesman Company had £20,000 worth of the shares, the

Nation Company £12,000 worth. *The Nation*'s shares were to be paid for with *The Nation*, valued at £7,500 and £4,500 in cash, part to be paid at once to provide working capital for the new company, and the rest when called for. In the event the balance was retained out of dividends which became due to the old Nation Company.

The immediate benefits of the merger were far from spectacular. Before the amalgamation of the two papers the *New Statesman*'s circulation was 10,000 or thereabouts, while that of *The Nation and Athenaeum* is said to have been about 6,000, but I believe that it must have been less than that, to account for the big drop in the joint circulations which followed, even if we take the loss due to overlapping readership into account. It is true that for a week or two the net sales of the *New Statesman and Nation* were over 18,000; but the average weekly net sale of the joint paper for its first year was about 14,500 copies. Since only one instead of two papers now had to be written, produced and printed, this was, of course, a gain. The net gain in revenue from sales was probably about £3,500 a year. But the gain in net sales is far from being reflected in the advertising revenue. In the year 1928-29 the advertising revenue of the *New Statesman* had slightly exceeded £10,000 and 1929-30 saw it only a little below that figure. In 1930-31 this fell to £7,000 and it only rose by £500 in the following year. If we suppose the cost of producing the *New Statesman and Nation* to have been substantially the same as the cost of producing the *New Statesman*, then the new paper was better off than the old by only £200 or £300 a year. But in fact the cost was not the same; during his first, inexperienced, year, Kingsley Martin was an extravagant editor; the paper was larger than it had been and the use made of the space was too extravagant. Martin subsequently became an economical editor, even at the expense of his contributors, although never like Orage. But even this first-year lavishness does not account altogether for the figures. What was happening? It is perhaps hardly necessary to say that this did not mean that the amalgamation had been a disaster: the great slump was to blame, the catastrophic depression which followed the breakdown of United States capitalism in 1929. The *New Statesman and*

Nation had been made just, and only just, in time: the competition from *The Nation*, combined with the slump, would have been crippling to the *New Statesman*; the competition from the *New Statesman*, creaming off the slump-reduced advertising revenue, would probably have killed *The Nation*. Their union had at least given them the strength necessary to meet the much harder conditions of the Thirties.

8

Waiting for Lefty

I<small>T</small> would have been difficult to find any editor in England whose methods differed more completely from Mostyn Lloyd's than Kingsley Martin. Lloyd was calm where Martin was excited; Lloyd was patient where Martin was impatient; Lloyd picked the job up every week and dropped it when the work was done; Kingsley Martin carried it about with him like a precious possession. The key-word for his three years on the *Manchester Guardian* had been Frustration. The *New Statesman* meant sudden and glorious release: this was it! This was Life!

His first and most unpleasant task was to choose between the *New Statesman* regular contributors and those of *The Nation and Athenaeum*, where duplication of work occurred. And it is representative of his state of mind about his paper that having decided, for example, to retain Constant Lambert's gramophone notes despite the fact that Lambert was never on time with his copy, Kingsley Martin was not above going in person to the composer's flat and standing over him while he wrote his piece.

It was inevitable that in making his choices he should make some enemies: Vera Brittain had been writing a Woman's Page for *The Nation*: it was unsuitable for that paper—Keynes detested it—and would have been even more unsuitable for the *New Statesman and Nation*. Kingsley Martin dispensed with Miss Brittain's services and she was not pleased. In the other choices which he made the new Editor showed that flair which Beveridge had detected in him, the rare journalistic instinct and judgment. It was manifest in the case of the City page: Kingsley Martin did not hesitate to put an end to Emil Davies's seventeen-year-old series of City pages in favour of *The Nation*'s Nicholas Davenport. Davenport was younger and he was the better journalist.

But although a good deal might be sacrified to good journalism, that is to making the paper consistently interesting and therefore attractive to a greater number of potential readers, there was one thing which could never be sacrificed, at least by the new Editor: Socialism. It was not a Party Socialism, although it entailed critical support of the Labour Party, and what some people thought a less than adequately critical attitude towards the Soviet Union; nor was it really any kind of *étatisme*. When Maynard Keynes, who was a leading member of the Liberal Party was still considering whether he should back Kingsley Martin's appointment as Editor of the united papers, he once asked him whether, supposing he got the paper, he would make it Socialist in policy. Although Martin could not be sure that Keynes would still support him if he said yes, he replied without hedging that he would. As it happened this was the right answer: Keynes was a Socialist in his advocacy of planning and if he was no worshipper of the State, nor was Kingsley Martin.

Although Kingsley Martin might make up his mind to be a Socialist editor, it does not follow that he knew, from the first moment, how to do it; he did not. Before he had his hand and eye in, his paper wobbled: its want of balance, its Editor's want of assurance, are still apparent. In its first months the *New Statesman and Nation* showed all too clearly that it was a union of two or more not entirely compatible elements. There is a good example of an entertaining lapse, which the Editor's inexperience as well as the difficulties of the task led to, in the rather absurd incident of letting Hubert Phillips write economic notes one week. Hubert Phillips was *Caliban*, the puzzle expert of *The Nation*, and he was taken over by the *New Statesman and Nation* together with his quite famous League of Nations column. An economist by vocation and training, he had been a lecturer in economics at Bristol University. But far from being a Socialist, he was a Manchester-school economist, a believer in *laisser-faire*, free-for-all liberal capitalism, a fact which Kingsley Martin had failed to grasp. Cole being unable, one week, to write his usual notes, Kingsley Martin asked Phillips to do them. He did so, in his own fashion, with the result that Keynes was on the phone a few minutes after reading that week's paper, wanting to know if the Editor had suddenly gone mad.

He had not gone mad; but whether deliberately, or by a process of evolution, he came to the conclusion that the policy, in politics, in social matters, and even in economics, of his paper, should be to point out that the emperor had no clothes on. A good example of this disconcerting practice is to be found quite early in his career as Editor. Ramsay MacDonald—whose outstanding quality as Prime Minister, a resonant voice, had not enabled him to solve the financial crisis which was paralysing his Government—was playing with the idea of a National Government as early as May 1931. In this crisis, J. M. Keynes contributed an article to the second number of the combined *New Statesman and Nation* which became famous—and to orthodox Liberal economists infamous—for he suggested a 10 per cent. revenue tariff. For this abandonment of Free Trade, which he had been guilty of simply because the only alternative (in any case out of the question) was all round wage-reductions, he was rebuked, in another *New Statesman* article, by Professor Robbins, and the correspondence columns of the paper were crowded with opinions of almost every notable economist in Britain. Liberal subscribers cancelled their subscriptions; liberal and Socialist ones took their place.

In 1930 the Swiss banker and economist, Felix Somary, had forecast that the decks would not be clear for dealing with the world crisis until three events had taken place: a banking collapse in Austria and Germany; bankruptcy of the Ivar Kreuger complex of companies; abandonment of the gold standard by Great Britain. By August 1931 there began to be horrified whispers in London that we were 'going off gold'. Kingsley Martin, being no economist, asked on the front page of his paper whether it would not be simplest and wisest to abandon the gold standard. He then went off to Berlin for a short visit, and to that city a letter from the economist H. D. Henderson followed him, protesting that to suggest that Britain should go off gold was a highly irresponsible thing to do and that such a course would ruin us. MacDonald, Snowden and Thomas were likewise of this opinion. The first thing the National Government which succeeded the Labour Government did was to go off gold. Nobody was a penny the worse, of course. H. D. Henderson became the new Government's economic adviser.

It will be useful before penetrating further into the most important decade of the *New Statesman*'s history to try to recreate the social atmosphere in which Kingsley Martin had to work and in which, under him, the paper flourished to an extent which will long remain one of the wonders of Press history.

In a way it would be true to say of the Thirties what Talleyrand said of the *ancien régime*, that those who never knew them do not know the joy of living: though it might be hell for conscientious intellectuals, it was hell with a way out. The young men and women of the Sixties are spending their youth at a time when the only great expectation is that of sudden, painful and probably universal death; when the noblest social theories have either been betrayed or have failed in practice; when science, which was to bring in the millennium, has in fact brought in an age of terror and of a shoddy, superficial prosperity which satisfies nobody; when the United States, once the White Hope of liberal and radical humanists, has become their despair; when the USSR, once the White Hope of Socialists and Socialism, has become their bane.

The movement—C.N.D.—which in the Sixties has captured the loyalty of the young people of goodwill who in the Thirties would have given their support to the positive ideals of Leftism, is a negative one, a protest against premature death rather than a promotion of the good life.

But there is something else: in the Thirties there was always the prospect, for progressives, of getting one day a real Labour Government with a strong majority and a clear policy of the kind created by Brailsford's *New Leader* and later Kingsley Martin's *New Statesman and Nation* out of all the Fabian, Guild Socialist and other Left-wing thinking and talking that had been going on for nearly half a century. When that happened, all would be well. But in the Sixties the Labour Government of 1945-50 is behind us; it accomplished a great deal of what the Left had hoped it would do; but all is not well and this time it is not possible to believe that another Labour Government will, in fact, make all well, if only because our problems have ceased to be those of national politics.

It is true that in the early Thirties the breakdown of capitalism inflicted severe hardships on the ordinary people: in the U.S.A. and Britain together, without considering the state of Germany, France, Italy and Spain, there were twenty million unemployed half-starving on a dole or private charity. But this very breakdown was, surely, what the radical young had been waiting for; it was the darkest hour before the Socialist dawn. Socialism, in 1930, was not, as in 1960, the name applied by the Beaverbrook Press to the policy of those rather timid liberals known as the Labour Party. It was the word for the Future, for the Ideal Realized, for national planned government by people of goodwill, even for Christianity in practice. It was a marvellous word of power, and it made a belief in a political solution of those problems which Capitalism had failed with such ghastly consequences to solve, not only possible but almost inevitable.

At this time, although the elders of the working class were still Socialists in the British Nonconformist Radical tradition which was anti-Marxist, or rather which was ignorant of Marxism, the intelligent young of the lower-middle and even middle classes—those of them, that is, who were capable of independent and disinterested thinking or feeling—were being clearly influenced, at last, by Marxist ideas. The two paramount influences were Strachey's *The Coming Struggle for Power*, and the books, articles, speeches, in short the 'agitation', of Professor Harold Laski. As a consequence it was argued, and became widely accepted in Britain as in France, that brain workers of all kinds—artists, writers including poets, philosophers, teachers, scientists—should enter into and become part of the working class and help the manual workers to oust the bourgeoisie from power. To give only one example, artists were to give their work a social content and a propagandist bent; and it came to be believed by many that without this quality their work would be worthless. With the rise to power of German Fascism, so much more dangerous than the established Italian variety, the need for this getting together seemed all the more urgent and a lead was given in France, where not only did intellectuals submit themselves to Communist discipline but all the parties of the Left united to form a Popular Front against Fascism, that is against the bourgeoisie in what it was hoped would be its last, militant, phase of power. There were, of course, some artists and writers who were hostile to this idea and rejected it. They were of two kinds: those who believed that the arts could not survive being deliberately 'used' in this way, such as Robert Graves; and those who were politically and socially Right, such as Evelyn Waugh. Towards the end of the decade we are discussing, Waugh expressed, with the brilliance and the humour to be expected of one of the two most talented of living English novelists, his contempt for this whole Left movement by making ferocious fun of those two socially significant poets Parsnip and Pimpernel.* It is none the less true that for thousands of hopeful people Parsnip and Pimpernel—Auden and Isherwood—were the, as it were, key intellectuals of a decade of striving for the good, the true and the beautiful. And although it must be said that, in the event, Auden and Isherwood removed themselves to America, rather than fight, although, too, the intellectuals of the Right often saw more clearly, realizing for instance that it was absurd to pretend that the working class was somehow morally superior to all other classes; it remains true that theirs was not the better part. For there was, in the Thirties, something repulsive in the very idea of a *young* talent at the service of the old Establishment. It implied a cold-heartedness and a cynicism which were not attractive in young people. Events, and the memoirs of the men who made them, have proved that the Thirties Leftists were very gullible; it remains true that idealism is proper to the young, and that cynical realism is an evil.

As Julian Symons has put it, it was better to be waiting for Lefty than to be waiting for Godot.†

Because the reader of the Sixties is equipped with hindsight

* In *Put Out More Flags*.   † In his *The Thirties* (see below).

and will, therefore, be ready to condemn as folly or irresponsibility some aspects of the *New Statesman and Nation* policy towards the USSR in the Thirties and Forties, I propose to deal here, in advance, with that Left-wing 'gullibility', which the *New Statesman* was not free from, a state of mind and spirit which the reader would have shared at the time unless he is a more unpleasant person than I take him for. Several writers have taken the exciting and, I still think, nobler decade of the Thirties as their subject, among them Robert Graves and Malcolm Muggeridge. But the best book on the period, because it is never written *de haut en bas*, is Julian Symons's *The Thirties*. I am going to make use of this book because it does a lot of my work for me. But first I must refer again to Arthur Koestler and his views of Thirties Leftism.

There was something at once amusing and outrageous in Koestler's sneers at the *New Statesman* for its Stalinist apologetics. For is he not in effect, saying: 'You bloody fool, fancy believing what I told you.' The sin of Kingsley Martin and those of his colleagues who were not opposed to his policy was the decent one of attributing their own integrity to writers who, working for the Communist Party, misled them. No doubt it is now clear enough that we ought not to have trusted them; but they were seductive and apparently honest writers and how were we to know the cynics from the idealists? The trouble was that an effort was being made to bring into politics idealists and an idealism incompatible with the low standard of ethics usual in that field. If we ourselves would not engage in faking news, inventing entirely imaginary political events, and misrepresenting people, what possible right have we to suspect other men, apparently activated by goodwill, of doing these things? By listening to the voices of the Beaverbrooks and the Rothermeres and their kind? But the young Leftists of the Thirties judged, and rightly judged, that such men were at best interested in preserving a bad old system, at worst prepared to support even such evil men as Hitler in doing so. Their word was worthless. The artists and writers of the Right saw this also—nobody handled the Press lords more mercilessly than Evelyn Waugh. But they were able, by virtue of a kind of premature elderliness, to extend the same contempt to the Left as to the Right.

Of course, it would have been better no doubt had the *New Statesman*, and the new statesmen, of the Thirties perceived that Russian National Communism was as evil in its means (it never was in its ends, which remained noble) as Fascism. It would have been splendid, of course, had Socialists contrived to create an international movement powerful enough to be effective against the régimes of violence and fraud on both Left and Right. Easy to say now, now that Koestler and Claud Cockburn, and indeed N. S. Khrushchev, have come clean. At the time it was simply out of the question since it seemed perfectly clear that Communists were aiming at the same goal as ourselves and were a great deal more efficient in moving towards it. The middle course which hindsight reveals as the right one would, at the time, have seemed merely to be going nowhere at all.

> The political-artistic movement of the Thirties thus slowly took the form of a pyramid. The broad base was formed by the million-strong intelligentsia, who may for convenience be called the Audience. Above them was a group perhaps 50,000 strong, of people who read some of the little magazines in which new writers were first published, and actually bought some of their books. This section of the pyramid was much younger than the base, and its social composition was complex. It included working class intellectuals, who believed that the proletarian novel and theatre were the coming art forms, but considered the work of the bourgeois poets as of some temporary interest; members of the lower middle class—that is those who had been educated at state or grammar schools, and in many cases had gone on to red brick universities; and a considerable number of professional men and women . . . who were looking for a link between art and society . . . they played a large part in making the theatre and the novel, and to a less degree painting and music, vehicles for social propaganda. . . .

Thus Julian Symons, in *The Thirties*; he tells us that this was in many ways the most interesting part of his pyramid, its members were the 'seeds of the post-war Welfare State'.

He calls them the Pragmatists; it is with them that we are concerned, for among them, and although it was often too mild for them, the *New Statesman* found its readers, rather than among the smaller group of perhaps 1,000 practising artists and writers who formed the peak of Mr. Symons's pyramid. He sees these Pragmatists, these *New Statesman* readers, boiling away like geysers, frothing anger at the Audience for its smug liberalism, and at the Artists for their social inadequacy. Finally, Mr. Symons sees this pyramid glued together by the threat of Fascism.

This is all true and very useful; the man who created the Pragmatist's *New Statesman* was Kingsley Martin, and far from complaining, at the time, that he was too 'committed' to the real Left, the activists among Left-wing writers were apt to complain that he was not committed enough to any-thing. Mr. Symons himself once wrote, in another but comparable context:

> It is all very well to say that this is the 'detached viewpoint', implies the reticence, etc., which is necessary for the artist *sometimes* (you pick your own times): the detached viewpoint today is too near the mud-brained Liberal-Labour viewpoint, in poetry as well as politics. Better the BU Quarterly* than the New Statesman. . . .

He has apologized for this, realizing that it was 'stupid, insensitive, downright wicked'. But it serves to make it quite clear that the *New Statesman* was much less 'gulled' than, for example, Stephen Spender whose account, in *New Writing*, of the Writers' Congress held in Madrid in 1937 should be read at the same time as the passage about the same event in his autobiography.

All this is an apology for those Thirties which were com-posed of political-artistic Audenism and Isherwood-ery, of *New Writing*, of the Left Book Club with its 60,000 members and 1,000 discussion groups all intent on stopping Fascism and ushering in the Socialist millennium, of the A.I.A., Unity Theatre and, finally, of Spain not as a mere geogra-phical expression but as the place where the struggle became military and where many of the young people who had been

* British Union, i.e. Mosleyite Fascist.

creating this special Thirties Leftism offered and lost their lives or limbs in defence of it; an apology therefore for what we might almost call the weekly organ of that Leftism, the *New Statesman*.

Martin was not taking over at an easy time, but while the problems facing the paper were hard ones they also represented a chance in a lifetime, and he took it. Some of the problems were business ones: the western world was afflicted by the worst slump in living memory, and this was making life difficult for John Roberts who, brilliant salesman though he was, could not check the fall in advertising revenue. Advertising is not a rational or logical science; if it were, then there would be more advertising when business is bad and less as it gets better. In practice, advertising expenditure falls as business declines; there are explanations, but no good explanations, for this. While Roberts struggled to win the paper the revenue it needed, Kingsley Martin had first to reconcile the *Nation*'s Keynesian liberalism with the *New Statesman*'s Fabianism, to produce a Socialism appropriate to the situation. He had to decide what line to take with the apparently paralysed Government of Ramsay MacDonald which had been in office since the 1929 election. While industry and trade ground almost to a standstill and unemployment rose into the millions, millions who half-starved on bread and scrape, this Government, far from seizing the magnificent opportunity to impose a planned economy on the nation which so badly needed it, a course which was being urged on it by its youngest and most brilliant man-of-action, Sir Oswald Mosley, did absolutely nothing whatever. MacDonald blathered, Philip Snowden gave an excellent imitation of the worst kind of Tory Chancellor of the Exchequer, and Socialist economics might never have been invented. Two leading Labour men were finally driven into resigning from the Labour Party and ruining their careers, by sheer exasperation. Sir Oswald Mosley, when his plan, rather like Roosevelt's New Deal of a few years later, was rejected, formed a new party which never, of course, stood a chance, moved right into Fascism on the Italian model, attracting a following of pin-headed louts of all classes, and became, for the rest of his life, a public nuisance instead of a public servant. More serious was the similar aberration of John Strachey, the most important intellectual of the Left during these years, whose *Coming Struggle for Power* was to exercise such a tremendous influence over all, or at least over many thousands of Mr. Symons's 'Pragmatists'. Strachey followed Mosley into the new Party: it was a perfectly understandable thing to do; these young men realized that action was needed and they believed they knew *what* action. When the New Party came to nothing, however, Strachey, who was at once as brilliant a man as Mosley, and a great deal sounder, turned briskly Left and found himself among Communists. Apart from the importance of his own writings, there was in the following years that of his influence, with Gollancz and Laski, as a selector for the Left Book Club, which seems to me to have been the most effective manifestation of Popular Frontism in Great Britain. But whereas Sir Oswald Mosley drifted further and further to the extreme Right, to be involved for the rest of his life in the more squalid kinds of rabble-rousing (and to very little effect), Strachey checked his own Leftward movement, made a superb recovery, and was able thereby to return, in due course, to politics and power, and to continue a valuable man both as a theorist and as a man of action. The magnitude of Mosley's fatal blunder can best be judged by considering the success of the Left Book Club which became Strachey's 'outlet' after he quitted the Labour Party: Victor Gollancz, whose idea it was, had expected a membership of about 2,000; what he got was a membership of 60,000.

In the matter of the domestic crisis, all the *New Statesman* could do was to keep reminding the Labour Party leaders that there was a thing called Socialism. As they took no notice of this, the crisis prolonged itself until it was solved, by Adolf Hitler, in the classic Marxist way. Capitalism repeatedly saves itself by taking the people into a war. As we shall see, when the crisis reached one of its peaks in 1931 and the National Government came into being, thus separating the Left wing of the Labour Party from the larger Right wing, the *New Statesman* could, by supporting and addressing itself to the Opposition in the House of Commons, continue to drive home those ideas which were realized when Attlee, the second leader (after Lansbury's death) of that Opposition, came to power in 1945.

Meanwhile, there was also a prolonged Imperial crisis, the matter of India and her independence. In this field Kingsley Martin made what is not sufficiently clearly seen as a major change in *New Statesman* policy. I have already suggested that there was such a thing as Socialist Imperialism, that the Webbs were imperialists and that so was Sharp. It was not so much that these Fabians objected to Indians or Africans having self-government, as that they seem to have objected to fragmentation of a Commonwealth which might, perhaps, be turned over intact to Socialism as one huge rationally governed unit. The model of how to make over an Asiatic empire to Socialism was before them; the Bolsheviks were, it seemed, doing just that with the eastern countries of the Russian Empire. This sort of thing would not do for Kingsley Martin who, as I have said, was never an *étatiste*. Sharp's anti-Indian feeling had been made very manifest in a long review, which became famous as a cause of ill-feeling, which he personally wrote of Katherine Mayo's *Mother India*; his review emphasized, with contempt for the Indians, all the faults of the Hindu civilization which that book exposed. *The Nation*, on the other hand, had been consistently pro-Indian and anti-Raj in its policy, and it was that policy which Kingsley Martin brought with him on to the combined papers; it was in his nature, his character and his education to do so. From the beginning he was on the side of the Indian Congress, of Gandhi and Nehru, and of working as quickly as possible towards independence of the African and Asian colonies. It seemed to him quite clear that these people had a right to govern themselves and to own their countries, and if there was a risk, as indeed there was, that they would fall into political errors of the kind which bedevilled Europe, it must be taken.

Important though the imperial problems were, however, it was the depression at home and all over the West which had to be given most of the paper's attention as it built up to a crisis in 1931. Young, inexperienced, and a newcomer to the job, Kingsley Martin had to decide upon a clear and definite policy for his paper. Remarkably, he succeeded; remarkably, because nobody else did; a glance over the Press for that year shows quite clearly that there was hardly another editor in the business with the least idea what to urge upon either Government or people. The quality of the *New Statesman*'s achievement in this respect can best be judged by reference to an issue of the *Political Quarterly* which appeared at this time and in which the Left-wing leading thinkers each analysed the crisis. It does not seem now that their views could have been reconcilable. The *New Statesman*'s editor contrived somehow to reconcile the opinions of J. M. Keynes, G. D. H. Cole and Davenport of the *New Statesman* City page, and to present a reasonably coherent policy. It was not only that there was a depression, not only that there was a sort of chronic crisis; there seems to have been a quite terrifying *muddle* and it is this, I believe, which accounts for the craven docility of the Press as a whole in accepting the more or less futile and quite ineffectual things which were at last done about it, as if they were strokes of political and economic genius.

It is difficult to see, from where we stand now, just why the crisis of the early Thirties paralysed the men who were supposed to be dealing with it. Difficult because, since then, the principal ideas of Keynes-ism, of Fabianism, even of downright Socialism, have made a partial conquest of the free-for-all Capitalist parties. Whatever Free Enterprise noises the British Conservatives and the two American political parties may make, and however hard they may strive to put the clock back to the days when a depression, like that of 1908 in the United States, could be regarded as if it were an act of God, like an earthquake, which we must put up with, they cannot really dismiss from their minds the knowledge that national economies, world economy even, can be controlled like machinery. Between the politicians of the Thirties and those of today lie Roosevelt's New Deal, the achievements of the USSR in planned economy, the achievements of the Nazis in controlling the German economy, the experience of half a dozen great nations in controlling the economy during the war. This does not mean that the economic know-how did not exist in the early

Thirties; it means that the Free Enterprise political parties were then still able to believe that they could get away with refusing to make use of this science, could still persuade the millions to starve in order to preserve for themselves an economic liberty with which they associated their privileges as a class. The same people are still in power all over the western world; but they have been forced to concede a great deal, and the relative prosperity of the working-class of the western nations is a product of their concessions. The *New Statesman* was outstanding in 1931 for steadily advocating the economic policies which have, in the event, proved successful in practice. In short, *New Statesman* writers knew what was wrong and how to put it right. In a sense this was not very difficult, because the real trouble was an arbitrary set of economic rules, the Conservative Doctrine rules which had and have no more validity than the rules of a game.

The Labour Government, instead of trying to apply a little Socialism to the country's economy, appointed an Economy Commission under Sir George May to suggest what could be done to Save the Pound. Because that is what the Government, hypnotized by the bankers, was trying to save, and never mind the people. The May Commission wanted economics of £100 m. in Government spending. In a world situation in which prices of raw material and food were very low, nevertheless the Conservative financiers only had their one, their usual idea—deflation. They had a good rationalization for their blind worship of the pound's status; unable to live on her own resources, Britain depends for her food and raw materials on trade; her trade depends on her credit; her credit depends on the strength and stability of the pound. Deficit budgeting, whether in the national or the private sector, for the sake of expansion, would damage the pound. Budget surpluses, or at least a balanced budget, were therefore essential to our ability to buy abroad. If we could not increase taxation, then we must cut expenditure. For example, reduce Unemployment Pay, the infamous dole on which three million families were half-starving.

If, said Keynes in his famous and heretical *New Statesman* article, we have to have cuts, why penalize the poorest? The paper suggested cutting arms expenditure to begin with: it is, of course, a fact that there is no more inflationary kind of expenditure, since in the arms industry no goods ever reach the markets to satisfy the demand created by money paid in wages and dividends. And why not increase direct taxation? The trouble as Keynes stated it, was essentially simple: goods were not being consumed; you were hardly likely to promote consumption by further reducing the money in the people's hands.

The Editor did not overlook the fact that the crisis was international: Bruce Lochart's *New Statesman* articles and later those of Elizabeth Wiskemann, on Germany were making it perfectly clear that unless Britain and the US put their own houses in order to the extent of being able to help Germany by debt remission and with massive credits, then Germany would 'adopt a Fascist solution'. The Germans had tried the May Commission methods, they had applied economies so stringent that the Germans were being ground by misery and want to save the mark, which was not being saved after all. Articles on France showed that though France had all the gold, she too had about a million unemployed, though she would, of course, never be in the parlous condition of Britain or Germany because she was fundamentally a much richer country. What of the extreme Socialist solution, which the paper did not advocate but which ought surely to be studied? A two-part article dealt with the new Soviet Five Year Plan, and with Stalin's exposition of it in the Supreme Soviet; the speaker, judged by his speeches, was presented as not merely a very able economist, but as one of the 'liberal' Communist leaders. It is mortifying to reflect that whereas this opinion of the old tyrant was based on carefully gathered information, the contrary one, which turned out to be correct, was based on nothing but emotion, on hate and prejudice. That contrary opinion of Socialism and the world's leading Socialist was being put forward in national newspapers which were obviously becoming daily more vulgar and irresponsible: their commercialization of an essential public service was deplored by Kingsley Martin, in one of the first leaders he wrote for his paper, as a serious danger to democracy. Serious-minded Liberal and Socialist journalists had not, in the Thirties, yet realized that the mass-circulation newspapers are read for the advertisements and as entertainment, and have not much more influence on the people's politics than the three-ring circus they seemed trying to emulate.

As soon as the May Commission's report was out, Kingsley Martin mustered all his forces in an effort to dissuade the Labour Government from letting itself be bullied or seduced into adopting the recommendations. The report contained the first suggestion of a National Government of all parties. Kingsley Martin, in his own attack on the report, pointed out that the Liberal and Labour Parties would be betraying all they stood for if they joined in a policy of taking from the poor to make things easier for the rich. Maynard Keynes's *New Statesman* study of the report, which inspired the Editor's attack, was entirely hostile. Keynes had forecast that the result of the cuts in Government expenditure would be a rise of 400,000 in the figure of unemployed and a fall in taxation yield which would absorb at least half of the £100 m. it was proposed to save out of the unemployed's bread and scrape. Conservative economists and financiers are very like seventeenth-century surgeons; their method of treating a man who is dying of a haemorrhage is to bleed him. Apart from the Socialists, Keynes was one Liberal economist who could see that there was something a little odd about this. Keynes concluded his analysis in the *New Statesman* by saying that the May remedies were not only undesirable, they would probably be impossible.

Mostyn Lloyd's *New Statesman* comment was political. He wrote that it was preposterous to ask the Labour Party, the Trade Unions, the working class in general 'to save a system which tantalizes them with goods they cannot get at'. G. D. H. Cole, having dismissed 'economy *à la* Sir George May' as 'unhelpful', called upon the nation to seize the opportunity created by the crisis to start planning its economy scientifically. It is clear, however, that he did not expect his suggestions to be adopted; he perceived that doctrinaire Conservatism and vested interests would be too strong for common sense.

They were, of course: MacDonald, Snowden, Thomas and

Lord Sankey, as well as a body of Liberal leaders, went over to the Tories—for that is what their conduct, whatever they chose to call it, amounted to. The *New Statesman*, if it did not, of course, hail this act of treachery as one of heroism, like the rest of the Press, did lean over backwards to avoid calling the act, and the actors, by the names which would have fitted them. It was this moderation, this rather easy-going cynicism about men, which so infuriated some of the paper's advance-guard readers, and which was to lead George Orwell, later in the decade, to write of 'papers that have the mentality of a whore, like the *New Statesman*'. For I do not think that this rather intemperate opinion can really have been intended as a comment on the Left-wing pro-Soviet orthodoxy which Kingsley Martin later adopted, for reasons which will be discussed in their place, and which was really imposed on him by the logic of the situation; the *New Statesman*'s mentality, in that case, should have been abused as that of a faithful and stupid wife.

The Editor found one consolation in the defection of the Labour leaders: it left the Party purer; there could now be a real Socialist opposition in the House of Commons, an opposition to which the paper gave strong support. It was unique in doing so. From the National, rather than the Party, point of view, the ratting of MacDonald, Snowden and Thomas was a disaster, since it made possible the application of the May recommendations which could not but make the world economic situation worse than ever. Supported by the Labour deserters, the National Government would be able to defend the pound at the expense of the unemployed.

Although *The Nation* element was less important than the *New Statesman* element in the *New Statesman and Nation*, the Editor, with Keynes at his elbow, had to make some concessions to Liberalism. He could not, for example, go quite as far as the Labour opposition spokesman, Dr. Addison, in the House, who announced that the whole thing had been a bankers' ramp. In any case Martin, with Cole to advise him, did not think it was as simple as that, though Cole's criticism did not fall much short of it. Nothing was to be gained by taking a conspiratorial view of recent history.

The paper's attitude to the crisis is summed up thus, on 5 September 1931:

> As the mist of religious enthusiasm with which the Government has been invested disperses, the situation appears every day more menacing. The policy of 'economy' will be bitterly opposed throughout the country, not only because people usually object to a forced reduction in their standard of living, but also because a very large section of the community sincerely holds that it is a mistaken and disastrous policy. When Parliament meets on Tuesday next there will be a clear-cut division—a division which must inevitably approximate more closely than ever before in this country to an undisguised class struggle. The pretence that this is a National Government is already wearing thin. . . . To attempt to rehabilitate England by cutting wages and the dole and reducing social services in order that profits may be larger is an intelligible, though in our view a fatal policy. But why call it 'equality of sacrifice'?

By 1932 the major issues with which the paper had to deal, apart from the continuing series of domestic and Imperial crises, were those of the moratorium on the German war debt and the associated Lausanne Conference; and Japan's Manchurian adventure. This Manchurian business, developing into Japan's general assault on distracted China, an attempt to create a vast Far Eastern empire, was of course the event which set the political fashion for the decade. This fashion can, given our post-war perspective, be simplified in broad terms. The Have-not Powers wanted empires for the same reason that the Have Powers already had them, as sources of cheap labour and raw materials, that is of wealth and power. The Have Powers had led the way in setting up Treaties and Covenants to prevent aggressive wars for the simple reason that, having what they needed, they had nothing to lose and everything to gain from keeping the peace. The Have-not Powers, having acquired the industrial strength necessary to wage a modern war, were signatories to the Treaties and Covenants, but had not, of course, the slightest intention of letting themselves be hampered by that. The would-be aggressor, Japan, in this first case, would find an excuse to attack, any excuse would do, and set about imposing its rule on the chosen victim. Liberals and Socialists all over the western world would then cry out for the League of Nations to act in restraint of the aggressor and defence of the victim. The *New Statesman* was usually a leader of the outcry. It must be said, however, that nobody seems to have given much attention to the fact that, although at first the League did, perhaps, have the means, given the goodwill of its members, to act in restraint of aggressors, it was progressively weakened by failure to act, so that very soon the League had no means of doing what it was called on to do. It had in any case one fatal weakness: it was boycotted by the United States (whose President Wilson had created it) in the name of that Splendid Isolation which the country had enjoyed for a century under the protection of the Royal Navy. Meanwhile, Right-wingers were urging that the League should do no such thing as the Left was urging it to do, but should allow the aggressor to get on with the job of 'restoring order' or with his 'civilizing mission' or whatever he pretended to be doing; and that the best thing *we* could do would be to quit the League anyway. There were Press campaigns in both senses, meetings, protest movements. The League remained inactive, serving as a useful forum for politicians to express the progressive ideas which they had neither the intention of putting into practice nor the means to do so. The aggressor triumphed. This was the history of the Thirties. Right-wing intellectuals saw in it the repetition of the eternal pattern of history and considered that all we should do was to defend our own empire, if necessary aggressively. Left-wing intellectuals, with their belief in world concord as the only possible future for mankind, and the League of Nations as the first, albeit feeble, manifestation of that concord, were led in their denunciation of and outcry against such doings, by the *New Statesman*. As these young men and women, mostly under Marxist influence, began to climb down from ivory towers and claim they were proletarians, the *New Statesman* became the leading organ of their protest against the sabotaging of peace and the future of crazy nationalists. As, however, they were also pacifists by conviction, there is, from where we stand now, a somewhat comic look about their conduct. I can write this without sneering, I was one of them, one of Mr. Symons's Pragmatists, in my late teens and early twenties. The *New Statesman* was the organ of our ambivalence and reflected it. But, as I shall show, half-way through the decade it gave us a clear lead by making a firm choice between two conflicting sets of principles.

It did not become the organ of the parallel literary and artistic advance movement; for that, Mr. Symons's Artists, the top people of his pyramid, preferred the Little Magazines, *New Writing* in due course, and the *Left Review*. The rear half of the *New Statesman* remained on the whole disengaged, and on the high side of middle-brow. Unlike the front half of the paper, it had, and for years continued to have, no whatness of its own, it did not look 'edited' and it lacked, at times, coherence. The fact is that it is very much more difficult to have a 'policy' for a literary and artistic review than for a political one. Or, rather, it is difficult to have such a policy if you reject, as Kingsley Martin did reject, the Marxist notion of the arts as political instruments, and if you are writing for a wide and diverse readership, not for some small coterie who will accept some special, usually ephemeral, theory of the arts; or who will believe that only the arts really matter. In short, the rather amorphous quality of the *New Statesman*'s hind-quarters was probably inevitable and it is quite probable that Kingsley Martin was perfectly right to interfere with it as little as possible. Its writers and reviewers might from time to time include a member of the young advance-guard; but on the whole they were 'uncommitted' men of letters and the arts. They included V. S. Pritchett, Peter Quennell, Gerald Bullett, Rose Macaulay. G. W. Stonier, who was still to be writing for the paper in 1963, had long been a contributor. Desmond MacCarthy and Leonard Woolf were, of course, still among the most important contributors.

In the summer of 1931 the Editor started a new feature, 'London Diary', signed Critic. Although some few paragraphs might be contributed by others—Woolf, for example, Herbert Agar, or Raymond Mortimer, the Editor wrote most of them. Members of his staff frequently brought him the material for a paragraph. Norman MacKenzie was later to contribute a good deal to London Diary, but whatever the source, it was the Editor who wrote this page. He might have blenched had he been told that he would continue to do so for thirty years. The feat of producing this page of paragraphs commenting on aspects of the news, with its light personal touch, its dry humour, its strong characteristic tone, for 1,500 weeks, is probably unique in the history of journalism. Nearly all such 'gossip', whether on the high level of Critic's or the base nattering about gaudy nonentities in the admass Press, though signed with one name is written by numerous hands. But Critic really was Kingsley Martin, and if he often welcomed a paragraph from a colleague, it received the typical Critic treatment before it appeared. Random sampling of the page over a period of three decades shows no flagging at any point. The tone we were familiar with until 1960 was found at once and never lost; vocabulary and manner of approach were modified to keep up with fashion changes in expression, but the manner is still the same at the end as at the beginning. A curious by-product of re-reading some hundreds of London Diaries is confirmation of my theory that the wisecracks attributed to men temporarily at the top—Churchillisms for example—are always the same ones, being attributed in each decade to some different 'character'. What Churchill is supposed to have said to Bevan, was in fact said by Mellon to Hoover, but before that by Clemenceau to Wilson. I am convinced that these dozen or so sayings (of the 'Here's sixpence, now you can phone *all* your friends' variety) have been used for centuries to trick out public character after public character, and probably originated with Pericles and Kleon, or perhaps with Pharaoh and Joseph. But 95 per cent. of the Diary was fresh as paint.

An important contributor of Diary material was C. R. Hewitt. He had been a constable in the City of London Police and became a Chief Inspector. He made himself an expert on the relationship between the citizen and the law. He took to journalism, was introduced to the *New Statesman* by Ernest Willison and in due course given a desk and a retaining fee. One of his most important contributions to the paper was the writing of a Supplement on crime and punishment in which suggestions were made whereby the Home Secretary could improve the quality of justice without amendment to statutes. Mr. R. A. Butler used this Supplement almost as a programme, taking it point by point in a major speech.

A new liveliness was introduced into the paper by the Editor's policy of letting contributors ride hobby-horses from time to time. He might insist on keeping W. J. Turner because he was a very good journalist, but he was willing to let Leonard Woolf conduct a one-man campaign against the BBC for broadcasting third-rate English music on patriotic grounds, and third-rate foreign music for fear of showing up the English composers. Several contributors had their special subjects. C. M. Lloyd hammered away at the manner in which Germany was being driven into dangerous political extremism by the havering of the Lausanne conferecs. And he led the fight against the economic imbecility of injuring our industry and commerce for the sake of refusing to trade with the Bolsheviks, as they were still being called.

The policy of publishing Supplements on special subjects was revived, although these were fewer and much less thorough than in the paper's infancy. In 1932 came an important one on Disarmament, not entirely successful. E. H. Davenport, however, the paper's 'Toreador' of the City page, by his discussion of the economics of disarmament made one thing clear: the dependence of capitalism on armament expenditure. Dorothy Woodman, describing the structure and anti-ethics of the armaments industry, made her first appearance in the *New Statesman*, so that she has now been writing for it for almost as long as Kingsley Martin himself. The contributor whose job it was to depict the next war in the Supplement made the same mistakes as the rest of us at that time: he greatly over-estimated the amount of damage which would be done by the bombing of cities; and he confidently asserted that gas, principally phosgene, would not only be used but would result in hundreds of thousands of deaths and in social breakdown.

That 'defence of', or 'apology for', Soviet Russia which became a 'mistake' of the *New Statesman* only after certain

very disingenuous Left-wing intellectuals had found it
expedient to change their own political colour, begins in
1931. Japan, having acquired Manchuria, created the
puppet Manchukuo and invaded Jehol, seemed ready to
pick a fight with the USSR. The British Right was
delighted at the prospect of gallant little Japan destroying
the Socialist experiment, and of the wicked Bolsheviki being
put down by the virtuous Samurai. It was the *New Statesman*
which pointed out how careful an adult and responsible
Soviet Government was being to avoid a clash, and how
such excitement as was to be found in Moscow should be
explained as a consequence of dread of the 'imperialist' States,
with Japan as their spearhead, launching an attack on the
Soviet Union. Liberal western specialists might not like a good
many of the things which they knew about the USSR;
but as it became clearer and clearer that the only hope of
successfully opposing Capitalism in its militant phase, that is
Fascism and Nazism, and of shifting the dead hand of
Capitalism in its older, liberal phase, lay in a firm union of all
progressives of the Left, then it became more and more
difficult not to pass over the sins of the USSR, the one
Socialist or potentially Socialist great Power, in silence. It
was, as a rule, not Kingsley Martin, but Mostyn Lloyd,
recently back from the USSR and greatly impressed by
what he had seen, who wrote editorial comments on the
Soviet Union. There was, however, an immense difficulty
for any honest and Left-liberal Editor in the fact that he
could not simply sweep aside the Soviet's much publicized
dread of the imperialist Powers, a dread which was to be
used, and abused, to justify the worst excesses of tyranny.
For such an Editor, and Kingsley Martin was of this kind,
knew perfectly well that the imperialist States *would*, in fact,
have liked to see the Communist Government destroyed and
would, had they dared and been able to indulge their real
wishes, have gone to war with Russia. This knowledge could
not but colour Martin's judgment of the Soviet Union for
many years to come; he was bound to take the view, for
example, that stories of the shocking behaviour of the Soviet
Government might well be nothing but Capitalist propaganda; and he was quite right, they were. Any resemblance

between these fictions, and the facts as subsequently revealed, is purely coincidental.

While, early in 1933, Mostyn Lloyd and Harold Wright, former editor of *The Nation*, were keeping readers warned of what the humbug and cowardice of the League Powers in the face of Japanese aggression could do to the world, more and more of the paper's attention had to be given to what was now happening in Germany. But the Editor was rapidly learning to keep his paper nicely balanced: the series of completely ridiculous Disarmament Conferences which were a feature of the decade and read like something out of *Alice in Wonderland*, were closely followed; proposals, first French and then British, for disarmament were supported, albeit without much conviction, which is not surprising when you consider the kind of proposals with which politicians wasted their time and our money. Typical was the British proposal for total abolition of military and naval aircraft with international control of civil aviation, *except that States were to be allowed to retain such military aircraft as they needed for 'police' purposes*. This, of course, simply meant that we, with our worldwide frontiers to 'police' (by bombing 'natives'), would be left with the strongest air force. Can any politician or any Service Chief or Civil Servant ever have seriously believed that other nations would agree to this sort of thing? The *New Statesman*, reflecting its Editor's pacifism, did its best to take this rubbish seriously, but could not resist satirizing it in a series of strictly anonymous sketches whose author was Gilbert Murray.

The prolongation of the unemployment misery of ten or twelve million victims among our citizens, victims of Neville Chamberlain's policies at the Exchequer, did not lead the *New Statesman* to take depression for granted. G. D. H. Cole used its pages to nag the Government for year after year, urging and arguing a policy of economically useful public works, the sort of New Deal socialism which was to be adopted in the United States when the universally detested President Hoover* was at last turned out of office by F. D. Roosevelt. Cole wanted this as at least a partial cure for unemployment.

* H. L. Mencken described this President as the most hated man in the world. Hoover later lost the world title to Hitler.

While the Editor's personal tastes and preoccupations for life (notably political life) rather than art are manifest in the increasing liveliness of the front half of the paper, they are also less happily apparent in the relative dullness, relieved by flakes of liveliness, of the hind-quarters, until the advent of Raymond Mortimer. 'Books in General' was now being written by Mercury Patten; Sean O'Faolain was occasionally brought in to help Connolly, Pritchett and Peter Quennell with the novel reviewing; and two young men, Stephen Potter and Arthur Calder-Marshall, made their debut in the paper in 1932. From time to time a strong stimulant was administered to the arts and letters section by a writer who really belonged in front: there was, for example, the case of Harold Laski's review of H. G. Wells's novel, *The Bulpington of Blup*. By the early Thirties, Wells was one of the sacred cows, despite his politics: Laski did what the literary critics would not have done, pointed out that the book was a muddle of confused feeling and contradictions in thinking; the review gave rise to months of correspondence.

A minor but favourite feature with which we are familiar in the *New Statesman* is 'This England'. As a feature it was started by the *Week-end Review*, but in 1933 Critic also began to make his last paragraph a short collection of characteristically English imbecilities modelled on H. L. Mencken's 'Americana'. At this time Critic was about 80 per cent. Kingsley Martin plus, after his advent as Literary Editor, 20 per cent. Raymond Mortimer.

When Hitler became Chancellor of the Reich the *New Statesman* was not, at first, particularly alarmed. Editorial comment (Mostyn Lloyd) was to the effect that the non-Nazi and slightly less pernicious elements in the new Chancellor's government would keep the extremists in check; and that a strong reaction from an at last united Left under Communist leadership would probably give the Nazis more than they bargained for. It is important at this point to remember that in 1933 it was not yet fully understood that nineteenth-century civilization had broken down; it was not yet possible for liberal men to admit that rationalism and scientific logic had led not towards the millennium of improved social and political behaviour, but simply to a rejection of the 'irrational' (chiefly religious) tenets which had been holding the old Adam in check, without the adoption of a positive humanism in its place. In 1933 most people still believed that certain horrors of social behaviour, for example the use of torture by police forces and of massacre by governments, were so much things of the past as to be no longer possible. Only cynics could foresee that the Nazis would keep no moral rules at all but would follow only the logic of power, rationalism without humanism. However, the Editor and his colleagues were quick to catch on: with the burning of the Reichstag and the exposure in some English papers—all had the facts but the Right-wing papers suppressed them—of a plan for a Nazi massacre of their Socialist and Jewish enemies, the tone of cautious semi-optimism was dropped, Hitler's promises dismissed as rhodomontade, and the very worst foreseen with some accuracy.*

To understand the *New Statesman* of the Thirties, and for that matter the Forties from the viewpoint of the Sixties it is necessary to understand its Editor's state of mind. Kingsley Martin, like thousands of other young men of his time, was reared in the no-more-war atmosphere, and above all in the strong and angry determination not to be tricked by an appeal to idealism into serving the wicked ends of militant capitalism. Although he was not an orthodox Marxist, he accepted a part of the Marxist canon, including the belief that wars were fought between Capitalist States for material advantages which would accrue to the masters of those States, but entail nothing but suffering for the workers. This state of mind spread downwards and outwards through the nation from the 'intelligentsia', far beyond even the lowest layers of Mr. Julian Symons's pyramid. Readers may need reminding that in the Peace Ballot organized by the Peace Pledge Union in the first half of this decade, *nine million people* in Britain signed a pledge repudiating war; and that in the Oxford Union a resolution was carried 'under no circumstances will we fight for King and Country'. The real point of this resolution has generally been misunderstood.

* *The Brown Book of the Nazi Terror*, which had much influence, was a Communist build-up. Yet what did it say which time did not make true?

The proposer of the famous Motion was C. E. M. Joad, and the 'King and Country' phrase was intended to make it clear that only the old-style 'Nationalist' war was in question; these young men were not, that is, absolutely repudiating war, they were repudiating jingoism. For most of the people who signed the peace pledge, this repudiation of war was an emotional act, they were not obliged to think about it; nor were they capable of thinking about it. The decisions in important matters made by most of us are not reached by thinking; thinking is rare; political thinking very rare. This being so, most people could at once repudiate war and demand of their government courses of action which would lead to war, for example that Japan be prevented from raping Manchuria, or Italy from mustard-gassing the Ethiopians. This does not mean that we were all dotty. In our ordinary lives we are accustomed to the threat of (police) force keeping order, and we know that it is comparatively rarely necessary for the policeman actually to hit anyone over the head. It was felt that a union for order of many nations must have an over-whelming moral effect. In short, there was much faith in the League of Nations, and the facts that the League had no truncheon to draw and that the 'moral' force of a police is really no more than an implicit threat of physical force, were overlooked by peace pledgers but not by dictators. If the speeches and acts of the men we and other Parliamentary nations sent to Geneva seem now like a farrago of non-sense, we cannot altogether blame our leaders; they were infected by, weakened by, our own ambivalence.

Kingsley Martin was a pacifist, but he was also a Socialist; he was therefore a hater of Fascist aggression, who saw that it was important to stop the Dictators in their careers of vio-lence before they involved the whole world in war. He was obliged by his own feelings to believe that the League of Nations might accomplish this by moral suasion and perhaps by economic sanctions. But the Japan-Manchuria affair and the behaviour of the League on that occasion greatly weak-ened the foundation of his support for it. Unlike the majority of his fellow-countrymen he was forced to think about what was happening, not merely to feel a succession of emotions. It began to look to him, as it had long looked to those people who take a strange pride in their cynicism, as if no member of the League would even dream of placing the interests of humanity above those of its own ruling class.

It is my belief that the almost startling success of the *New Statesman*, from the Thirties onward, can only be explained by reference to the fact that its Editor, having thought instead of felt, took a clear decision, as I shall show, between two opposing principles, and out of that decision gave his paper a 'hard' policy. The rest of the Press, as far as I know without exception, simply went on behaving like its own readers, went on waffling, went on advocating mutually incompatible policies, or else advocating the basest solution to every political problem. The admass Press, that is the ordinary large-circulation daily newspapers and some of the Sundays, made the usual mistake, the mistake which leaves them utterly without influence despite enormous circulations, of taking their readers for moral imbeciles. The 'quality' Press indulged, for the most part, in that kind of pharisee-journalism which consists in advocating policies that confer on their advocates the right to feel holier-than-thou, without regard to the practical possibilities.

The triumph of Japanese arrogance over League impotence left Kingsley Martin and a handful of other intellectually honest men facing the fact that it was going to be very difficult to continue being both pacifist and at the same time to advocate world order; to continue to be against duelling *and* against giving the policeman a truncheon. He perceived that it is too easy to be a high-falutin' idealist refusing to lower one's political nose from its elevated position. His thinking self put a proposition to his feeling self: *Yes, what you would like to do ideally is very nice indeed; now consider what, in fact, can be done.*

But the failure of the League in the case of Japan was not in itself enough to make him lose all hope of the Covenant. It was just possible that their very failure might have the effect of forcing League members to sink their differences, put their particular interests second, and combine in face of danger. The second great test of the League Covenant came with Mussolini's attempt to build a second Roman Empire in Abyssinia. The League's second great failure forced the *New*

Statesman to decide between two principles and, as I have said, to adopt a 'hard' policy. But for the time being and whatever painful struggles he was having against some of his deepest conscientious convictions, the Editor continued to make the *New Statesman* lean over backwards in the pacifist-rationalist cause. For example, when in 1933 Hitler seemed willing to accept the British plan at the Disarmament Conference, editorial comment (Mostyn Lloyd) was:

> In effect she [Germany] gives us five years to prove the sincerity of our professions. This is a challenge which on the face of it is perfectly fair. Many will dislike and fear it; the Nazis have inspired an immense distrust in their neighbours. Nevertheless it must be taken up. The alternative is more armaments and attempts to coerce Germany, which might have a temporary success, but would lead to general disaster in the end.

The paper acquired a new literary distinction at this time when David Garnett started to write the 'Books in General' page. The succession of Literary Editors will be dealt with in its place; Garnett was, as editor, one of the failures but, as contributor, one of the successes. Garnett, like his predecessors and successors on that page, was a man who, while he might be politically advanced in a crisis, was in fact bored by politics and was, therefore, not 'committed' in the post-war Sartrian sense of the world. In fact the whole of the artistic and literary rump of the paper continued, with individual exceptions, to be in the hands of uncommitted men and women whose political motto might have been *Surtout pas de zèle*. It was when, later, the front-half zeal began to permeate the whole paper that the intellectuals, by that time wearying of their own zeal, were infuriated by what they no longer saw as a virtue and started to abuse the Editor in very immoderate language.

Through 1933 and 1934 it was possible for the *New Statesman* to continue in the hope, waning all the time, that pacifism was still realistic, and this despite what was happening in Germany and at Geneva. The rantings of the sawdust Caesar in Rome could, with a little goodwill, be laughed or shrugged off. The paper had long been banned in Italy, for saying that Mussolini had had Matteotti murdered, which was of course true; it was to be banned in Germany as well. English intellectuals had long had an affectionate admiration for Italy and Italians, and it was difficult to imagine that very civilized people taking their absurd Duce too seriously. At one point the Duce with his largely rhetorical 'six million bayonets' could be seen as a relatively desirable check to the other lunatic in Berlin.

Thus, as late as March 1934, the paper was giving strong support to Viscount Cecil in his appeal for more funds for the National Peace Ballot, while Mussolini was starting to whoop it up in Rome for his projected conquest of Abyssinia. During the spring a note of increasing alarm was sounded in editorial comment, most of it written by Mostyn Lloyd or by Brailsford. Some hopes were placed in Anthony Eden, who had gone to Rome to talk with Mussolini; but the note of conviction is lacking. In July the Editor commissioned Brailsford to write an article to make the choice we faced a clear one: 'Mussolini or the League'. (In 1962 we were talking of 'Salazar or the U.N.' in something of the same spirit.) Brailsford did not concern himself solely with Abyssinia, a country whose social shortcomings its Left-wing friends were obliged to glide over, but with the consequences which must necessarily follow a discrediting of the League:

> . . . a League which has failed to cope with Mussolini singly would lack the prestige and authority to deal with the complicated dangers his audacity may unleash.

The *New Statesman* urged, persistently and repeatedly, that our whole policy must be bent to the saving and strengthening of the League, for the alternative was chaos.

The policy actually followed by the governments of the European democracies was fraudulent. Their words in the League were flatly contradicted by their acts as individual nations; the *New Statesman* exposed, with foreboding, that Britain, France, Belgium and Czechoslovakia had stopped arms deliveries to Abyssinia. As the Duce continued lashing himself into a warlike fury, Critic concluded that he was 'not far from the borders of insanity', but saw a faint hope in the fact that Italians showed distaste for the prospect of war and that anyway their soldiers would all be afflicted by dysentery. Munichism appeared, *avant la lettre*, in the daily Press: the Government was urged to bring pressure not on Mussolini to desist from his violent courses, but on Haile Sellassie to hand over his country to Fascist Italy. Critic picked this out to deplore it. It has since been forgotten that Neville Chamberlain learnt his appeasement from the Press lords, as the people learnt theirs from the same source and from the pacifism of the Left-wing intellectuals, filtering down through the pyramid. It is possible to see Kingsley Martin's pacifism beginning to fail in August, when the *New Statesman* was advocating that Abyssinia must be allowed to import arms to defend herself. The change was not approved by those of his friends, notably C. E. M. Joad, who were active in the pacifist movement.

It was the Editor's practice to write his leading article in the small hours of Wednesday mornings and to send it to the printer by special messenger. It was during a conversation with Joad on Tuesday, 19 September, that he realized that he had come to a decision between his conflicting principles. He told Joad that it was now necessary for the Labour Party to support sanctions against Italy. Joad pointed out that this could lead to war, and was, therefore, an abandonment of the pacifist position. Kingsley Martin knew this when he sat down at one o'clock on the Wednesday morning, to write 'Socialists and Sanctions'. The Covenant of the League was so important that we must even go to war in defence of it, the salvation of Abyssinia from Italy being secondary to that.

In short, Kingsley Martin had become willing to give the policeman a truncheon; and by that change had given the *New Statesman* a 'hard' policy in what was to come.

9

Eng. Lit. and Plain Writing

A STUDY of the *New Statesman* since its foundation until
now reveals a curious inequality of sophistication as
between the political and literary halves of the paper.
As I hope to show, this is not merely a matter of changing
editors. Until some time in the late Twenties the political
half of the paper is 'superior', tough, cool, even a little aloof,
and sophisticated in the sense of being almost excessively
deft and professional. Thereafter, it becomes much more
'human', at once gentler and angrier, more involved and less
judgematical, more emotional and less complacently in
command of its political temper. Obviously, this has a great
deal to do with the advent of Kingsley Martin and, with him,
a number of new men. But there is more to it than that. An
editor of a paper which suddenly begins to be very successful
is in much the same case as the leader of a nation, or an army,
which suddenly finds itself on a career of triumph: he seems
to lead, but is in fact being driven. This is very far from
meaning that he is a puppet; for he is driven only in the sense
that one's head is driven by one's body; that is, it finds the
ways to satisfy the body's needs and aspirations. A successful
editor is a man who can sense his readers' preoccupations
and express them.

But the curious and more interesting aspect of the change
I am here concerned with is this: that in the literary half of
the paper it was, in a way, reversed. The comparison must
not be pushed too far, but in the *New Statesman* literary pages
the tone, from easy, intimate, not very serious-minded,
becomes tougher, more professional, altogether harder-
minded. I think that these two changes reflect large-scale

social phenomena quite as much as they reflect the minds and spirits of the men who gave them expression.

The *New Statesman* had four Literary Editors during Clifford Sharp's term of office as Editor: J. C. Squire, Desmond MacCarthy, G. W. Stonier (*de facto* not *de jure*), and Ellis Roberts. These men seem to have had very little in common. Squire was a poet, extraordinarily versatile, a fine all-round journalist and, as everyone knows, a brilliant parodist. MacCarthy was primarily a critic of the theatre. Stonier a professional journalist. Ellis Roberts has been described to me, by V. S. Pritchett, as 'a curiously priest-like figure'. He was a High Anglican man-of-letters. The tone of the *New Statesman*'s literary pages was, nevertheless, very much the same during the whole period covered by them as literary editors, and the reason lies not in what they were but in what they were not: they were not rebels, not originators, they all worked within a certain convention, a set of rules, even MacCarthy.

The fact is that before the 'change' in the late Twenties or early Thirties, reviewing and even criticism were gentlemanly, amateurish however skilful; after the change they became either commercial, or academic and professional. To put it without refinements, the literary and arts pages of the *New Statesman* were, before the change, produced by various men who, however different from each other as individuals and however much 'personality' each may have had in his way, were all of one variety of the species *homo sapiens*, which is now almost, though not quite, extinct: the Man-of-Letters.

The man-of-letters is a peculiarly English variety of mankind, although he occasionally occurs in New England too, and he often bears an Irish name and may, rarely, be a Scot. Whatever his early schooling may have been, he was formed by one of the older universities. He was the kind of man who might be poor but who often had some private means and who, in due course, received invitations to country-house parties and accepted them, finding himself at ease in such company, or at worst getting over his uneasiness with the gentry on the second day. It is highly significant of the kind of man he was that he might well end his career as a knight. His reading was very wide, but rarely deep: he might have the air of a scholar and write like one. On the whole he avoided literary enthusiasm though, if Irish, he understood how to be enthusiastic without offence. His writing was technically adroit, urbane, polished, above all, charming. He had lovely literary manners, his critical judgments were, as a rule, rather too easy and generous. He somehow, and often despite what he actually said in so many words, contrived to convey that literature is really not terribly important thank God and is, in fact, a sort of superior game, a kind of super-chess. It was this which gave his work, for all its professional preparation and polish, that deadly gentlemanly touch of the amateur. This touch implied that critical writing, *belles lettres*, the practice, after a thorough grounding in the theory, of Eng. Lit., was, like cricket, somehow better if it avoided professionalism.

The tone of the *New Statesman* literary pages from the beginning under Squire until after Ellis Roberts's time was, to borrow an adjective which has a clear, received meaning when applied to a school of poetry, Georgian. There was nothing singular or even deliberate in this: no widely read weekly had any other style. And it is not, either, that the more advanced writers, the popular or the original, were unnoticed. They were noticed, they even appear, and they are admired and praised. But just a little bit *de haut en bas*, almost as if they were performing seals. And the reason for the long duration of this kind of 'Establishment' writing in the *New Statesman* as well as in other English journals, long after it had ceased to be appropriate if it ever was, is quite clear. The practitioners of criticism were all trained in a gentlemanly tradition and this tradition, with its characteristic style, served them in lieu of a 'policy' and therefore eased their task, gave them rules of manner, in the place of rules of judgment, which were wanting.

But why not have a 'real' policy? I have tried to discuss this from one point of view in another chapter: I do not think that a widely read review of literature and the arts can possibly have a 'policy'. To do so means either writing for writers or putting your critics and reviewers into the strait-jacket of a strict social theory (*vide* the book reviews in the *Daily Worker* or *The Tablet*). But there was another reason. Unlike France, England does not produce schools of writers foregathering to discuss their work, to form philosophies of their work, to be very *sérieux* about their work. If English writers foregather at all, it is probably to discuss the iniquities of publishers, to gossip about people, to eat and drink. In the past, English writers even foregathered to play cricket.* And they wished, when not actually writing, to be men-about-town or country gentlemen.

But though all this is true it is not enough; for while the *New Statesman* Literary Editors had the faults they also had the virtues of their gentlemanliness: they were not, on the whole, jealous; on the contrary they were generous-minded and constantly on the watch for new talent among the young; even the young who did not hold with the urbanity and imperturbability of the ruling University style. This was particularly true of Desmond MacCarthy, who watched for and sought and found new contributors for the paper. And it is for this reason that any list of contributors to the *New Statesman* literary pages is at the same time a very nearly complete list of every considerable literary talent from 1913 to 1963. I doubt whether the distinction of this list can be equalled by any other weekly journal; it is surely unique.

Only in Squire's case did the Literary Editor edit the whole paper for any length of time, although his successor, Desmond MacCarthy, was sometimes obliged to make good, with Mrs. Vincent's help, the Editor's shortcomings when Sharp neglected part of his work. Squire was perfectly capable of being Editor-in-Chief; he was one of the most accomplished and versatile journalists of his time. What is more remarkable is the way in which the political pages of the *New Statesman*, when he alone was in charge, retained the character which Sharp had given them. This is so much the case that one seeks an explanation, for it is hardly enough to say that the two men had worked together on the paper for two years. The key to this consistency lies in the quietly exercised influence of Sidney Webb. When Sharp was present Webb's touch was light; while Squire was virtual

* In the famous and too much quoted cricket match in A. G. Macdonnell's *England their England*, a work of the rankest flattery, there are portraits of both J. C. Squire and Desmond MacCarthy.

editor, Webb's touch became just a shade firmer. But this is not the whole story, for Squire himself contributed largely to his paper's political pages during the war years, and it is a remarkable fact that his political and his literary writings do not seem to be by the same hand. Perhaps his gift for parody, which is in some sort a gift for imitation, came in handy and enabled him, when writing on politics or the news in general, to *be* Sharp. Squire writing on books was the not-too-deadly-serious gentleman essayist, nothing if not urbane; shift him to the front of the paper and he becomes a hard-minded Fabian liberal.

Squire left the *New Statesman* after the war to become editor of the *London Mercury*. Desmond MacCarthy, who had returned from his duties with the ambulance corps and was again writing for the paper, was appointed in his place. The 'Books in General' page had become the Literary Editor's personal territory and most of the *New Statesman* Literary Editors did, in fact, write that page. MacCarthy did it as well as it has been done except, for my own taste, by Victor Pritchett.

In view of the 'image' of himself which MacCarthy presented, and of the tales which are told about the man, it might have been expected that while he would do his own writing week after week to the very high standard he himself had set, he would not be very good at organizing that of other people. In fact, however, and apart from his reliance on Mrs. Vincent to organize his time, he was a very good editor indeed. Not only was he very thoroughly 'in touch' with the whole world of letters and the arts, he had a magnificent eye for new and coming talent; he spotted newcomers while they were still at their universities, and was quick to nobble them for his paper. As a selector of reviewers, he had a flair for knowing what a man would do well and seeing that he did it. The *New Statesman* owed both Cyril Connolly and Peter Quennell to MacCarthy. Probably no writer has ever reviewed novels so consistently well as Connolly did it in the *New Statesman*. He was at once penetrating and hard in judgment, gentle when the author he was dealing with merited gentleness; he was exceptionally good at picking out *kitsch*, a thing which Time is usually better at than any critic. When Bland reviewed novels in the *New Statesman*, all the novels were good. Connolly did not make the most facile of highbrow mistakes, that of finding them all bad. In expression he was, from the first, lucid; and though he took the work seriously he was the most entertaining of reviewers. Of other *New Statesman* novel reviewers only Rebecca West has come up to his standard, and then not consistently.

MacCarthy, of course, had his faults as an editor, especially from the contributors' point of view. When George Stonier joined the paper, he became MacCarthy's assistant. One of his jobs was to choose the poetry to be retained out of the much greater quantity which was sent in. MacCarthy would allow a pile of some poet's work to accumulate, occasionally deciding to print a poem and then taking one from the pile. The first the poet knew of the fate of the work which he was apparently posting into limbo, would be the arrival of a proof several months—or even years—later.

MacCarthy gave up the literary editorship of the *New Statesman* to write for the *Sunday Times*. The daily and Sunday 'quality' Press has repeatedly recruited the ranks of its writers from the *New Statesman*—Desmond MacCarthy, Cyril Connolly, Peter Quennell, Raymond Mortimer, John Raymond, T. C. Worsley, R. H. S. Crossman and Desmond Shawe-Taylor are among those who worked under Kingsley Martin before being seduced away by other editors.

Having lost MacCarthy, Sharp appointed G. W. Stonier to 'look after' the literary side under his, Sharp's, supervision. Poor Stonier had a terrible time, for there were weeks when he was obliged to edit the whole paper, answer the letters which the Editor had neglected or carelessly thrown into the waste-paper basket, and see the paper to bed almost single-handed. However, after some months Sharp, or it may have been John Roberts, was approached by an old Fleet Street hand, Clennell Wilkinson, who wanted the job of Literary Editor. It was fairly obvious that he had not the qualities for the job, but he came offering a valuable consideration. If he was given the job, he could undertake to get a weekly article from Hilaire Belloc, who happened to be his brother-in-law. As he was an experienced practical

journalist it seemed quite a good idea to accept his proposal.*
Sharp and Roberts decided to do so. But although he could
do the office work, and although he brought Belloc with him,
he was quite unable to judge other contributors' work at the
New Statesman level. Belloc had undertaken to write his
weekly page for six months and he did that; but when he
ceased to write for the paper there was no reason to keep his
brother-in-law. Once again Stonier had to carry the can.
Relief came with the appointment, as Literary Editor, of
Ellis Roberts. He had worked for some years on the *Church
Times* and he had been editor of the *Daily Chronicle*, so that
presumably he had a 'name' which might be of value to the
paper.

Ellis Roberts was not only a Man-of-Letters; much worse,
he was, or he saw himself as, a Literary Figure. He wore a
cloak and a wide-brimmed hat of the kind associated, I
understand, with the highest Anglicanism; he was vaguely
Chestertonian in appearance, manners and tastes; he was
vaguely a Socialist. He was a competent literary critic
without an original idea in his head, and one whose judgments were invariably secondhand. He was a perfectly
professional journalist, however, who wrote his stint, saw
that others wrote theirs, and kept good time. He had no
distinction and too much "personality"; he was a born
frequenter of literary coteries. He was out of place on the
New Statesman. Yet his professional reliability as a regular
copy-producer must have been valuable at a time when
Sharp had been shipped off to the United States, and
Mostyn Lloyd, who had neither time nor inclination to
bother with arts and letters, was editing the paper in a three-
day week. Still, it was an odd appointment, and even odder
was the fact that he was conceded his demand for £1,000 a
year, a salary out of all proportion to what anyone else was
getting. Appointment and salary were so eccentric, in fact,
that gossip suggested that Sharp had been drunk when he
came to terms with Ellis Roberts. This is to underestimate
the value of Ellis Roberts and also to misunderstand the
nature of Sharp's alcoholism; his journalistic judgment was

* The appointment was never ratified by the Board of Directors. This
was an interregnum.

not impaired; and as to the money, John Roberts must have agreed to that. Stonier tells me that Sharp could write a perfectly good leader after drinking more than a bottle of whisky; and that the appointment of Ellis Roberts was much discussed in the office before it was made, with John Roberts (no relation) in favour of it. I think that it is clear what John Roberts, as manager of the paper, wanted: a Literary Editor who could be relied on to do his job without the supervision which Sharp could not, now, be trusted to provide.

It should be emphasized that Clifford Sharp had not become a helpless sot. He was, as it were, drunk but not incapable. He was still good for his leader, for his paragraphs of comment, or for a review. But he was not running the paper, and therefore not developing it so that its growth potential could be realized. Occasionally, even, Sharp would come into the office late on the evening before press-day, carrying a bottle of whisky and accompanied by his mistress carrying half a bottle of the same; they would retire to the residential flat upstairs, drink the bottle and a half of whisky and enjoy each other's company in the customary way; meanwhile, Sharp was presumably thinking out his leader, for he would then sit down and write it and so have it ready for the printer the next day. But he was otherwise rarely at the office; it was difficult to get decisions from him, and he seemed to have lost his power of sustained purpose, if not his skill. In such conditions the steadiness of Ellis Roberts, his professional reliability, must have been of some value, even if 'that priest-like figure' had no other great qualities.

By the end of 1929 the long-suffering Board of Directors had had enough of Sharp; I have already described how reluctant they were simply to get rid of him, and how his editorship had been tapered off rather than terminated, by giving him a sabbatical year. He owed this to John Roberts, for the Board, at the end of its patience, had written to Sharp: '. . . that the contract between yourself and the Company should, for various reasons, be terminated'. He was given the chance to give notice to the Company, but the choice of being sacked if he preferred it. John Roberts got this softened to first six months', then a year's, leave, with a general understanding that Sharp would not, in fact, return. When Ratcliffe, having with Orage found Sharp destitute and drunk, cabled the Board for permission to advance Sharp money against his shares in the *New Statesman* Company, the Board (and this time John Roberts agreed with his directors) insisted that the shares be transferred to them before money was advanced. In view of their long record of patience and generosity, it seems that Sharp must have tried their tempers beyond bearing. Incidentally, Lloyd, when appointed Acting Editor in his place, was paid £1,000 a year.

Kingsley Martin inherited Ellis Roberts from Sharp. It was obvious to him that this man was not the Literary Editor he wanted for the newly amalgamated papers, and for the journal which the new Editor had it in mind to create. It was one thing to decide as much, quite another to get rid of Ellis Roberts. There is a strange tale of Mrs. Ellis Roberts invading the offices late one evening when all but the young Editor, brooding at his desk over his paper, had left. He was warned by her and by diverse literary pundits that if he dismissed the Literary Editor he would not only ruin the paper, he would render the Company liable to an action at-law of the most serious kind. It may have been the quality of Mrs. Roberts's wifely loyalty which kept the Editor respectfully silent: he is said to have uttered not a single word from beginning to end of this scene.

Once again the *New Statesman* was without a Literary Editor, and the work of organizing that department fell upon Stonier. Kingsley Martin arranged for Harold Nicolson to write 'Books in General' for six months, but Nicolson could not undertake the other duties of literary editorship. Nicolson's weekly essays have all the clear distinction which still makes his article what one turns to first in *The Observer*; he was urbane, but his urbanity has a different quality from that of the early twentieth-century man-of-letters, for it is free from cosiness and complacency; he had (and has) the gift of making it clear that he was conveying a personal reaction to a book, a personal judgment; and that he did not imply universal 'civilized' validity for his personal judgments.

During this interregnum it was decided to offer the literary editorship to David Garnett. It seems to me to have been a curious decision; Garnett's talent was a very singular and peculiar one; his books, all of them small masterpieces, are exceptionally personal and intimate, and one would have thought that their quality implied in the author's character a natural inability to run an office, to give out rather than take in. He accepted the appointment, but he was not a good editor. His own writings for the paper gave it further distinction; they could do no less. He was somewhat eccentric in his choice of books to discuss, but that was not necessarily a disadvantage. But otherwise he was the antithesis of MacCarthy, taking no trouble to seek and recruit new talent or to do any other of the jobs proper to his office, and leaving the donkey-work entirely to Stonier or to whomever would do it. Kingsley Martin describes Garnett as a 'sleepy' editor; and there is, of course, in his books a dream-like quality which is delightful but which does not suggest the business-like manager of journalists.

To save Garnett from the misery of a job he disliked and the paper from the difficulties in which his business ineptitude was involving it, it was agreed that what the Literary Editor needed was six months' leave, which was granted. Raymond Mortimer had written criticism for the *New Statesman* since 1922. But as that paper refused to allow him also to write for *The Nation*, whereas *The Nation* left him free to contribute to other papers, he had transferred his work to *The Nation*. He had also been writing for *Vogue*, at the time a very 'smart' journal, interested in the arts and rather high-brow. In the emergency created by Garnett's 'sleepiness', Mortimer was asked by Kingsley Martin to take Garnett's place, 'temporarily'.

With the advent of Raymond Mortimer came the first stage of the change which was to emancipate the literary pages of the *New Statesman* from 'gentlemanliness': there was still no hard policy, nor was it possible, for the reasons I have given, that there should be. But what becomes manifest is a coherent and consistent tone. George Stonier who worked with both men for years considers that both as a writer and as an editor MacCarthy was the best Literary Editor the *New Statesman* ever had. Victor Pritchett, who was to succeed Mortimer, places him above MacCarthy. Referring to the 'tone' which dominated the literary and arts half of the paper under Mortimer, and identifying it as 'Bloomsbury', Pritchett says:

> Raymond Mortimer embodied this Bloomsbury spirit and was, to my mind, the most brilliant literary editor the paper ever had. He was a curious mixture of liberalism and ruthless intolerance, especially towards the literary puritan-ism growing up in Cambridge. . . .*

The 'Bloomsbury' tone was, of course, strengthened by the fact that most of the old *Nation* literary hands had come over to the *New Statesman and Nation*. But it was chiefly owing to the new Literary Editor. He was contemptuous of the Eng. Lit. professors—can the *furor Leavisiticus* which burst about the paper in 1962 with the terrifying explosion of a bursting paper-bag have been what the Communists call a *revanchiste* movement? Professors, he thought, took no trouble over their writing because having, as a rule, a captive audience, they were not obliged to compete for attention. Raymond Mortimer believed that a writer should aim to please—I think that is the sense in which he meant it—in the way that any tradesman whose work has an aesthetic attribute, a cabinet-maker or a potter for example, should aim to please; this is a different thing from the adoption of a set of writing-manners, the felicities of a gentleman-of-letters.

In Raymond Mortimer, Kingsley Martin had found a man whom he could leave alone to get on with the job and who gave his half of the paper a consistent tone. His sympathies and interests were very much broader than would now be the case. The young and not-still-so-young writers now most to the front are singularly narrow, consciously and deliberately provincial. Raymond Mortimer was a Francophil whose mind and ideas had been shaped by French culture and French literature. He was passionately interested in the visual arts and in music, consequently in all the subjects he had to employ people to write about. Know-ing something about them, he was fully competent to judge the work of art and music critics, which many Literary Editors are not.

* In a private communication.

Before David Garnett's six months' leave was over, Kingsley Martin had decided to keep Raymond Mortimer if he could. Garnett was not pleased when told of the change: but he was asked to continue to write 'Books in General' and for the time being he did so. In due course, however, Mortimer took over this major task of the Literary Editor's work himself, and Garnett ceased to write for the paper except as a reviewer.

No Literary Editor could have differed more widely from Garnett than Mortimer. He applied, he even devoted, himself to the work. He knew every literary talent, new or old, rising or setting. He took enormous trouble with the work of the writers he found and employed. Cuthbert Worsley, who worked with him for years, says that a session with Mortimer over a piece of 'copy' was like a university tutorial. Raymond Mortimer says that he learnt this method and this thoroughness from Desmond MacCarthy. With the manuscript before him and the author in attendance he would take it almost phrase by phrase: 'You say here so-and-so and so-and-so. Do you *really* mean that? You are quite sure that that is the best way of expressing your thought?' He detested sloppy writing, careless writing, the have-a-bash school of writing which has since become fashionable.

Edward Sackville-West, who had worked for the *New Statesman* under MacCarthy, and who was, I suppose, Assistant Literary Editor, although it has proved difficult to pin a label on him, was Mortimer's first assistant. If Edward Sackville-West was not, himself, ever considered for the editorial chair in the literary and arts department, it was because he was too mild, too unwilling to assert himself. But he was the most valuable second a Literary Editor could have; he had his own routine and ways of doing things, and the advantage of having been there first. But when he ceased to be Assistant Literary Editor, though continuing to write for the paper, Raymond Mortimer recruited Cuthbert Worsley in 1937, and Worsley was made his Assistant Literary Editor. But Mortimer, like most very able men, was not good at teaching routine to his assistants, or explaining what he was doing and how he was doing it, and he was apt to prefer doing, himself, what could have been delegated.

This was to have consequences when Worsley had to take over from Raymond Mortimer.

The Editor's policy of non-interference with the writers' and artists' department, and Raymond Mortimer's firm grasp of his work, had one disadvantage: it perpetuated and perhaps emphasized the division between the two halves of the paper which I have already pointed out, and which was to persist until the advent of John Freeman as Editor and with him a new and deliberate policy of integration which will be discussed in its place. During Mortimer's long and successful term as Literary Editor, Kingsley Martin is said sometimes to have admitted, with mock sorrow, that he was really the Editor of two papers, not one. The two editors had their offices side by side and frequently consulted each other, but this was not enough. The Editor's supervision of the second, the literary and arts review, was diffident and tactful, as was sensible since he had at last found a Literary Editor of outstanding ability and versatility. He exercised remarkable restraint even in the important matter of the overall political policy of his paper: from time to time he would appear in the Literary Editorial offices, look wistfully at the long shelf of newly arrived or long published Left Book Club volumes, and say, tentatively, 'Surely one or two of them must be worth reviewing.' That was as far as he went, except on one or two special occasions. There was the time when he sent a note to the Literary Editor saying that while aware of the importance of Kafka to the modern novel, he would suggest confining references to that novelist to every *other* week. And there was the time when he burst into the Literary offices in a rage: Worsley, who had taken over dramatic criticism from MacCarthy when MacCarthy had to cease writing it for the *New Statesman*, had seen the first Brecht play to be produced in London and pronounced Brecht to be a bore. Worsley, with his knowledge of the history and material of German theatre, insisted that Brecht was not only a bore but a plagiarist. Kingsley Martin complained that you could not call the great Marxist poet and playwright a bore and that his office was besieged by infuriated German refugee Marxists clamouring for Worsley's blood. Worsley asked the Editor if he had himself seen any Brecht on the stage. Kingsley Martin, taken aback, hesitated, then burst out laughing: he had not. And he told Worsley, 'I'm sorry, carry on. If you think Brecht is a bore, say so of course. I will go down and do battle with his disciples.'

Mortimer claimed that Kingsley Martin's non-interference with the literary and arts part of the paper was balanced by his own constant interference with the political side. If this was designed to influence the paper's politics in favour of Mortimer's old-fashioned Liberalism, it failed. But it would not be true to say that the Literary Editor was hostile to the paper's Left-wing attitude, although he did from time to time contrive to make fun of it in that part of the paper which he controlled, a *tour de force* on his part, and a test of tolerance on the Editor's, which must both be very exceptional. However, Mortimer had no difficulty in getting on very well with Socialist intellectuals whatever his feelings towards Socialism; he worked harmoniously with Harold Laski and with G. D. H. Cole, and he had a great admiration for R. H. S. Crossman, whom he considered a most brilliant reviewer of books. His own recruits to the *New Statesman* were not politicals: it is not clear whether he was responsible for bringing Pritchett on to the paper; but Desmond Shawe-Taylor, admirable whether as 'Peter Galway', reviewer of books, or as a music critic, was Mortimer's 'find'.

The worst crisis of Raymond Mortimer's editorship occurred when a German bomb more or less destroyed the contents of the offices at Great Turnstile. It is always the case that a certain amount of material for a literary review is held in proof until the occasion to use it occurs. The original manuscript or typescript will probably have been returned, with proof for correction, to the author. All this pending material was destroyed and for that week Mortimer and Worsley were obliged to bring a paper into existence out of thin air, harrying authors for carbon copies which often did not exist, and conjuring material out of limbo.

When Worsley returned to the paper after the war, in 1945, he again became Assistant Literary Editor, but found that Raymond Mortimer had got into the habit of doing almost all the work himself. Then, in 1946, Mortimer accepted, from the *Sunday Times*, an offer which would enable him to earn what he wanted in return for only a single article a week, so that he would be free to write original work or to do nothing at all if he liked. Worsley took over the job of Literary Editor, but he was at first handicapped by the fact that Mortimer had not delegated responsibility or much of the executive work, believing, perhaps, that Worsley had not the editorial temperament. However, he did the work efficiently and as he, in his turn, needed an assistant, Janet Adam Smith, who had been assisting J. R. Ackerley, Literary Editor of *The Listener*, was engaged by the *New Statesman*.

Worsley's real interest was the theatre; he liked nothing better than writing dramatic criticism and wanted to concentrate on that. It was decided that he should run the Arts and Entertainment pages of the paper, and meanwhile the Literary Editorship as such was offered to Victor Pritchett who, again, had long written criticism and reviews for the *New Statesman*.

Victor S. Pritchett was, perhaps, the first man to fill a major post on the *New Statesman* who had not been shaped by the Public-School-Old-University machine. But like Garnett, he was an imaginative writer, not a 'managerial' one. Moreover, he is a comic writer of very rare talent; his *Mr Beluncle* will, in due course, take a much more important place in our literature than is at present accorded to it. When he discusses a book, Pritchett makes the operation of taking it apart in order to look at it extraordinarily interesting; he has, as critic, the qualities of the born teacher who can capture and hold the attention and make even the indifferent find what he has to say important. For me, at least, his series of 'Books in General' raised that page of the *New Statesman* to a new high level, but above all it changed the tone of the page in a sense initiated by Raymond Mortimer but going much further. It was really Pritchett who made 'Books in General' fit the times by being 'scientific' without, however—and here he seems to me unique—paralysing his own feelings about books or writers: his analyses are works of 'science', but they are inspired by a convincing warmth because he is *sérieux*.

169

Unfortunately, Pritchett detested the executive part of his job; being a conscientious man he did not simply neglect it or forget that it was there to be done; but he never enjoyed it, he wanted to write and he liked writing for the *New Statesman*, but he wanted someone else to do the office and contact work. In due course this was arranged.

The only way I can think of to express what I feel and believe to be true about the change from the old to the new style in the literary pages of the *New Statesman*, is to say that Letters, Literature—note the capitals—the gentlemanly convention of critical writing as an indoor sport is replaced by, simply, plain writing about things. Plain writing is much more difficult than fancy writing. It is fair to say that when Squire was first writing 'Books in General' he, too, was not an 'exclusive' writer, did not turn a cold shoulder on the un-initiated, the non-University reader, by maintaining a sort of cosy, intimate tone. In plain writing the critic makes far fewer assumptions about the nature and background of his reader's mind; he tries to write for everyone who has a certain standard of reading and intelligence, not just for a group of people whose reading and intelligence are of a predetermined, known pattern. As a matter of fact this new plainness was an achievement more considerable than it seems to be, because get-together cosy-complacency is a besetting sin of English literary 'schools' in so far as they exist at all. The young writers of the Thirties, for all their political radicalism, committed this sin so gravely that their books and articles are full of what one might almost compare to family jokes. I have no doubt about the reason for this: the English are only with great difficulty and deliberation a city people; their civilization is not naturally metropolitan. They like villages and village gossip and the taste is very oddly reflected in their writing; they like clubs, and although they do not form coteries as obviously as the French do (but how differently in spirit), their clubs are, in fact, cliques. To keep clear of this kind of thing is extremely difficult for most English writers, whether they be creative or critical writers; and those who achieve emancipation are the outsiders, the eccentrics.

The extreme case of plain writing, not in place here since

it is not reached until the Sixties, but useful by way of demonstration of the trend I am trying to describe, is deliberate vulgarization, even proletarianization, of terms. The French led the way, of course; a lot of Sartre is written in street jargon and is, consequently, not translatable into English but only into American, since Americans have a livelier demotic speech. In the *New Statesman* it is reached in the Arts and Entertainments pieces of Rayner Banham, and occasionally in Clancy Sigal's reviews. Some of Rayner Banham's work is done almost in the with-it coffee-bar jargon of the period; he goes so far along this way that he is no longer writing 'English', but English as she is spoke. This makes his work even more ephemeral than most journalism, but it has one immense advantage: it enables him to make use of a whole group of states-of-mind expressions of immediate, contemporary validity, as ephemeral as the language he employs but as rich in immediate meaning and significance as they are fashionably wanting in precision.

The broad-brimmed hat and flowing tie also vanished from the treatment of music and painting in the *New Statesman*. But in ways different from their removal from the lay-figure of the literary critic and reviewer. Music seems, for the time being, to be a branch of science, of *n*-dimensional mathematics. For many years Turner wrote about music in the *New Statesman* on the assumption that everyone listened to it and was middle-brow musically literate. This does not seem to me to be true now, and I would guess that the *New Statesman*'s music writing in recent years has been written for and read by the especially, rather than the generally, interested. When, in the Twenties, a *New Statesman* critic first attended a jam-session he dismissed the whole of jazz as contemptible. No journalist who could be writing for the *New Statesman* today would dream of doing such a thing. The popular has become important; and as each new vogue of it is treated seriously by intellectuals, it ceases to be popular. The movement of culture has been reversed: it travels upwards. As for painting, since I know nothing about it and am incapable of understanding a page of art criticism, or even of getting to the end of it, I am singularly ill-equipped to write about the paper's art critics. But John Berger, one of

171

Worsley's 'finds', has obviously solved a difficult problem by having the good fortune to be a Communist and therefore to have a clearly defined point of view to write from. Whether it is the best point of view from which to judge a picture is not clear to me.

Pritchett's style, as Literary Editor, was then at once simpler and much more 'nervous', leaner, more muscular than the old style. It is probably quite unfair to accuse the men-of-letters of frivolousness about their subject because they did a certain amount of 'charming' fooling with ideas and language; but Pritchett and those who write like him are *sérieux*, and to that extent they are un-English. They came just in time: the downfall of the arts is artiness; the downfall of critical writing is urbanity, is complacent charm. The abandonment of charm, the purification of judgment and of expression by a scientific ambience also has its dangers, as is clear from the excesses of M. Alain Robbe-Grillet and his disciples in France. But for the moment we are safe.

During and after Pritchett's term of office, Worsley continued to write the paper's dramatic criticism. Meanwhile J. B. Priestley had been invited to join the Board of Directors when a new director was required. The invitation was one of the things about which Kingsley Martin and Raymond Mortimer had not seen eye to eye. Mortimer did not consider Priestley, who had no respect for highbrows, to be the kind of director the *New Statesman* needed. But this was to identify himself with the *New Statesman*, whereas the only valid identification was, of course, with Kingsley Martin. Priestley had, at all events, become a director. His success as a playwright had made him very much a man of the theatre; he did not like Worsley's dramatic criticism. He tried to persuade Kingsley Martin to replace Worsley, and he enlisted the support of John Roberts in this undertaking. The pressure on the Editor was heavy and sustained and it failed completely. Kingsley Martin's loyalty to his writers was as great as his confidence in his judgment of their abilities, and Worsley did not leave the paper until he was offered more money to go to the *Financial Times*.

MacCarthy; Raymond Mortimer; Cuthbert Worsley; and there were others who made a name for themselves on

the *New Statesman* and were, in due course, tempted away
from it by offers from other editors, which the paper,
prosperous as it had become, could not afford to match. This
business of running, as it were, a training establishment for
distinguished literary journalists, and distinguished political
journalists too, was one of Kingsley Martin's most remarkable achievements. The *New Statesman* has, since 1930, been
as great a school of good journalistic writing as was the
Manchester Guardian in the first decade of this century. It is
not, of course, invariably money which tempts a man away
from the paper on which he has made his name; he may feel
the need of a change after ten, fifteen or even more years in
one niche. But the fact is that no weekly, however successful
as a business undertaking, can possibly compete in the
matter of salaries with a newspaper like the *Sunday Times*,
or the *Financial Times*, or for that matter the *Daily Mirror*,
whose revenues are out of all proportion greater. Such a
newspaper can probably offer thousands for hundreds, or
almost. In the case of political journalists, like R. H. S.
Crossman for example, there is also the desire to be addressing a larger audience, to be preaching to the unconverted
for a change. This is a less potent force in the case of the
literary journalists: one *New Statesman* writer shocked and
astonished an editor of the *Daily Express* by refusing an offer
to work for that paper. It was not his refusal of the vast
salary which disturbed the poor man; it was the refusal to be
impressed by the idea of writing for four million readers.
Indifference to numbers above one million is, in our time, a
kind of subversiveness.

After Pritchett as Literary Editor—he still wrote 'Books in
General' as a rule—came that period in the paper's history
when one was apt to be asked, 'By the way, you write for the
Staggers. Who *is* the Literary Editor?' This was during the
reign of Janet Adam Smith. She was appointed when Pritchett gave up, and she had, in fact, been doing the executive
part of the work for some time.

As an editor Janet Adam Smith was well-informed about
the world of literature, a good and highly critical judge of
poetry, so that during her term the standard of the poetry
printed in the *New Statesman* rose to the strictly 'literary

review' level; and she was very efficient in the managerial side of her work. It seems to me that she did not allow herself to write enough for the paper. Even when Pritchett was not still writing 'Books in General' and she might have done so—as she occasionally did—she was apt to efface herself in favour of a specialist. It was done for the sake of the paper; but because of this too modest loyalty to the cause, she failed to impose herself on the paper, she did not succeed in becoming a 'name' to its readers, perhaps because she did not wish to do so. During part of her term of office she was assisted by John Raymond; he had been recruited, for the brilliance of his writing, by Worsley. It is by no means clear that this made her task any easier. Theirs were not compatible natures and they cannot be said to have composed a team. Janet Adam Smith was quiet, academic in the best sense, reserved, clear-headed and naturally industrious. She had the qualities of the distinguished mountaineer that she was (and is, for all I know). John Raymond did not have the qualities of a mountaineer. The paper never had, and did not now, impose any kind of 'policy' on its literary contributors; but there was an incompatibility between new statesmanship and John Raymond, and he was not an easy man to get on with. When Janet Adam Smith told the Editor—it was a blow—that she wanted to give up the job a year before he had expected her to do so, there was nobody obviously suitable to replace her.

Literary Editors good at all the parts of their job are not as thick as autumn leaves in Vallombrosa; they are rather more difficult to find than good Prime Ministers. Walter Allen, whose work as a literary critic is distinguished by thoroughness and whose name has been made as critic and historian of the English novel, had been working for the *New Statesman* for some years: he wrote reviews, knew many of the contributors, was friends with the staff people, understood the workings of the paper, and was very much an *ami de la maison*. He had been living with his family in Kent, but had moved to the West Country where he would be at peace to write his critical and imaginative books. This, however, put him out of reach of London. To offer him the Literary Editorship would entail asking him to move back near or into

London, and there was some hesitation to do that. It seemed to the Editor and his advisers that Walter Allen would probably make a good Literary Editor, but this was not in the nature of things certain; and to ask him to move only to find that he was not happy or perhaps not at his best in the work, would be a serious matter. In the end Kingsley Martin made the offer and Walter Allen accepted it.

Once again there was proof that a man learned and absorbed in literature and the arts generally, a critic of distinction and a novelist in his own right, does not necessarily make a good Literary Editor. Needless to say, as a writing-editor Allen was good; as a judge and buyer of other people's work he was knowledgeable. But in accepting the appointment he had done what thousands have done before and more will do again; misconceived not so much his abilities as his ambitions. He must have thought that he would do the executive part of his work with the necessary zest; he discovered that it bored him beyond bearing. I think it possible that Walter Allen discovered that, after all, he did not enjoy, and therefore could not properly exercise, power; he could not assert himself, and if a man of character cannot assert himself it is probably because he does not want to. However, Allen stuck gallantly to the work until somebody could be found to replace him.

IO

Lefty

BEFORE the *New Statesman*'s progress through the Thirties can be followed and understood it will be necessary to remind the reader of the history of that epoch. I shall offer no apology for devoting almost the whole of a long chapter to what we may call the paper's foreign policy: it was in the Thirties that it became impossible for any serious English journal to give the best part of its attention to purely domestic affairs. The Webbian *New Statesman* was no longer a possible paper: Britain was no longer a mighty oracle giving laws to the world out of a cloud of industrial smoke—the image is Evelyn Waugh's—but a small part of a violently changing and extremely quarrelsome world with which she could plead but to which she could not dictate; she was no longer a sort of Lady Catherine de Bourgh among nations, scolding the lesser breeds into peace and prosperity. The physical break-up of the British Empire did not come until the Forties; but its moral failure can be dated a quarter of a century earlier.

The *Pax Britannica* had been not merely broken in 1914; it had been shattered for ever. Since there was no world empire to keep the world's peace, and since the United States persisted in a selfish isolation and an attitude of holier-than-thou, hope of establishing and maintaining the peace among nations was invested in the League of Nations and the Covenant of the League. But at a time before the H-bomb had been invented and when, therefore, it was not impossible that war might still be a profitable policy for a nation on the make, the members of the League were not on an equal footing. As I have said, there were Powers, like Britain, France, Holland and Belgium, which had all the territory and resources they wanted and wished only to be left in peace to enjoy their property; and there were other powers, such as Japan, Italy and Germany, which had malthusian or industrial or economic problems which, they believed, could best be solved by creating empires for themselves. I include Germany since that is what she was to come to, to be driven to; at the beginning of this period she was still the Weimar Republic and not, apparently, bent on any kind of imperial adventure. It is fair to say that although on moral grounds it was to everybody's advantage that the peace be kept, it was also the case that peace suited the Have Powers better than the Have-not Powers.

When Japan got away with her mayhem, her success in defying the League was of the first importance because it showed other would-be aggressors that they, too, could get away with violent assault. In 1935 Mussolini led Italy into an empire-building war against Abyssinia; again the League was expected by men of peace to assert itself and put a stop to this; again it failed to do so. A possible reason for these failures will appear in the course of the chapter. The next major failure of the League occurred when a group of Spanish Army officers led by General Franco invaded Spain from Morocco with the object of destroying the Republican democracy which had been set up in that country and replacing the elected government with a Fascist dictatorship on the Italian model: the League policy of 'non-intervention' was so manipulated that it enabled the Italian Government to send between 50,000 and 100,000 men to Franco's aid, while depriving the Spanish Government of weapons to arm the Spanish people. Up to almost 1936 it was reasonable to hope that the League of Nations could, given the goodwill of member governments, be made effective; thereafter, it became rather silly to hope anything of the kind, but a lot of people none the less, went on hoping for reasons which will appear.

The real weakness of the League of Nations must be sought in the relationship between the Governments and the peoples of member States, which were complicated by the existence of the Russian Communist Government. Right-wing Governments of member States were afraid and distrustful of their own Left-wing masses: if they combined to act against the Fascist, i.e. extreme Right-wing, imperialist adventures of aggressor States, they would automatically be helping not only their own Left-wing opponents at home but the dreaded Communist Russians. Moreover, they would not be effective, militarily speaking, unless their respective peoples were willing to arm them; and Left-wing movements in their own countries were very reluctant to entrust 'Capitalist' Governments with armaments. Respectable but Right-wing Governments dedicated to Capitalism could not help seeing that the Fascists were, in some sort, their natural allies. And they might also feel that if the aggressive nations could be allowed to conquer territory not within any of the established colonial empires, they would be less dangerous to those empires. There was yet another weakness in the League, also deriving from the relationship between Governments and peoples inside member States: a liberal government or movement in a Have-not State could not make the concessions required to keep the peace without running the danger of being overthrown by its own people roused to violence by a demagogue.

Coming now to the case of Britain, with which the *New Statesman* had to deal: although its Governments were 'National', i.e. Conservative, the majority of its people were more or less Left—Labour and Liberal votes outnumbered Conservative votes if counted in bulk and not constituency by constituency. The articulate and therefore leading Left group was Mr. Symons's 'Pragmatists'. The *New Statesman* was, as I have suggested, their organ. What, then, was their state of mind?

In a period, like our own now, of taking it morally easy, it is difficult to convey with conviction that the abandonment of conscientious principles may entail great difficulties. There were very many men and women of the British Left whose social conscience played as important a part in their lives as did the Christian consciences of their Nonconformist grandparents: as we shall see, Kingsley Martin was very much such a man. He was far from being the only one. It was, for example, once said by Stafford Cripps that the support given by a citizen, or a newspaper, to any Government, should always be conditional. The British Left was pacifist by conscience and in that respect Kingsley Martin was passionately in sympathy with it; as we have seen, he served his country in war but as a pacifist nursing the wounded, not as a fighting man. But there was much more to this Left pacifism than conscience. All feeling, thinking men in Britain had suffered a tremendous revulsion against the idea of war because of the unspeakable horror from which the world had emerged in 1918. Men and women of the British Left swore a mighty oath that never again would they be tricked, misled or inveigled into a 'nationalist' war. Their feeling was given expression by the war poets and the war novelists whose bitterness and revulsion were extreme. Although similar feelings were to be found in Germany and France, which had suffered more than Britain, German pacificism was becoming masked by resentment at the way they were being treated and by thoughts of revenge; while in France idealism never stands much chance against a 'realism' which readily degenerates into cynicism. The French accept that force is supreme; the English are always hoping that this need not always be true.

The pacifism of the British Left, and of a good deal of the British Right, was reflected in the *New Statesman*. It is a mistake to see an editor as a creator of opinion; he is, if good at his job, a man who finds terms to express an opinion already there but inarticulate. He is the head finding ways to express what the body desires. In the course of the years 1930-36, the British Left moved slowly and reluctantly away from its pacifism into a state of mind and spirit in which war was at last accepted as the only means to arrest the Fascist career of international crime; in the course of this movement the Left tried hard to maintain its position in the matter of barring anything like an old style 'nationalist' or patriotic war, and it maintained that what it would fight for, if absolutely necessary, was the enforcement of the League Covenant. Inevitably, the Left several times found itself in what, coldly analysed, were obviously ridiculous positions; for example it was to demand loudly that the dictators be 'stopped' while refusing the means to stop them. This reflected the difference of opinion, already described, between Left 'Pragmatists' and the masses who more or less followed or agreed with them, and Right Governments.

The *New Statesman* gave expression to the evolution of Left feeling and thinking during this era. Its Editor was gradually driven by his own thinking into abandoning his pacifism, yet remained always reluctant to become really bellicose. Nothing is more difficult than for a thinking, feeling, intelligent man raised by Christian parents, to be really warlike. Consider, for example, the test-case of Germany's re-occupation of the Rhineland with soldiers, a breach of treaty. The *New Statesman* line when that happened was far from warlike: even had it been possible to take action against the Nazis, it would have been unreasonable. Hitler was here receiving the benefit of the British sympathy for the old Weimar Republic; he had to be treated as simply the head of the German Government and not yet as a monster. At that time Kingsley Martin had a German-Jewish refugee doing some typing for him, and when he dictated to her his article on this event, she broke down and upbraided him: she told him that the line he was about to take in the *New Statesman* had already cost the European liberals their lives or their liberty, that Kingsley Martin and his kind did not understand about Hitler, and that if the Democracies did not resist him now and regardless of conventional 'rights' in the Rhineland, they were doomed. The Editor was far from being unmoved; as far, indeed, as from being convinced. The *New Statesman* rejected this kind of extremism on two grounds; that to prevent the Germans from taking over a piece of Germany was a ludicrous idea; and that in any case there was not the remotest chance of Britain fighting such a war:

> Hitler's re-occupation of the Rhineland was nicely calculated to create confusion among the League powers. The French stand firm. They demand Germany's withdrawal before discussion. If Locarno goes, they argue, all security goes. Hitler will know that the *fait accompli* always pays, that the solidarity of the League powers is a myth. He will be encouraged in a new advance which will be beyond his frontiers. The French have submitted to a series of illegalities; somewhere they must stand firm and they have

decided that it must be now. British opinion on the other hand deplores the violence of Hitler's methods but accepts his moral right to occupy the Rhineland. It tends, too, to accept with far too much simplicity the reality of the new peace he offers. We discuss Hitler's offer in our leading article and suggest that it would be folly to reply merely by a *non possumus* to Germany and that the sane policy would be to invite her back into the League on terms which will do justice to her and ensure that she is a better neighbour.

14 March 1934

Did the Editor really believe that his suggestion was practical politics? Yes; by this date Hitler had not fully revealed himself; all English Left intellectuals had a guilt feeling, probably quite unjustified, about the Versailles Treaty; it really did not seem to them that at this stage Hitler was doing anything worse than accomplishing, though truly by a distasteful violence, what they themselves had said should be done. It was passionately hoped, and *therefore* believed, that negotiation within the League would make violent courses in future unnecessary. Our 'Pragmatists' had not yet realized that civilization had broken down; it is doubtful if they could conceive of a national leader who was *wantonly* warlike, who, for psychological and even mystical reasons, actually preferred to gain his ends by war even if there was a good chance, as there was, of getting them by negotiation. I believe that it is possible to see, now, and despite the arguments of Mr. A. J. P. Taylor, what no man of goodwill could see then, that no negotiations, no concessions whatsoever would have prevented Hitler from going to war, because he did not go to war simply to gain material ends, he went to war because he wanted to feel a hundred feet tall.

At this stage in the paper's history, the London Diary assumed a new importance for both Critic and his readers. Although the *New Statesman* was abandoning the woolly pacifist line, and was slowly and reluctantly assuming the hard policy of resistance, even at the risk of war, to the Rome-Berlin Axis, as it was called, it was not possible for the Editor simply to shed his past principles and forget them. His personal conflict was prolonged; he was not, for many years, able to feel sure that the *New Statesman*'s abandonment of pacifism was right. He began to use his personal page in the *New Statesman* as a sort of catharsis so that while the leading article for the week might be urging a policy which was likely to lead to war, and consciously faced the risk of war, London Diary would put the pacifist case forward yet again, making pacifists feel that although the paper had gone over to the other side, it still argued the respectability of their case. To some extent Critic made public confession for Kingsley Martin in the London Diary. By bringing the strife of his mind and spirit, shared with tens of thousands of men and women of the Left, into the *New Statesman* he gave an important part of that paper something of the quality of a work of art. As a rule the journalist is a pundit or a reporter, not an artist; the artist puts his personal conflict into his work, and it is that which gives the work its commanding quality; the journalist does not. Martin did, and as a result the paper became increasingly identified with him, so that only by writing about the Editor can one convey anything at all about the *New Statesman* in the Thirties. The wonder is that the *whatness*, the essential *New Statesman*, was not destroyed; it remains intact today, under a new Editor. I say it is a 'wonder', yet on second thoughts perhaps it is nothing of the kind; I have already suggested that the successful editor knows how to make the most of the essence of his paper; it is a difficult thing to explain. At an editorial meeting there will be some on the staff who can decide what line to take on a given matter by their own good judgment; but there will be others, or there should be—Norman MacKenzie, of whom I shall have more to say, is a good case in point on the then editorial staff—who somehow know not only what they think, and what the others think, but what the paper, in order to remain new statesmanly, must 'think'. If Kingsley Martin made the *New Statesman* an extension of his own mind and spirit in matters of public importance, he also knew how to become the servant of that longer-lived entity, the whatness of the *New Statesman*.

This self-dedication had practical results; the Editor's exposure of his own moral dilemma infuriated some, offended some, but gave guidance to many who were in his own case. Had he inherited a vocation for ethical preaching?

It is surely possible, and it accounts for the fact that many readers found the tone of the paper intolerable; they were the readers who would have found a strict Protestant sermon equally so. I said in Chapter 1 that the tone of the *New Statesman* is in the direct line of descent from those Protestant clergymen who made such a tremendous impression on Hippolyte Taine, who called for a higher moral conduct by way of reasonable argument and without recourse to mysticism. This, precisely, was what Kingsley Martin did; and the analogue with the Protestant clergyman can be rounded off, for he declared himself a sinner, worthy only to give guidance to fellow-sinners because he was at least a thoughtful and self-conscious one.

What is remarkable is that the London Diary was still written with the light touch, the wry irony which had been the making of it, and Critic's state of mind was not conveyed by any heaviness of expression, any breast-beating. It became, and it long remained, the most popular feature of the paper; and it was certainly a circulation builder. To make that clear, to convey the practical business results of the Editor's 'artistic' honesty, I shall have to hark back a couple of years, and give a page or two to the progress of the *New Statesman* as a commercial undertaking.

*   *   *

During the year 1933 the average weekly net sale of the *New Statesman* was 13,991. At the beginning of 1934 Gerald Barry, then Editor of the *Week-end Review*, asked Kingsley Martin to lunch with him one day and told him that Samuel Courtauld, owner of the *Week-end Review*, was tired of losing money on it and was about to withdraw his support. Barry had Courtauld's authority to offer the *Week-end Review* to the *New Statesman* for £1,000. Although John Roberts, when consulted, was able to tell Kingsley Martin that the *Week-end Review* was losing money indeed, it was not costing its backer enough to worry him seriously; it had a very loyal and even enthusiastic body of readers, and evidently Courtauld had some reason other than financial for selling out, since there seemed to be a fair chance that, in another year or two, the review might begin to pay its way. In fact what

Gerald Barry was offering the *New Statesman* was something of a bargain. A snap decision was required because Courtauld was unwilling to back even one more issue. John Roberts, consulted, had to balance the pros and cons in his head: increased weekly sales lower cost per copy of production, but there would be some loss of old *Week-end Review* readers; how many? The larger circulation would help to sell advertisement space, but would it justify an increased rate? Roberts advised buying, and took over the negotiations with Barry. He paid a deposit of 10 per cent. of the purchase price, but then another potential buyer, who planned to keep the *Week-end Review* alive, but who had broken off negotiations, now suddenly resumed them. A settlement one way or the other was required on the very day he did so, for otherwise, with Courtauld refusing to pay for another issue, the *Week-end Review* would simply lapse because the day happened to be press-day for the *New Statesman*. The *New Statesman* agreed to withdraw, but at six that evening Gerald Barry telephoned to say that his negotiations with the other people had again broken down or fallen through. Roberts closed the deal and in the next number of both papers, the last of the *Week-end Review*, the amalgamation was announced.

The circulation of the *Week-end Review* was probably about 6,000 a week. The average weekly net sales of the *New Statesman and Nation, Incorporating the Week-end Review*, for 1934 were 18,033. Now this is remarkable, for when two papers are amalgamated there is nearly always a very substantial loss of those readers of the old, now incorporated paper who find they do not like the new, incorporating, one. In this case the total loss was not much more than a thousand. Kingsley Martin's paper now embodied the spirits, as it were, of the departed *Athenaeum*, *Nation* and *Week-end Review*, as well as the spirit of the very much alive *New Statesman*. In 1934 this, as it were, omnibus weekly got a new home. It had started life in one room of the Norfolk Street offices of the National Committee for the Prevention of Destitution; it had spent its childhood and adolescence at 10 Great Queen Street; it came to maturity in the new offices at 10 Great Turnstile.

We can now come back to 1935: in that year the net sales

rose by more than 2,000 to over 20,000. In 1936, the key year of the paper's 'conversion' from pacifism, and of the Fascist attack on the Spanish Government, it rose by over 4,000. It is quite clear that Kingsley Martin's way of editing a weekly was immensely successful. And this success in selling the paper was reflected in the advertisement revenue: the figure for 1933-34 was £9,855; for 1935-36 it was £11,184; for 1936-37, £13,352. The policy which the *New Statesman* had adopted and which, clearly, was broadening its appeal, can be described by printing a letter to the Editor which tells us something about the policy which had been abandoned as well as the one which had been adopted:

Jan. 4 1936

Sir,

Mr. Clive Bell . . . continues to point out with the maximum of logic and the minimum of tact, that a true pacifist (i.e. one who is not prepared to fight in any circumstances) cannot, under existing conditions, be a supporter of the League of Nations.

May I tell him why I—who presumably come under the category of 'Young Patriot'—piped up in Mr. Geoffrey Dawson's triumphant 'cackle'? Not, let me assure him, because I want to have a crack at the 'wops'. But because I firmly believe that the only chance that now remains of preserving peace is the rapid development of the League of Nations into an effective instrument of (collective) policy, strong enough to restrain an aggressor by the threat of sanctions, and backed by overpowering (international) force.

The only alternative seems to be a war of final destruction within the next five years. To abandon Abyssinia at this juncture would be to destroy the League and to give the 'All Clear' signal to Hitler for 1937.

In a world as insane as this one there is no room in practical affairs for the Christian pacifist or indeed for any theoretical idealist; but the rationalist still has a part to play and may once again save the sum of things. . . .

[The rest of this letter is concerned with detail, not principle.]

ROBERT BOOTHBY

The French House
Lympne, Kent

Robert Boothby's policy was the *New Statesman*'s. But even that small measure of buck-passing implicit in the idea of vesting the League with everybody's responsibility for civilization was not much use when it came to Spain . . . the Civil War.

The Spanish Government which had come into power in February 1936 was a manifestation of the Popular Front policy which was supported by the *New Statesman* as another means of preserving the humanist society from the new mechanized barbarism. The whole movement, French in origin and represented in France by the government of Leon Blum, owed its precarious being to a closing of Socialist, Communist and Liberal ranks against Fascism and was wrecked by the Communists who, ever since the split of the Social Democratic revolutionary movement into Bolsheviks and Mensheviks, had been more hostile to the Socialists and Liberals than to the Conservatives and Reactionaries, largely because Socialism, which might conceivably succeed by parliamentary means, would take all the wind out of Communist sails. But for the brief period of its existence the Popular Front was dominated by Communists because they were the most disciplined and organized of its members, and anyway knew just what they wanted, which the rest did not. Its principal manifestation in Britain was Gollancz's Left Book Club, likewise dominated by Communist or crypto-Communist ideas. John Strachey was its principal spokesman. In Spain the Popular Front Government had succeeded one dominated by Gil Robles in the service of the ultra-reactionary Spanish Church and the big landowners.

The Popular Front Government was composed of Communists, Socialists and middle-class Republicans. These three groups were far from being in accord. Their strength lay in the support, if they could get it, of the Workers' Alliance, itself a collection of political dissenters of all opinions. There were two difficulties, as well as the usual ones, in uniting the Spanish Left, difficulties peculiar to Spain: the influence of Bakunin had left her with some powerful and numerous Anarchist Trade Unions; and her Marxist purists were fiercely hostile not only to the

Anarchists but to Stalin and the Government of the USSR. They were, in short, Left-wing Deviationists or Trotskyists who detested the developments of the National Communism of Russia and her Empire, and the growth of a class system by the elevation of Stakhanovites. These intractable revolutionaries also repudiated any alliance whatever with 'bourgeois' Liberals. The (Moscow) Communists, on the other hand, were at this time ready to co-operate with anyone, from Anarchists to Parliamentary Conservatives, with a view to turning and destroying their allies as soon as they were strong enough to do so.

So much for the Left. On the Right were the Church, the billionaire religious Orders, the big landowners, the industrialists, the financiers and the sentimental monarchists; finally, the *Falange Espanola* movement of Jose Primo de Rivera, son of the former dictator, and now the saint and martyr of such well-to-do young Spaniards as cannot quite stomach the Francist Fascism into which the Falange has developed, but are, by virtue of their wealth, hostile to the Left.

As late as May 1936 it was possible for the *New Statesman* correspondent in Spain, Geoffrey Brereton, to write, after interviewing virtually all the leaders on both sides, that the Right groups formed 'a heavy, inert mass which by sheer bulk will get in the way of the Left, but which is bound ultimately to be swept away'. He excepted the Falange from this contemptuous dismissal. The Falange was an ostensibly syndicalist movement and as such it could call itself anti-Capitalist for the sake of attracting some of the workers, which it did. They were not very many, though, the Falangists tended to be woolly-minded young men of goodwill from the upper classes. Here are the *New Statesman*'s (Brereton) conclusions on the state of affairs in May:

> It is fairly evident that the Spanish Fascists are in full retreat. Their desperate acts defeat their own ends by irritating public opinion against them. If Spain ever again had a Right-wing government solidly supported by all ranks of the army and police, the tale would be different. The time for that, however, has passed, and with it a great load has been lifted from Spain.

It is a fact which I can vouch for that never—thanks to this illusion which Brereton shared with the Spaniards—has any people been happier than they were that late spring and early summer. One found oneself in an atmosphere of laughing optimism and goodwill, of bliss-was-it-in-that-dawn-to-be-alive. Probably the Spaniards were no more generous in victory than other people; they had suffered a great deal and for a long time at the hands of the old Establishment. 'Life being what it is, one dreams of revenge', and revenge on the institutions of the Church was taken by brutally ill-treating more or less innocent individuals and perfectly innocent buildings. It was not this which provoked the Army to reaction; it was the danger of Socialism succeeding.

Not nearly enough attention has been paid to this truth; it is important because the same danger, that of Socialism succeeding *peacefully* and therefore unobjectionably, was what paralysed the hostility of Right democratic governments to the Fascists who, if one came down to brass tacks, might be their natural allies in the maintenance of Capitalism.

The *New Statesman* was not to know what the generals had in mind. Brereton, writing from Spain, was in a state, as so many of us were, of Popular-Front euphoria, manifest, for instance, in Alexander Werth's *New Statesman* contributions at this time. Writing from Paris in the same week as Brereton's piece of optimism appeared, on the subject of Leon Blum's Popular Front Government, Werth concluded in exactly the same spirit as Brereton:

> France today is a land of hope, though of hope mingled with a thousand apprehensions. But the apprehensions are old; the hope is new.

Quite so. What the *New Statesman*, ignoring the jeremiads of orthodox Marxists, could not quite bring itself to realize, was that the bourgeoisie would have recourse to arms in defence of its privileges, and would even, at the top, prefer Hitler to Socialism—perfectly naturally, of course. Yet there were warnings enough even in Britain. Letters to, among other papers, the *New Statesman* repeatedly exposed the bias of the London police in favour of the Mosleyite Fascists, for example, a bias long protected, with his characteristic blandness, by Sir John Simon, although he was ultimately driven to appear to condemn it. Nor was this the only warning, and the *New Statesman* drew attention to the significance of the restoration to office of Sir Samuel Hoare who had been kicked out of it by the righteous and futile indignation of the Left when the unfortunate man was driven into cooking up the Hoare-Laval sell-out of Abyssinia by the clamorous pacifism of that same Left.

Kingsley Martin's 'Geneva Diary' of late 1935, is so evocative of the long crisis of the Thirties that it is worth reprinting almost in full:

Geneva, Tuesday

. . . Rumour was naturally mainly concerned with the private doings of the Committee of Five, and by night some of the better informed journalists were convinced that Great Britain had put forward an actual proposal for an 'international mandate'—whatever exactly that may mean. I have, however, the best authority for knowing that this was an intelligent anticipation rather than a fact. The truth is that the Committee approached the Italian Government to ask why it turned down the Paris proposals and what it would like better. The implication is, of course, that it is willing to offer them something more than the Paris proposals which were flatly turned down by Mussolini, though they went far beyond anything that could be justified by the Covenant, which makes the League Powers jointly responsible for preserving the political independence and integrity of all Member States.

*   *   *

There is now at least a possibility—and, I think, one must say a danger—that some such scheme involving probably a foreign 'gendarmerie' mostly Italian, will be offered to Mussolini and accepted by him. For last month the Duce was convinced that he had nothing to fear from the League whatever he did. Three weeks ago he told a well-known American journalist that the League could do nothing to him, and pointed in proof to its behaviour in regard to Japan and to German rearmament. Lord Beaverbrook, I understand, told him in Rome that British opinion was against any sort of interference, and the Duce believed Lord Beaverbrook in preference to Mr. Eden, who warned him of the true state of feeling in England. Today he must be disillusioned. Even Lord Beaverbrook has deserted the Duce. 'Conciliation' is for the first time being tried with the ultimate threat of sanctions behind it. And today he may hope for terms that would mean victory. I say that I fear this, for it would surely be the worst thing that could happen. If France and Great Britain agree on terms with Mussolini, they can force the other members of the Committee of Five into agreement. (Incidentally, I am told on good authority that the Vatican has brought influence to bear on the Spanish Government to push Señor Madariaga, the Chairman of the Committee, into supporting proposals of this sort.) Then the Committee could force the rest of the Council into line and confront Abyssinia with these proposals as a League recommendation. Even if the Emperor could be bullied into acceptance, his chiefs would certainly refuse—if they did not cut his throat first—and we might even see the spectacle of Italy carrying out a punitive expedition into Abyssinia with the apparent approval of the League. That would indeed be peace (with Italy) at any price—at the price of war with unoffending Abyssinia, at the price of all honour and good faith, at the price of ending any genuine collective system in Europe and telling all dictators they could do as they please. Mr. Litvinov actually refused to serve on the Committee of Five because he foresaw this kind of manœuvring, and was unwilling to be involved in any effort to force an unjustifiable settlement on Abyssinia. This disastrous outcome is, I say, a possibility. The safeguards against it, such as they are, are the strength of world opinion against Italy, the intransigence of Mussolini, and the fact that Mr. Eden has a reputation to lose and would, one hopes, refuse to go all the way in such a dirty deal.

*   *   *

The only obvious alternative is that the Committee of Conciliation will fail and that economic sanctions will be enforced when the Duce begins hostilities. It now seems certain that this will not be until the Assembly has dispersed. The rains in any case have been unusually heavy and much of the ground the Italian troops would have to cover will be swamp until October. There is apparently no hope of preventive sanctions under Articles X or XI. If, after hostilities have actually begun, Great Britain proposes economic sanctions, I have no doubt about the support of France and the other League Powers. Experienced League journalists tell me they have never seen such cohesion at

Geneva before. Everyone is against Italy; Baron Aloisi met with not a shred of sympathy when he marched out of the Council last week, and Italy's arrogance has completely isolated her. The document demanding Ethiopia's expulsion, backed by data about Abyssinia's internal conditions and by pictures of atrocities (which could easily be countered by far worse illustrations from the record of Italian Fascism) merely disgusted everyone. The French will resist, but will follow a British lead. M. Laval himself said so a few days ago. In the last resort the French know that Great Britain is a better ally than Italy. A half promise from Great Britain is worth nine signed treaties with Italy!

*   *   *

When it comes down to brass tacks all the League Powers will co-operate in economic sanctions. The possible loopholes are Germany and the United States. Germany has, I understand, been approached by Great Britain and given some assurances. But it is thought that she is playing a double game and may also give assurances to Italy. The points to be remembered here are (a) that Italy cannot afford to pay for much and that even Germany will need payment; (b) that Germany can supply coal and perhaps a few other things that Italy wants, but not any large proportion of the hundred materials for war which the League Committee of thirteen experts recently enumerated as essential for a country making war; and (c) that Hitler is not at all ready for war himself, and is above all things now anxious to keep on good terms with Great Britain. As regards the United States, public opinion has been greatly misled about the meaning of the recent Neutrality Act. This Act was the result, very largely, of the Senatorial Commission on the Traffic in Arms which has led to a demand in the United States that never again should there be a trade in arms, or in contraband in general, which will involve the United States in disputes with belligerent countries. Therefore the new Act forbids the export of 'arms, munitions and implements of war' to any country at war. This, coupled with the statements of Roosevelt and the State Department that the United States would never put any obstacle in the way of an attempt by the League to enforce peace, means that if economic sanctions are applied the United States Government will not make a fuss should American citizens, sending contraband at their own risk, find it seized on the high seas. It may also mean that after a

191

time popular feeling in the United States would lead to an actual refusal to allow American ships to carry those articles which the League declares to be contraband. But in any case it seems to mean that the United States would not help Italy.

*   *   *

I must add two conversations overheard in the lobbies.

Journalist A. 'I'm told that even Baron Aloisi cannot talk frankly to Mussolini. He has been so long a dictator that he listens to no one—scarcely even to his generals.'

Journalist B. 'Yes, and the Italians here all look sick. They have discovered that public opinion really exists, and that it's all against them!'

Journalist A. 'That's true. *They have not an ally left to betray.*'

The second conversation runs:

X. 'All the real business here is done in private rooms in the hotels where the delegations are staying.'

Y. 'That's why the British delegation is staying in the Beau Rivage. It has the largest bed-sitting rooms in Geneva— which illustrates the British genius for compromise.'

CRITIC

In short, the ruling middle classes everywhere were closing their ranks against the threat of eviction from power by the 'people'. Realization of this was fogged, however, by a hope which now looks rather fatuous. The key Popular Front country was France and Kingsley Martin reinforced Werth —actually he was the *Manchester Guardian* man in Paris—by H. N. Brailsford, whose articles on Blum's Popular Front New Deal were enthusiastic. The Roosevelt New Deal, as reported for the paper by Ratcliffe, had been another apparent gain for the liberal Left. G. D. H. Cole was encouraged to ask yet again, 'What about a New Deal for Britain?' He, after all, had thought of this Left-tending compromise in the first place and the *New Statesman* might have claimed to have found and published the political and social solution which Roosevelt used in America and Blum in France. But the British Right is always the most resilient in the world. It is pneumatic; throw it out, it bounces back. The Conservatives and Liberals in power continued to bear, with perfect stoicism, the sufferings of the unemployed;

the national adversity under their leadership was making
some strange bed-fellows, and we find the *New Statesman*
discovering that Winston Churchill, hitherto the *New
Statesman*'s ugliest bugbear, was really rather a fine fellow
whose principal political handicaps were 'his intelligence and
the misfortune of being logical'. His logic had not appealed
to the *New Statesman* in the past.

The first reference to the trouble in Spain came on 18
July 1936 in an editorial comment on the murder of Sotelo,
the Conservative leader, the arrest of 150 Falangists in
Madrid, and the suspension of the Cortes for one week. Only
a few days before the actual invasion from Morocco, Mostyn
Lloyd, writing editorial comment, was sceptical about the
danger of civil war. The worst the Spanish Popular Front
government had to fear was 'Right-wing gangsterism'. The
scale of the gangsterism became apparent the following week.
The Editor himself concentrated, then, on exposing the
sinister significance of the atrocity-propaganda which
Rothermere was publishing in the *Daily Mail*, at that time
a pro-Fascist newspaper. In this and in the *New Statesman*'s
righteous outcry over the abuse of the non-intervention
policy, there is a curiously unreal note: probably one of the
major weaknesses of British Socialism is that it does not altogether believe that the enemy will do what theory, and for
that matter, commonsense, says he must do; it was as sound
for Rothermere to support the Fascists as for Italy and
Germany to give Franco an air force, which logical act in the
class-war was denounced in the *New Statesman* by Brailsford.

Here appears the really great difference between Kingsley
Martin as Editor and Clifford Sharp. When, in the early
Twenties the Italian industrialists and landowners had been
scared by the complete absence of violence, and the ease,
with which Italian workers in the north had taken over
factories and continued to operate them; and when, meanwhile, peasants in the south, led by the priest Sturza who
founded the Popularismo movement were taking over the
land; they had realized that Socialism might succeed, and
they smashed it by violence. The tools they used were, of
course, the Fascist bands and, a little later, Benito Mussolini.
There was, in the *New Statesman* comment at the time, no

sign of illogical and indignant astonishment that men of the Right should be as ruthless as one had long announced that they certainly would be. Clifford Sharp's cold realism has been miscalled cynicism. It was nothing of the sort, it was simply fact-facing. But fact-facing about the wickedness of men is something the English detest. The *New Statesman* under Kingsley Martin might face this fact, but must nevertheless and always preach righteousness, for therein lay the sole hope. In his capacity to be surprised and angry when the man whom he expected to punch him on the nose punched him on the nose, Kingsley Martin had something in common with a far wider British public than Sharp could ever have aspired, with his cold acceptance of facts, to captivate. When, for example, Mussolini employed an American gangster named Duomini to murder the Socialist barrister Matteotti for making a fool of the Duce in parliament, to Sharp this was simply what one would have expected of the Fascist leader; whereas to Martin, while it might be what one would have expected, it remained nevertheless incredible until it happened, and then it was outrageous. This was precisely the *New Statesman* attitude to the use (from the Socialist viewpoint, abuse) made by Conservative Governments of the non-intervention policy during the Spanish war.

This policy had been started by the Popular Front Government in France at a moment when its application would have favoured the Republican Government and not the rebels. That is to say, non-intervention was devised to help the Left. When, by reason of the massive support given to Franco by the pouring of a large Italian army into Spain, and by the German Government with its air force, the balance shifted in favour of the rebels, it should have been clear that the same policy would be used by the Right-wing friends of the rebels, such as the British Government, to help General Franco. Perhaps because of its origins in dissenting Christian sects, the British Left tends to feel that its enemies are not only wrong, they are blasphemously wicked. Because he can put other considerations above his own interest, and because his inheritance and training make it difficult, even impossible for him *not* to preach righteousness, Kingsley Martin assumed almost always in his writings that other men should do so. No doubt they should, but they don't. In the long run however, *New Statesman* writers were forced to see that the whole policy of non-intervention had become a plain fraud, and to attack it as such. But in doing so it moved one more step away from pacifism and even reverted, for some weeks, to a kind of Marxist opportunist imperialism: if our Government allowed Fascist powers to control Ceuta, what use would Gibraltar be as an imperial bastion? In an article entitled 'NOT OUR CONCERN', the Editor wrote:

> The second lesson for the Left, when this crisis is over, is that it must reconsider its whole foreign policy. It may still continue to hope some day to build, as we have urged in this journal, an honest League of like-minded States within the present League of quarrelling sovereignties. But clearly, to talk of the collective system today is academic.
> . . . Labour was forced by its own past declarations to announce that it would not co-operate in re-arming or fighting, unless the government showed that it intended to stand by the Covenant of the League. Today, with the tragic spectacle of Spain before its eyes, British Labour is surely in a position to say: 'Here is Fascist aggression of the most terrible kind. We are prepared to run risks to save Spanish and French democracy and we believe the bold course is also the safest. . . . But if, after abandoning democracy as you have abandoned the League, if after allowing the democracies to be destroyed piecemeal and the world to be given up to the Fascists, you then expect us to join in a fight for the remnants of the British Empire in some quarrel you muddle us into, we shall not be with you. Your policy was isolation when there were causes worth fighting for and a good chance that if we honestly stuck to our obligations and our professions we should not have to fight at all. But now, in a hopelessly weak moral and strategic position, with our friends abandoned and all the values we cared for betrayed, it is our turn to be isolationists. We recall the words of Sir Samuel Hoare. Your cause will not be our concern.'

The only strong and 'Great' Power the world's Liberals and Socialists could look to in their passionate desire to see the Spanish Left victorious over the Falange, the Moors and the Italians, was the USSR. That country was not an ally which Kingsley Martin, or most of his contributors, particularly fancied. In September, for instance, he wrote an article on 'The Moscow Purge', subsequently and magnificently denounced in the *New Statesman* by H. N. Brailsford. The paper had already wounded the feelings of those readers who felt that in this crisis Communism had better be sacrosanct, by announcing that it was not 'convinced' by the confessions of Zinoviev, Kamenev and other Old Bolsheviks whom Stalin was busy getting out of his way. The *New Statesman* was as anxious as anyone to believe, with Mr. Pritt, K.C., who was present, that the trial had been fair and everything above board. But it really would not do.

> Clearly if they were going to plead guilty and ask to be shot they had no need of a lawyer to do it for them. It is their confession and decision to demand the death sentence that constitutes the mystery. If they had a hope of acquittal why confess? If they were guilty of trying to murder Stalin and knew they would be shot in any case, why cringe and crawl instead of defiantly justifying their plot on revolutionary grounds? We should be glad to hear their explanation.

The articles conclude that there may indeed have been a plot; that the G.P.U. tended to regard all criticism as treachery, that such criticism was a product of the discontent with Russia's increasing Nationalism manifest in its acceptance of the non-intervention policy in Spain.

Touching this matter of the Moscow purges, the Editor had had a curious and significant conversation with the man whose machinations were supposed to be Stalin's justification. In April 1937 Kingsley Martin was in Mexico and he went to see Leon Trotsky. The exile was beautifully housed, looked very dapper and was working on a book to be entitled *The Crimes of Stalin:* 'He looked like a Frenchman, not, I decided after a few minutes, a French politician, but, in spite of his neatness, a French artist.'

Kingsley Martin formed the impression of a man who was vain and very able, of fierce will and unruly temperament. A man, moreover, who always saw events in relation to his own career and was incapable of objectivity. He was charming and friendly and had a high opinion of the *New Statesman*'s honesty and radicalism. It occurred to Kingsley Martin that Trotsky had read the *New Statesman* article in which the evidence at the Moscow trials had been treated with scepticism. He got Trotsky to talk about the 'proofs' he had promised that this evidence was all faked. Trotsky did talk, volubly, but not really to much purpose. When Kingsley Martin put it to him that it was strange that none of the accused men had behaved like Dimitrov and, since they were going to die anyway, 'have gone down fighting and appealed to the public opinion of the world', Trotsky became excited and even abusive, rather than lucid in explanation. He wanted to know how much 'Mr. Pritt, K.C.', had been paid to report the trial as a fair one. The Editor defended Pritt as an honest man, and he and Trotsky had a 'regular wrangle' about this. 'To see him get up and shout abuse at Mr. Pritt was revealing.' Trotsky clearly thought that any-one who had a word to say for Stalin or who did not de-nounce the whole trial as a frame-up, was in the pay of Moscow.

The conclusion which Kingsley Martin came to after this interview is important because it must have been one of the influences which shaped the *New Statesman*'s attitude to the USSR during the next two years:

> When I wrote that I did not know whether or not to believe in the confessions, I meant exactly what I said. It seemed to me the only honest thing to say. Trotsky, like other people, interpreted my scepticism as a vote against Stalin and tried to remove any lingering doubts. But I came away from our talk rather less inclined to scout the possibility of Trotsky's complicity than I had been before, because his judgment appeared to me so unstable and therefore the possibility of his embarking on a crazy plot more credible. . . .

Neither then nor later did the *New Statesman* accept Stalin's case; but nor would it simply reject it. There may well have been a conspiracy against Stalin and the Soviet Government; the court confessions of men like Radek may, after all, have been genuine. Nobody knew, and there was a serious danger that 'Capitalist' exploitation of this uncer-tainty would be used to break with the USSR which, whatever its faults, was a strong ally against the warlike

Fascists and Nazis. If the western democracies and the USSR quarrelled openly, there would be nothing left to restrain the Fascists from plunging the world into war.

> Every effort is of course being made to exploit this proof of difficulty and violence in Soviet Russia. It is grist to the mill of the Conservatives . . . there is a great deal amiss and political liberty has a long battle to fight before it becomes a reality in Soviet Russia. But that makes no difference to the fact that Russia is a Socialist country with an over-whelming desire for peace.

This *New Statesman* attitude, critical but patient, was to infuriate the extremists on both sides. To those who, as the paper put it,

> finding few investments for their spiritual capital, have staked their all on Soviet Russia and may feel spiritually bankrupt when the dividend is beneath expectations,

anything but a fanatical insistence that there was nothing wrong with Russia was plain treachery. To those who knew what was going on in Russia, or what the Stalinist Communists were doing in Spain, anything but open denunciation of these evils was, as George Orwell was to say, 'to have the mentality of a whore'.

The *New Statesman*'s handling of both pacifism and this question of the shot-gun wedding between Soviet Communism and the Western Popular Front, was consistent. In a single issue of the paper Critic, applying the method he had devised to deal with his own conflict, might point out that war over Manchuria, Ethiopia, the Rhineland, albeit apparently justified, would probably turn into just another, conventional 'Capitalist' war, while a leading article would suggest that the point had been reached at which resistance to Fascist aggression must stiffen even to the point of war. Similarly, in dealing with Communism, the *New Statesman* favoured the alliance between Socialism and Communism because it was expedient, but did not hide from its readers that the Communist ally was no gentleman.

This firm line—I call it so by comparison with the want of or excess of 'realism' in the rest of the Press—was severely tested in the matter of George Orwell's Spanish articles.

Kingsley Martin himself twice went to Spain during the war; he talked with Republican leaders and he saw what one could see. Orwell, on the other hand, saw what one was not supposed to see and what most men could not see: that imperialism is imperialism whether its bosses are Russian Communists or British adventurers or American bankers. It was in Spain that he conceived his loathing for Party-line Communism. He perceived, what, by the way, any experienced British trade unionist could have told him, that if Russian Communism was at war with Fascism it was much more whole-heartedly at war with Social Democracy, with Anarchism, with Liberalism, with any kind of Leftism which did not entail toeing the Party line; above all with the pure Communism of the Trotskyist World Revolutionaries. And as the Communist Party had got control of the Spanish Government, assisted by the fact that Negrin's Government could look to no power but Russia for arms, it was able to wreak its will on its supposed allies. Orwell came back to Britain with a series of blistering articles attacking the Spanish Government and offered them to the *New Statesman*. Kingsley Martin did not disbelieve what Orwell had written, but he decided against publishing it. In Spain there was a fight between Fascism and Democracy and the latter must be supported; if neither triumphed, but Communism came out victorious over both, even that would be better than a Fascist victory. In short, the *New Statesman* had become a 'committed' paper while recognizing that, Fascism defeated, we might then have to fight for our principles against the worst elements in Communism.

The domestic scene was not neglected during the international uproar. Outstanding during the Thirties were the articles written for the paper by Harry Roberts, whose journalistic skill and first-hand knowledge of social conditions among the poor and those pauperized by the seemingly interminable industrial depression, were matched by the warmth with which he espoused other men's troubles. Roberts was one of those rare doctors who become a legend among their patients: he created and ran a vast practice in the East End of London and his work for his patients was very far from being confined to clinical treatment. The conditions in which millions of the English lived at this time, and which came as such a shock to so many of the middle class when the war evacuation scheme revealed the truth, can have come as no surprise to those who read Roberts in the *New Statesman*, though his writing was not confined to social questions. He was enormously versatile, and his books on gardening, for example, written after he had moved into the country and taken to that craft, are still useful. The Editor was also and always busy recruiting new talent for the paper. It was not easy; the experiment of getting Bertrand Russell to write a diary in place of the London Diary while Kingsley Martin was on holiday was not repeated. But Sagittarius sent her first contribution to the paper in December 1934, and by the middle of 1935 had become established as the staff satirist. Readers who are not familiar with her admirable satirical verse are referred to the specimens of it which I have reprinted in *New Statesmanship*, published at the same time as this book, and by the same publisher. Her achievement was an astonishing one. I cannot think of any other journalist who, for twenty years, has written every week a poem faultless in form, pointed in satire and sharp in wit. Sagittarius is Mrs. Hugh Miller, *née* Olga Katzin, of Russian-Jewish origin. She was not 'committed', she had no formal political affiliations, and her work consisted in exposing social and political evil to ridicule and, in the course of so doing, in entertaining her reader. She succeeded triumphantly.

In 1935 R. H. S. Crossman started to write for the *New Statesman* as a reviewer. He became a staff-member and was paid a modest retainer. His influence on the paper was to become steadily greater for a quarter of a century but was never to become decisive. In 1937 he wrote an article, 'On Losing Elections', in which he revealed himself as much a practical politician on the home front as Kingsley Martin had recently shown himself to be on the international front: Crossman had just been defeated in an election because 11,000 'natural' Labour supporters simply did not trouble to vote; yet he remained opposed to the policy of a Popular Front which the Labour Party was rejecting. The Popular Front was a gimmick, and Communists were not to be trusted;

the way to overcome Labour apathy in the constituencies was to develop a Party machine at least as efficient as the Conservative one. Later in the same year Crossman contributed articles from Germany; one from Swabia made it clear that he was going to be a great asset to any paper he wrote for. His curt summing-up of what Nazism had done to the political life of ordinary Germans was brilliant:

> To remain an active Nazi today a German must retain or artificially induce the hysterical obedience of the pubescent convert to religion. If he cannot do this he sinks into the cynicism of premature old age. There is no third alternative.

Crossman introduced into his political writings a wit, a sparkle, and that touch of 'perversity' which stimulate, by momentarily shocking, all qualities which had become rather rare in British journalism. This, from Crossman, could have been from Bernard Shaw:

> . . . decent Englishmen have been brought up by the press lords to be crisis minded and to equate sensation with news. And so, poor things, they live in a world of sudden inexplicable shocks to which they can only react with pained and helpless surprise.

Crossman's was a new influence on the paper; stronger than this, however, by their hold on the Editor's mind, were three older ones: Harold Laski who had been Kingsley Martin's close friend since L.S.E. days, who was (if he can be said to have had one) Kingsley Martin's political mentor, and who became the human link between the *New Statesman* and the Left Book Club; John Strachey, but not so much the man himself as his *The Coming Struggle for Power*, which influenced the thinking of the whole Left wing; and H. N. Brailsford, for whom the Editor had the greatest admiration and respect both as a man and as a journalist. Brailsford was, like Kingsley Martin, a man whose politics were founded on ethics, who was driven by a thirst for righteousness. As editor of the I.L.P.'s *New Leader* he had, with Wells, Shaw, Bertrand Russell, Julian Huxley and others as contributors greatly raised the standard of Left-wing journalism. Kingsley Martin held, and still holds, Brailsford to have been the greatest journalist of this time. It was Brailsford who, during

1935, repeatedly confronted the readers of the *New Statesman* with the real nature of Mussolini's Government, and with the incompatibility between not only the democratic ideal and Fascist opportunism but between Fascist imperialism and British imperialism; he saw the importance of exposing the fatuousness of the British Right, which seemed unable to recognize a man and a régime which were doing what, in their heart of hearts, they would have liked to do, as their most dangerous enemy. In 1936 and 1937 Brailsford wrote the best of the paper's interpretations of what was happening in the Spanish Civil War. But it was also Brailsford who, demonstrating that the *New Statesman*'s committal to the Communist alliance remained conditional, wrote the finest denunciation of the Moscow Stalinist purges.

Another very valuable man recruited to the paper in 1935 was Aylmer Vallance, who became contributor, chief sub-editor and editor *de facto* in Kingsley Martin's absences. Vallance was one of the most agreeable, as he was one of the kindest and best, men I have ever known; it was impossible not to develop a strong affection for him. He had been assistant editor of *The Economist* and editor of the *News Chronicle* and was an immensely skilful and versatile journalist, one of the real masters of the trade, who could do and do well any of the tasks connected with the production of a newspaper or a weekly journal. His dismissal from the *News Chronicle* occurred in circumstances which are well known in Fleet Street, are funny, scandalous and will not be repeated here.

One of Aylmer Vallance's qualities was calm; cool good sense distinguished his attitude to both problems and colleagues, and this quality was to become very important indeed. The advent of Richard Crossman not simply as a writer for the *New Statesman* but as a member of its editorial group had a singular effect in the paper's office: it was as if one of the elements which composed the Editor's inner ambivalence has been suddenly externalized, personalized. Crossman's political thinking was of a kind which Kingsley Martin knew and half-suppressed in himself in the course of compromising with his feelings and his upbringing. In Crossman it assumed a strength and a clarity extremely hard to resist; for there is a good case for saying that he was, intellectually, superior to any man who had yet served the *New Statesman*, the best mind which new statesmanship had produced. Thus the conflict which had, hitherto, been inside the Editor's own mind, was now to some extent brought into the open. Crossman exerted influence in favour of ideas and policies to which the Editor himself would have come much less readily or would, although they were in some sense his own, have rejected. This generated tensions in the office and the atmosphere was at times electric, threatening storms. It was in such moments that Aylmer Vallance's calm, his ability in and insistence on keeping all discussion at the level of cool and reasonable argument, became of the greatest possible value. Nor was this all: as a teacher he was a man above rubies; he was the mentor in journalism of John Freeman, now Editor of the paper, who acknowledges his debt to Vallance in the warmest terms. My own first work for the *New Statesman* was done under Vallance's wing; he is the only man in the sort of position he occupied who, in my experience, could make you feel grateful for the rejection of a piece of work, could make you realize, more by his manner than by what he said, that he was saving you from publishing something unworthy of the high standard you had set yourself. This quality in Vallance gave you a particular respect for your own work in the *New Statesman*. This attitude on the part of writers was not a new thing: it is a fact that most of them did, because of the standards set by Kingsley Martin, treat their work for the paper with particular care. But Aylmer Vallance made it easier and, somehow, more natural to do so; you felt under an obligation to his sympathetic care for your own reputation as a writer.

Vallance was often thought to be a Communist sympathiser, but he had no 'faith' in political solutions to social problems; he had the appearance and manner of a Scottish laird, and he would have made an excellent editor of *The Field*, having a passion for and knowledge of field sports. He was a wit, he had a rare gift of friendship, he liked wine, women and fly-fishing. He had served in the Army and in the coming war he was to do so again as a colonel in

Intelligence. Early in 1936 he went to the United States for the *New Statesman*, and he wrote a vividly evocative description of the American state of mind in that election year. As a Socialist he was skilful in presenting not the academic case but the ordinary man's; he seemed to reveal the whole rottenness of the capitalist sub-structure without saying a word against Capitalism.

Recruitment of fresh talent had by 1936 restored to the paper much of the sustained brilliance which radiates from literary and journalistic stars and which had so distinguished it during its first year. The literary editorship during this period has already been discussed. Regular reviewers now included David Garnett, V. S. Pritchett and Cyril Connolly. Since Robert Lynd was still writing for the pleasure of very many readers, the paper still had a survivor from the period of the whimsical essayist, but the general tone was harder and, perhaps, grimmer. Bertrand Russell and Leonard Woolf wrote regularly for the paper, Edward Marsh, Aldous Huxley and Harold Laski less regularly. Lawrence Easterbrook's long series of articles on farming and farm-life conditions began at about this time; they were some of the best things of the kind ever written.

It will be obvious to anyone for whom these names have meaning, that however 'committed' the political forequarters of the *New Statesman* had become, the arts and letters half of the paper was still completely disengaged. There were sometimes to be heard loud complaints that as a review of literature and the arts the paper had no policy. This sort of criticism was misconceived: a literary review can, as I have suggested, only have a 'policy' if it is published for a coterie. If it is not consciously *avant garde* because it may not displease its more conventional readers and anyway wishes to cover a wider field; if it is not firmly 'square' because it wishes to notice and encourage the *avant garde;* if it is not affiliated with some group of literary idealists such as Leavisites, again because it must by its nature and claims be more catholic and therefore more useful to a larger number of readers, it cannot have a 'policy'. The best it can do is to employ the most competent and talented writers to do its reviewing and to write its criticism, under the guiding hand of a literary editor who at least knows what is going on in *every* coterie and outside all of them. The only common attributes one can find in *New Statesman* writers on the arts, literature and science is their liberalism and their quality as professional writers at a high level of both intellect and technical skill.

In 1937 and 1938 the *New Statesman*'s adoption of a Popular Front policy combined with full support for the League of Nations, as a means of averting a war with Fascism by being prepared to fight one, gave the paper increasing influence and stature and, incidentally, made it ever more profitable business; the rise in circulation was both swift and steady, from 24,000 in 1936 to 29,000 in 1938, with advertising revenue rising in the same steady line, with no sign yet of an exponential bend at the top, to £15,000. But the Editor and his political contributors were approaching another crisis of judgment and conscience.

The justification of the 'Pragmatists' policy, to which the *New Statesman* gave expression, was simply this: Until 1936 it was reasonable, as well as hopeful, to believe that the Fascist dictators could be checked and an 'imperialist' war averted if a large enough group of nations working within the League offered a firm enough resistance to their arrogance. But since, instead, there had been one show of weakness after another, from 1936 onwards, while it was still psychologically *necessary* to the Left to believe in collective security, it cannot be said to have still been reasonable. In 1937 and 1938 the Editor did a good deal of speaking in public in favour of this policy, which the *New Statesman* continued to advocate, usually with some earnest Liberal on his right hand, and Harry Pollitt of the British Communist Party on his left. But, in common with many men of his persuasion, he was less and less able to believe in what he was advocating. By 1938 it had become all too clear that there was not going to be any effective collective security and for one outstanding reason: there was not going to be any alliance between a British Conservative Government and Stalin's USSR.

If this was true, and it seemed quite clear that it was, then there was a grave danger that the policy which the *New Statesman* advocated would lead not to 'stopping Hitler' by a mere threat of war but quite simply to war of the old-fashioned 'capitalist' kind, of the kind in which thousands of people on the Left had sworn never again to be inveigled; against which nine million Britons had signed the famous Peace Pledge which had the *New Statesman*'s support; and which the undergraduates of the Oxford Union had repudiated in a resolution denounced by 'patriots' as infamous. Given the improbability of alliance between British Right and Russian Communism, it even became possible to accuse the *New Statesman* of old-fashioned war-mongering and, in fact, the psychologist Edward Glover did just that. Yet it was not possible for the Left, for the Labour Party, for the *New Statesman*, suddenly to abandon the one policy which had given hope of keeping the peace of the world and which, even now, remained the only hope, however slight. On the other hand it was not easy for a man of Kingsley Martin's kind, brought up so to respect the truth that he must proclaim it when he believed himself to be in possession of it, to continue in the same course.

A hint of the editorial difficulty in this dilemma appears in March 1938 when the *New Statesman* used a front-page headline for the first time in its history. The headline was: FIVE MINUTES TO TWELVE. Is there now, the Editor asks, any hope of preventing general war? Ceuta will soon be a fortified post in German and Italian hands, so that our failure to lead the League in resistance to Fascism in Spain must end in our loss of control of the Mediterranean. Austria has fallen to Hitler and Czechoslovakia has three million Sudeten-Deutsch who will of course support Hitler. Hitler will, therefore, probably repeat his Austrian coup in Czechoslovakia:

> Mr. Chamberlain must make up his mind. If he intends not to stand with France or look after the British Empire in Spain, that would be intelligible as a way of keeping out of the war for the moment. With a Nazi Europe and a Mediterranean lost, England could look forward after a troubled time to a future as a second-class power. If Mr. Chamberlain is prepared for the results of isolation, let him say so. We for our part, *regarding war as the greatest of all catastrophes and recalling the results of one war to prevent Germany from holding the hegemony of Europe, would applaud and support such a decision.*

We have never advocated it in the past because we do not
believe that Mr. Chamberlain, Lord Beaverbrook or anyone else in the British ruling class really intends or can be
induced to intend anything of the kind. It has always been
axiomatic in British policy that we should stand by France,
and if France is involved we believe that Britain is involved
too. If that is the position it is incumbent on Mr. Chamberlain to say so and to make it clear that *we are involved if
Czchoslovakia is attacked.* There is still a chance that some
hesitating States such as Poland would remain within the
British, French and Russian orbit, and that Germany would
not think the risk of war worth undertaking. . . .

The italics are mine; the ambivalence is self-evident. But in
the same number appeared an article by H. N. Brailsford,
'Where to say Halt', which is probably the clearest exposition
of the crisis ever written. For Brailsford it was not merely
Britain's status as a Great Power which was at stake but
something very much more important and less ephemeral:

> If Western Civilization means to make any stand before all
> the strategical keys are in its enemies' hands, it must call a
> halt before Prague and Barcelona. . . .

But there was, in the *New Statesman*'s view, one concession
we could and even should make to the enemy: the Sudeten-
land should never have been included in Czechoslovakia in
any case. The Sudeten-Deutsch should be reunited with
their fellow Germans.

Both the Editor and Brailsford made it clear that in their
view effective resistance depended on the Soviet alliance.
This was so obvious to them that the paper suffered obloquy
for its sake, and the stupid abuse of the ex-pinks who had
worked their passage back into political 'respectability' when
Stalin's oriental behaviour gave them the chance to deny
their past. They were, by the way, just about the same people
as had howled with indignation when, in his *Practice and
Theory of Bolshevism*, Bertrand Russell had, after a visit to
Russia and talks with both Lenin and Trotsky, criticized
the USSR for police-state practices which, he foresaw,
would lead just where they did lead. The *New Statesman*
believed in the Russian alliance, but with its eyes wide open:
it was a case of setting a relatively 'good' thief to catch a

robbery-with-violence thief. And at least the USSR had, like France, declared its intention to honour its obligation to defend Czechoslovakia. What about us? Because, and the *New Statesman* was clear about this, *if we were not to have the USSR as our ally, we had better not fight at all.* It is important to bear in mind that this point was made quite early in the crisis.

The London Diary for this and subsequent weeks makes fascinating reading: no law is laid down; no didactic advice offered to the Government; Critic 'talks' intimately, an anxious friend, to readers with whom he shares his perplexity and who cannot fail to see that he is in the same state of mind as themselves, that he no longer has any certainties left. It is journalism at its most honest, and at its most moving.

But these analyses of perplexity were followed, towards the end of March, by some firmer guidance. The *New Statesman* suggested what 'we', i.e. the Left, should do to avoid simply being dragged into a war for mere national survival after everything worth the frightful price of war had been lost in advance. Most of 'our rulers', that is the Conservative Party and their lapsed Liberal and Labour hangers-on, seemed clearly to prefer to give the Fascists what they wanted rather than fight beside Soviet Russia. But there were some, led by Winston Churchill, who saw that the Fascists were the greater danger to the British Empire. We of the Left could and should support these Churchillians without hesitation, for in an alliance with them lay the only remaining hope of peace.* But what kind of peace?

That question was answered in the same number by J. M. Keynes, in an article entitled 'A Positive Peace Policy', and which, I am bound to confess, *now* reads as a repetition of ideas which seemed to have already proved unworkable. An effort is required to recall that they had not, in fact, been tried. Keynes wrote that Chamberlain's peace policy was merely negative; as such it was ephemeral and would ensure that 'when the time comes we shall have no friends and no

* It might be reasonable to claim that this lead given by the *New Statesman* to the Labour Party was what led in due course to the Labour Party forcing Churchill on the Conservatives after Dunkirk. In that case the nation's debt to the paper is colossal.

common cause'. Keynes's positive pacifism was to consist in the forming of a much more closely bound league within the League, based on Britain, Franco and the USSR and including Scandinavia, Czechoslovakia and others, armed, ready to take action against the aggressor, but also calm and, within reason, placatory.

Perhaps, at the time, this seemed possible; now it seems quite clear that it just 'wasn't on'. Keynes himself admitted in this same article that we were suffering from 'paralysis of the will' which he described as 'the worst of diseases'. We kept saying that the dictators must be stopped, but we did not move a finger to stop them, though we had the means to do it. I suppose that the received explanation would be that we had the disease even worse than Keynes perceived. My own belief is that the Right in all Europe and America too had no real wish to 'stop' the dictators who were doing what in defence of their own position they had long wanted done by somebody: smashing Socialism. As between two opposed tyrants, the Right must prefer the Fascist to the Communist, just as the Left must prefer the Communist to the Fascist. The policy of Chamberlain and Daladier was the mirror-image of the *New Statesman*'s. *New Statesman* Leftism was prepared deliberately to take the risk of support for a Russian Communism it now understood and detested; the Right was prepared to take the risk of supporting a Fascism to which its attitude was remarkably similar. Keynes had one other justification for his and the *New Statesman*'s attitude: he did not believe that the Nazis would, in the last analysis, be willing to fight us; the vital thing was to put on a bold collective security front and do nothing to let Hitler think that we did not mean what we said.

But that understanding had been weakened in advance by Brailsford's admission that we had no moral or political right to restrain the Sudeten-Deutsch from rejoining the other Germans. And in the following months it became clearer that if the Sudeten-Deutsch asserted themselves there was nothing Czechoslovakia could do about it; if she tried to, if she refused to let Hitler's people go, were we to fight for her 'right' to hold an alien people against their will? It was not a strong moral position and early in August the paper began to hedge a little. The line taken was this: if the Czechs cannot make such an offer to the Sudeten-Deutsch as will reconcile them to the existing frontiers, then 'the question of frontier revision should at once be tackled'. The strategical value of the Bohemian frontier should not be made the occasion of a world war.

In so far as the Editor was influenced by other men's opinions in his decisions, Brailsford's views had more weight with him, at this point, than Keynes's. The policy of agreeing to frontier revision was not Keynes's. He and Kingsley Martin were in constant touch, exchanging numerous letters. On 27 August 1938 Keynes wrote to Kingsley a hastily scribbled note:

> Having put on my mantic robe my further reflections on Cz-Slo are—
>
> Hitler's speech at Nuremberg will be violent and amount to a quasi-ultimatum demanding a revision of frontiers.
>
> After many parlez-vous this will be granted. He will again win the appearance of a major success. And it will be without war. What we ought to work for is a maintenance of Cz-Slo's integrity without frontier revisions. As a preliminary we ought formally to ask Germany her intentions and demand an international conference. If he refuses, invite collaboration of U.S.A.

But by this Keynes meant that this should be our 'front'; in fact we should be perfectly prepared to concede frontier revisions. He said as much in another letter in which he describes frontier-revision as 'the cleaner and *safer* remedy'. The Editor did not have much taste for this sort of double-talk. On the very day that the above note was written the *New Statesman* was saying:

> It should be remembered that Czechoslovakia is now almost surrounded by enemies, for though Hungary has undertaken not to attack Czechoslovakia no one believes that Hungary would be more friendly or less avaricious than Poland in the event of a German attack. The U.S.S.R. is a long way from Prague and its help would necessarily be limited. The U.S.S.R. will not make any move unless France moves, and the French could do little to help the Czechs though French mobilization would, of course, force Hitler

to place a large part of his army on the western front. Mobilization would almost certainly lead to general war. Nothing we or anyone else could do would save Czechoslovakia from destruction; it would be a question of a counter-attack on Germany. . . .

The wording is discreet, but in fact it was a break in the firm line. Early in September the *New Statesman* was firmly back on course with:

In the last resort there is no doubt that Britain as well as France and the whole democratic world would stand by the Czechs.

Whistling in the dark? It is perhaps significant that in mid-September we find R. H. S. Crossman taking over the editorial commenting on the Prime Minister's flight to Berchtesgaden, acknowledging that Chamberlain had virtually a mandate from the whole British people to avoid war, and finding this 'disturbing': for it seemed that what can only amount to a new Hoare-Laval type of scuttle 'might be regarded as a contribution to permanent peace'. Even half the London Diary was taken over by Crossman that week; it seems that, for a few days, the Editor felt paralysed by his own honesty in admitting what the whole intelligent world knew in its heart: that nobody could now help the Czechs, an admission from which Crossman had done all in his power to dissuade him.

However, as soon as the Chamberlain-Daladier capitulation to Hitler, entailing a brutal sell-out of the Czechs, was an accomplished fact, the *New Statesman* supported the National Council of Labour in its declaration that this deal was a 'shameful betrayal', and rounded on Chamberlain for doing what did, indeed, run counter to the policy the paper had been advocating for years, yet what it might seem to have justified by its single lapse into pessimism, into a devastating honesty. The front page on 24 September carried an editorial called 'The Murder of a Nation'. It was unsigned, but there could be no question who wrote it. Nor did Kingsley Martin seek to hide behind the editorial 'We', for at the same time he sent a letter to the *News Chronicle*, in which the Prime Minister was very roughly handled for his treachery to democracy. For this he was attacked at once in a letter, probably 'inspired', written to *The Times* by an officer of the Conservative Party. The letter had been sent to the *News Chronicle* whose editor, Gerald Barry, having consulted Kingsley Martin, had refused to publish it on the ground that there was now no point in dragging up the *New Statesman*'s one short lapse from the Collective Security line. Kingsley Martin made a spirited defence of himself in *The Times*, but he did not answer the accusation that he had been the first to 'abandon the Czech cause' by saying, as he might have done, that he was expressing fear of a contingency rather than advocating a policy.

This was simply, of course, the penalty for that editorial candour which, entailing the conveyance of his own mood to his readers as if he were talking with a circle of intimates, people who would know how to discount a moment of depression or cynicism, had been so successful. What, after all, had the Editor implied in his admission? His exasperation with the fact that the Government was doing nothing to secure the one condition on which defence of the Czech democracy was possible; it was Crossman who had realized that this mood ought not to be given public expression.

Far from being weakened by the fact that the Editor's personal conflicts were apt to be reflected in the *New Statesman*, the paper's appeal was strengthened, for the whole intellectual Left, all Mr. Julian Symons's 'Pragmatists', were in the same boat with him. This is obvious from the paper's still rapidly increasing circulation. It is usually the case that the circulation of a weekly journal can only be largely increased by lowering the height of its brow. Kingsley Martin kept the high standard maintained by his predecessors, yet found a way to make a wider appeal. The attitude of the kind of people he had rallied to the paper can be communicated in extracts from two letters to the Editor published shortly after Munich, one from a distinguished archaeologist with Marxist leanings, V. Gordon Childe; the other signed by Lancelot Hogben, J. F. Horrabin and Raymond Postgate. Gordon Childe wrote:

> I confess to having been convinced that another war 'to make the world safe for democracy' could only have the same

disastrous results as the last and must, in fact, destroy all that in Britain still deserves the name civilization. The actual device adopted to avoid such a war, however, threatens to destroy that civilization no less surely, if less dramatically. Great Britain is, it would seem, not merely to tolerate the violent—and for the aggressor costly and even perilous— dismemberment of Czechoslovakia. She is to assist the Nazi tyranny in imposing that dismemberment on the last out- post of formal democracy in Central Europe and to guar- antee the political neutrality of the rump, presumably against Russian help, while its economic subjugation is peacefully completed. This bit of 'foreign policy' must have internal repercussions the effects of which are perhaps already percep- tible. . . . German intellectuals who hailed Hitler as their saviour from Marxism are now helpless to protest against the consequent sterilization of science and art. British intellectuals who preferred peace in alliance with Hitler to war in alliance with the U.S.S.R., may all too easily have cause to wonder whether the bombed ruins of London and Berlin would not have been better than the skeleton of civilization condemned to stagnation by the denial of free enquiry. Still, it may not be too late to arouse the anti- Fascist forces to defend the spirit of British traditions in the interval of precarious 'peace' so perilously purchased by the betrayal of the Czechs.

The letter was a product of a bitterness which spread wide and deep and of which the *New Statesman* became a vehicle. Had this not been so, then it would have been very difficult even for Winston Churchill to lever Chamberlain out of the office to which he clung like a limpet; and had he not been removed it is probable that, with a Conservative Party terrified of any kind of alliance with the Left behind him, the end would have been that of France. The last five lines of the letter were the line which the *New Statesman* was, in fact, taking, but a paragraph from the other letter mentioned above clearly expresses the frustrating hopelessness of the situation:

A war over Czechoslovakia with Conservatism in the saddle would be a war to crush a rising competitor in the Imperialist game. Once it is started, all opposition to an Imperialist settlement would be swamped in the need for 'national unity'. Faced with this dilemma the only policy which a British Socialist party can logically pursue is to challenge Hitler's war bluff and Chamberlain's peace bluff by persisting in the demand for an immediate world conference to build a lasting peace on four foundations. . . .

We need not consider the four foundations; it is more interesting to wonder whether the signatories, whether the *New Statesman*, still seriously believed in any such possibility? Or were they not advocating this policy because it was all that was left for them to do until the war, which despite such homage paid to goodwill they knew must come, broke out and left them with a clear and simple decision to take?

Throughout 1938, letters reflecting this unreal opposition between what one was bound to say and write, and what one knew, went on. The note of bitterness is as clear as the note of shame. And in the first war number of the *New Statesman* there is, despite his pacifism, a note of something like exhausted relief in the Editor's:

One of the things that one will never forget about these days is the contrast between the great loveliness of the summer and the pall of horror accompanying it. On the first night war was declared, I looked up at the captive balloons, silver in the sunset, and thought that it must be a peace gala that we were celebrating. Even as night fell and the black-out became complete, London remained peculiarly lovely. The dark deserted streets in the moonlight had a mysterious new beauty and it was not until one sat down behind one's own blackened windows that one realized that we had entered upon a period beginning, as in August 1914, with a new sense of purpose and comradeship, but with the knowledge that we have in front of us a vista of monotony and tragedy which, whatever our personal views or occupations, will test nerves and endurance to the limit. At this stage in the war there are certain psychological compensations for many people. We have watched the degradation of standards in Europe, the growth of barbarism and the systematic use of cruelty as a political weapon. Many of us have longed to stop it, as it could have been stopped long before it reached the supreme barbarity of war. Now that the worst has happened there is some slight compensation for the moment at least in the new sense of purpose that the war gives.

11

The New Statesman's Three-front War

THE *New Statesman's* war, like that of most people and institutions, can be divided into two parts: the first, a period of confusion and anxiety when it did not even seem certain that a real war would be fought at all and when, therefore, there was a spasmodic temptation to revert to that pacifism which still nagged at the conscience; the second, when the paper's determination to extract some good from the monstrous worldwide evil of total war, led it to fight, in its pages, a social war on three fronts.

It will be recalled that the war began with propaganda, a series of leaflet raids on Germany which were denounced by the more ferocious element of our population as a lot of nonsense, but which were welcomed by the *New Statesman* as 'a right and imaginative stroke of good augury for the future'. This hope that the war might be fought in a highly civilized fashion was not allowed to fade even with the sinking of the *Athenia*, the paper taking the line that this might have been 'a rash initiative on the part of an individual U-boat commander rather than an indication of Germany's policy'. For the first weeks of the war the paper reads a little like Clifford Sharp's *New Statesman* of August and September 1914: it follows events as an observer and commentator whose patriotism must not be allowed to interfere with his objectivity, and meanwhile is clearly determined to put a stop to that nothing-matters-but-winning-the-war-let's-have-no-politics ploy into which the Conservatives would surely try to blackmail the whole nation in their usual single-minded conviction that they alone know what is good for us ... and above all for them. The resemblance of the old and new *New Statesman* at this point and for a few weeks only is striking. It demonstrates remarkable consistency of aim. We find G. D. H. Cole doing, for example, what Webb had done in 1914 and 1915, holding a watching brief for the workers who might be exploited in the name of king and country; and insisting on the maintenance of democratic control. As it happened, the influence of Winston Churchill was, in due course, to ensure this. The readers of the *New Statesman*, including the leaders of the Labour Party, had been reassured about this by a remarkable interview or, rather, dialogue in the paper between Winston Churchill and Kingsley Martin (January 1939) which might have been designed to point out that this man, the one and only politician in whom both Right and Left could find a war leader, need not be judged by the Labour Party on the undemocratic acts of his past, and that his very traditionalism, romanticism, Englishry, made him a good House of Commons man with no inclination for the sort of dictatorial paternalism which Neville Chamberlain had shown every sign of favouring. In this dialogue—a new journalistic form which was to be copied by lesser editors after the war—it was established that Churchill would, even in wartime, respect the House of Commons, maintain the freedoms which it guaranteed, tolerate free criticism of the executive. Churchill restated in the most downright terms a number of basic principles: he was convinced that a Democracy would, in the long run, prove to be more efficient and able to endure longer than a Fascist State and he repudiated the idea that a country could defend itself without carrying the war offensively into the enemy country. But there was as yet no question of Churchill. The 'real' Tories, with their complacent and apparently immovable leader Neville Chamberlain, would, it seemed, as soon have been led by the Devil as by him. Thus, Cole was making a point of great importance when he wrote that it was the duty of the Opposition

> . . . to secure, to the utmost of their power both that our economic methods of carrying on the war are so conceived and executed as to do as little damage as possible to our democratic liberties and indeed enlarge those liberties wherever an opportunity can be made. It is their duty to ensure not only as much equality of sacrifice as practicable under war

conditions, but also a constructive movement towards turning our 'Plutodemocracy' into something much nearer to a real democracy in the economic as well as the electoral sphere.

If this was not exactly the policy of the official Opposition in so far as there was one, it did become the policy of the Left rank and file, of progressive trade unionists, of the 'Pragmatists' now for the most part in the fighting services or in Civil Defence; they created the 'climate' in which the outcome of the 1945 General Election was inevitable and the programme of the Government it put in power almost a foregone conclusion.

Although the *New Statesman* began by putting a good face on the *drôle de guerre* of 1939-40, the Editor, the principal contributors and the editorial staff were all more or less uneasy. The reasons for this uneasiness can be found in the article 'Retrospect' by Kingsley Martin. They were supporting a war they had done all in their power to avert, and which was being fought in the very conditions they had declared to be utterly unacceptable to the people, and which they felt we could not win since we were allied with neither the USA nor the USSR. Hitler, having easily conquered Poland, was now making peace-loving noises. We could not rescue Poland. Why go on with war at all? But the paper would not have anything even remotely to do with the ludicrous Communist somersault which had followed the Nazi-Soviet Pact. The new Communist denunciation of the war as merely 'imperialist' was making things impossible for Socialists, who probably felt that it always had been and yet must be fought because the enemy imperialism was so much worse than our own. The Communist appeal to pacifism was particularly cynical, since it had been Hitler and the Communist Party between them who killed the pre-war pacifism of the Left.

It remained true that there seemed to be nothing we could do to help Poland or the Czechs, and therefore no point left in the war. Meanwhile, the paper was as jaunty as it could manage to be. It took up small sensible causes at home. Raymond Postgate ran a little campaign to win the people a modicum of light in the streets at night, quoting the Mayor of Barcelona who had said that more of his citizens were killed by black-out accidents than by bombs; profiteering in sandbags was exposed; price stabilization was supported; evacuation stories were printed, of a kind to off-set the class-hatred variety which were going the upper-class rounds: thus, from the London Diary:

> . . . I know of one case where a family with an income of 46s. a week is trying to satisfy the appetite of a secondary schoolboy of 17. Last Sunday the parents arrived in a nice car, and having shared the Sunday dinner, thanked the foster mother for the trouble she had taken and gave the boy 6d. pocket money. The foster mother remarked that the boy would need a hair-cut. 'Oh, he can take that out of the pocket-money,' replied the father, and drove off. . . .

In the literary pages, Zoshchenko's satirical stories continued to appear. W. J. Turner asked for wartime concerts, and in due course got them, and expected the level of taste in all the arts to rise as a result of the war. He was right; it did, at least so long as the war lasted. The most improbable people showed a new taste for the substantial in art and letters, as if the war were being taken as a warning that time was rationed and tripe a waste of it. David Garnett reverted to the gossipy paragraph style for 'Books in General', the style which had been Squire's in the early days. Cyril Connolly, Anthony West, Peter Quennell, John Mair and John Betjeman continued to review books.

But this superficial tranquillity could not last. In response to Hitler's peace propaganda, Lloyd George made a speech in the Commons on 3 October which was virtually an appeal to stop the war while it was still possible to do so. It was a sensible speech, but pronounced by a man who had destroyed his credit with the nation by his want of personal integrity and by his pre-war support of and admiration for Adolf Hitler. Nevertheless, Kingsley Martin, who was in touch with the old leader, was more or less in sympathy with his pacifism. But Kingsley Martin and his staff had reached by this time the point of knowing that peace with Hitler was not possible; what they hoped for was that democracy would put up a counter-case in what was an ideological war, thus helping to rally, once again, those League and Left forces which Chamberlain had alienated. Thus, the *New Statesman* editorial comment was cautious: Cole wrote it and he went no further than to say that, '. . . it would be most unwise to reject outright an offer to discuss peace which has not yet been received and whose nature is still unknown'. He added: '. . . before the frightfulness—the real war—is begun in earnest let us lose no opportunity of talking people to people, and making sure there is no other way out'. However, in the same number of the *New Statesman* appeared Bernard Shaw's exceedingly downright but, as usual, perverse 'Uncommon Sense About the War'.

When he received this letter the Editor had it set in type. He was dining with Maynard Keynes on the evening when he received the proof from the printer and he happened to have it in his pocket. He showed it to Keynes and he was astounded at the violence of the economist's reaction. Keynes declared that the *New Statesman* could not possibly publish this subversive document and when the Editor insisted that it could and would for after all Shaw was Shaw, Keynes even threatened to resign from the Board. Kingsley Martin being, apparently, unmoved by this, Keynes urged him at least to take Foreign Office advice before printing the letter. The Editor telephoned the Foreign Office and was told that, as far as they were concerned, any letter from Shaw should be published; they did not even ask to see the letter. Kingsley Martin removed one dangerous passage from the letter, and published it. Shaw, delighted, wrote to Lady Astor that the war was now virtually over. Among other things, the letter held up our war aims to ridicule and it suggested that not puny Britain but mighty Stalin would be 'taking Hitler by the scruff of the neck' and putting him in his place. In all such crises Shaw was an Old-style Fabian in that he saw order as being imposed from above; the only safe peace was an imperial *Pax*, in this case all the safer for being Socialist, the *Pax Sovietica*. But he subsequently admitted that in this case he had been wrong. Keynes persisted in opposition and wrote to Kingsley Martin as follows:

Dear Kingsley,

My opinion is:

(1) That the article is mischievous and that your editorial judgment should be against accepting it;—I think it would do harm both ways—both to the chances of success in peace and the prospects of success in war, and (2) that in any case you ought to take the advice of the Censor before publishing it (this applies not to the whole of the article but to one or two extensive passages in it).

If after re-reading it you want to proceed with publication, I agree with you that others should be consulted*— the available members of the Board immediately and the other two as soon as possible. I should also attach importance to the opinions of Lloyd and Raymond.† If I am in a minority, I still reserve my liberty of action but should if I ——‡ it resign from the Board.

From your own standpoint I believe the article would do great harm.

Yours,

J. M. KEYNES

The Foreign Office must have backed Kingsley Martin either because it was important to show the world a fine example of the freedom we had declared ourselves to be fighting for, or, possibly, because the Foreign Office really agreed with Lloyd George and Shaw, as perhaps, and despite what he had said in the House, did the Prime Minister. The accommodating way in which the Nazis had taken Stalin's imperialist moves in Poland and Finland supported the Shavian argument that Hitler, afraid of the USSR, was now ready to talk peace seriously. In an editorial about the argument, 'The Right Reply to Hitler', the *New Statesman* said:

> Hitler's proposals are vague, insincere, and perhaps meant only for propaganda? Very well, then, we should reply, as Mr. Lloyd George wisely says, with propaganda which is more subtle and sincere . . .

setting the tone of an editorial which, though it did not

---

* They should have this letter of mine as well as the article.
† Mostyn Lloyd and Raymond Mortimer.
‡ Illegible.

support Lloyd George and Bernard Shaw, did show that the paper was doubtful about continuing with the war. Mr. Chamberlain having failed to take the Shavian line, Shaw commented in the *New Statesman*:

> Germany having just conquered Poland, Mr. Chamberlain demands that any [peace] conference must proceed on the assumption that Poland has just conquered Germany.

The strongest attack on Shaw's position, or rather on the irresponsible-seeming perversity of his terms, was made in the *New Statesman* itself by Desmond MacCarthy; it was the second time these two new statesmen had conducted a public row in their journal. Keynes, too, reproached the paper for its policy in its own columns. So did Princess Antoine Bibesco, who had once made a practice of inviting herself to the Editor's famous Monday lunches at which leading men in all fields foregathered. This lady wrote, that the only thing which was clear to the *New Statesman* reader was that, 'War was desirable till it occurred and peace is desirable now that war has arrived'. Her letter was printed, but with a sharp editorial comeback: 'Princess Antoine Bibesco should talk sense, even in wartime.'

The Editor's temper was, no doubt, being tried by the vexations of the *drôle de guerre*. It became sunnier, as did the nation's, when the position was clarified by the light of London on fire. When the bombs began to fall the intellectuals of the Left were immensely relieved—barring the few who had saved their skins in the manner satirized in the *New Statesman* by Anthony Powell:

> A literary (or left-wing) erstwhile well-wisher would
> Seek vainly now for Auden or for Isherwood.
> The Dog-beneath-the-skin has had the brains
> To save it, Norris-like, by changing trains.

All but these few were at last exposed, with everyone else, to danger of death, and at last faced by a relaxingly simple situation. The London Diary became high-spirited:

> I boast [wrote Critic] of being the only man in London who has been bombed off a lavatory seat while reading Jane Austen. She went into the bath; I went through the door. . . .

and

   . . . But the real moral is that it is fatal to go on considering this war as an interruption to normal life. In that case everything seems intolerable. . . . But if you think of this as a new kind of world altogether and do not expect anything to be normal, life to those who have not suffered bereavement and who have a job may be tolerable and even exciting.

At this point in the war it became possible for the Editor and his advisers to evolve, out of the policies which the paper had created for itself during the Thirties, a war policy, or set of policies, which could be consistently followed.

Because the war had been forced on us in the worst possible conditions and on the terms which the *New Statesman* had defined as those on which war was not worth fighting, it was all the more important to extract some kind of good out of evil. We had not got the kind of war which the Editor had reluctantly come to believe justifiable; the only hope was, therefore, to transform the war we *had* got into the justifiable war we might have had, the war which would end not in the triumph of a nation or group of nations over another but in social revolution and the union of mankind.

There were three fronts on which this new statesmanly war could be fought: the home front; the imperial front; and the European front. On the home front the war in the *New Statesman*'s pages was waged principally by Harold Laski. Like Sidney Webb in the First World War, he believed that the war could be made the social ally of the working class, and what he wrote about was how this could be done, how the working class could, by, as it were, making their support for the war leaders conditional, win not only the war against the enemy abroad but also win some campaigns against the enemy at home. In one sense the position of the working class and of their allies in the middle classes was much stronger than it had been in 1914. With the advent of Winston Churchill to the supreme office, an advent which the Labour Party was responsible for, Labour's own leaders were strong in the Government. Moreover, they had nevertheless asserted their political independence and given, as it were, a guarantee that they were not going to do a Ramsay

MacDonald, by refusing to serve under Chamberlain or Halifax.

But although Labour Party leaders are sometimes more or less Socialist out of office, they tend to be much less so when in office, especially when they are under Conservative Party leadership. As the whole Left movement knew to its cost, Labour Party leaders are rather easily cajoled and flattered into becoming more royalist than the king. It will be remembered that in 1914 the *New Statesman* had not found it possible to condemn the German Social Democrats for supporting the Kaiser and the Junkers; for they must defend German civilization against the Russian barbarians. But in 1939 excesses of patriotism among working-class industrial or political leaders would be much more dangerous because between the two wars Capitalism had shown that its strength lay in its cosmopolitanism while Socialism had shown that its weakness lay in its nationalism.

Harold Laski and G. D. H. Cole were not left alone to wage the social war at home, under Kingsley Martin's leadership. Much of what R. H. S. Crossman wrote for the paper, until he went to the Department of Political Warfare, had the same general tendency. Crossman even tried to persuade Herbert Morrison to be a Socialist at the Ministry of Supply. He wrote an article exposing, with his customary lucidity and economy, how the Ebbw Vale steel plant, a substantial part of the nation's steel-producing capital, had fallen or been wangled into the hands of moneylenders, to wit the Bank of England and the Prudential. The interests of these financiers were not very likely, as Crossman showed, to coincide with those of a nation in dire need of an expanding war economy, and should not the Minister of Supply remember that he was a Socialist and hold an enquiry into this? When Morrison claimed that it was not his business to go poking into the backwaters of capitalism, Crossman argued that in the name of national efficiency it was.

This, then, was the *New Statesman*'s policy at home as soon as the Luftwaffe had convinced its Editor that the war would, indeed, have to be fought: it must preach the advance into Socialism, first in order to win the war because Socialist economics were more efficient than Capitalism; and second in order that the outcome of the war should be a Socialist Britain.

The leader in the *New Statesman*'s social war on the imperial front was Noel Brailsford. He had, of course, been long writing for the paper and the war did not call for any change in the line he had always taken, which was, briefly, the old *Nation* line: let us set the colonial peoples free to govern themselves; and, notably, let us give India back to the Indians.

Whether we consider the empire, or the non-British world beyond the empire, what I think can fairly be called the *New Statesman*'s noblest attribute was its internationalism, its Socialist oecumenicalism. For centuries the peoples of the world have suffered and been kept in misery and want by two kinds of war: the religious and the patriotic or nationalist. It is as certain that nationalism and religion have directly caused the worst afflictions of the human race, as that love of one's country and religious feeling are nevertheless amiable qualities often and perhaps usually to be found in the most admirable of men. This antithesis is a great misfortune, for it makes it in the first place very hard for men to denounce nationalism or religion without being themselves denounced as treacherous and wicked; but, what is worse, it makes it easy for scoundrels, hypocrites, cynical careerists, acquisitive businessmen, and demagogues generally to cover their evil-doing with a cloak of patriotism or religion or, usually, both. Until the fourteenth century, all Europeans were of one faith, and nationalism was unheard of. The bio-psychological fact that men are attached to their calf-country made it possible for men who took and held land by force to persuade the local natives to identify large chunks of private real estate as fatherlands. They were enormously helped in this by the rise of numerous Protestant sects which made it easy to destroy Christianity as a unity. In only five centuries, nationalism, including religious nationalism than which nothing could be more ridiculous, has come to seem the natural and inevitable condition. The man who tries to transcend it must have courage of the highest order, because his opponents are often among the most honourable, brave and agreeable people of his community, and the cause which is opposed to him carries a banner most of us feel to be sacred, and wears an aura of heroism almost irresistible. The man who insists that the cause of mankind as a whole is a nobler one than the cause of any single group of men, is apt to suffer ridicule, hatred and contempt as at best a crank and at worst a traitor. I do not, therefore, hesitate to call the *New Statesman*'s internationalism noble.

New statesmanship, as Kingsley Martin understood it, aimed at world unity, but it must be voluntary, and it followed that all men must be free, if they wished, to be nationalists before they became internationalists. This happens to be fairly orthodox Marxism as well. And in this Kingsley Martin, and Brailsford of course, differed altogether from the old *New Statesman;* for the Webbs and for Clifford Sharp, world order was much more important than the freedom of the lesser breeds, so important that it should be imposed imperially. This is also my own belief, but that is by the way. It was easy for the Webbs and Sharp to be didactic about this because they knew nothing whatever about anyone but the English. Writing in the *New Statesman* on its twenty-fifth birthday, Bernard Shaw, reminiscing about the Fabian past, said that the Webbs were totally ignorant of foreign affairs and cared nothing about them; the same might have been said about colonial affairs. Britain, for them, was not an empire; it was a municipality.

Brailsford's line in the wartime *New Statesman*, when he wrote on India, his most important topic, was to expose that clumsy stupidity with which the Indians, surely our natural allies against Nazi racism, were being mishandled by our rulers. This, too, was part of the general policy of so voicing the feelings, resentments and aspirations of the common people everywhere, as to turn the war into that war for social revolution and the total destruction of Fascism—and crypto-Fascism—which had been the only one the Left had ever been really willing, if necessary, to fight; and which it had in fact first fought and lost in Spain.

One of Kingsley Martin's most amiable qualities as an editor was his loyalty to his men. As a general rule he suffered no interference from the Board of Directors, though on rare occasions a single director, or a caucus of two, would take against a contributor and try to force the Editor to get rid of him. They invariably failed. Maynard Keynes was perhaps the only director of the company who tried, time and again, to influence Kingsley Martin against a contributor; in his case the bugbear was Brailsford. As early as 1937 Keynes had written angrily to the Editor stigmatizing one of Brailsford's articles as an example of 'drivelling irresponsibility'. He maintained this hostility and could, for example, write:

> Brailsford . . . seems to me to have every defect—almost incredibly misinformed and ill-informed, carrying credulity to the point where it is almost certifiable, extraordinarily tenacious in a frightfully boring sort of way. . . . It is astonishing how often things which get the paper into general low repute and mockery (which are usually attributed to you and for which you, deservedly perhaps, get most of the blame) turn out to be from his pen. . . .

This was provoked by one of Brailsford's leaders on the struggle between the Indian Government and the Indian National Congress. Later Keynes explained his exasperation by saying that he was so sick of India that he would be glad to see us out of it at any price. He agreed that Brailsford was generally on the right and generous side of every question, but claimed that he had an unfortunate gift for 'making the better cause appear the worst'. Although Keynes's hostility was sustained and obstinate, the Editor did not allow it to influence him in the slightest. Nor was this simply a matter of emotional loyalty to Brailsford. Kingsley Martin had chosen him to do a certain job and in a certain way; he knew that this choice was the right one, and he was not to be moved from it, even by so powerful a personality as Keynes.

It is a fact that Brailsford was a hundred-percenter; on all levels and on all matters, the Indians were right and good and the Raj was wrong and bad; he made it almost as simple as that. A man who writes, as Brailsford did, with his heart, does not always write also with his head, and it is certain that much of what he wrote for the *New Statesman* would never have got into the paper when Clifford Sharp was Editor. It was not new statesmanly in the sense that Keynes understood that word. But Kingsley Martin was determined to make his support of the Indians from the heart as well as the head, because he had discovered, what other Englishmen of goodwill working with or friendly with Indians have discovered, that feeling counts for more in that country than in the West and that, in dealing with Indians, it is useless to mean, and do, coldly well; you must also feel warmly. Even supposing that Kingsley Martin had been persuaded of the cold truth of Keynes's case, it would have seemed to him beside the point: Indians must be free, free even to be corrupt and inefficient if they must.

As the war progressed and fewer hands became available, the task of Kingsley Martin and Raymond Mortimer became more and more difficult. But they were helped and encouraged by that curious wartime improvement in public taste which had been forecast by Turner in the matter of music, but which was manifest in the other arts and in literature. For the taste in journalism was also affected. In 1939 the *New Statesman*'s circulation had been 29,000; by 1942 it had risen to 42,000.

One problem of wartime contributions solved itself admirably: the *New Statesman*'s military notes published unsigned every week were exceptionally meaty, curt and well informed, and this for an excellent reason. Aylmer Vallance, having been recalled to the Army, was serving in Intelligence with the rank of colonel, acting as liaison officer between the War Office and the department of Political Warfare. He had, therefore, to be kept very fully informed on all military matters. It was he who was writing the *New Statesman*'s military notes. The War Office knew all about this, of course. It may have been responsible for the fact that the Editor had no trouble with military censorship during the whole war: a military spokesman was said to have remarked that at least there was no danger of Vallance giving away military secrets inadvertently.

Great events were not allowed to crowd out lesser matters. Perhaps 'lesser' is the wrong word; the fact is, the *New Statesman* kept a remarkable sense of proportion and never forgot that we were not just fighting, we were fighting for certain values and that the quality called 'culture' was not less but more important now that it was threatened by men who had openly declared their hatred of it. Arthur Calder-Marshall and Stephen Spender carried out an inquest, perhaps rather prematurely, into the politico-literary aspect of the Thirties. A whole precious page was given to C. E. M. Joad's review of Bertrand Russell's *An Enquiry into the Meaning of Truth*. Raymond Mortimer, whose industry was fabulous —so that he was writing, at times, at least half the literary and arts section of the paper—ran a series of 'Books in General' ('Cross Channel') on the French classics reassessed. The *New Statesman* went vigorously to the defence of Michael Redgrave, Beatrix Lehmann and other actors and musicians when they were barred by the B.B.C. for adhering to the pacifist People's Convention.

It is in the great tradition of the Press to draw the attention of legislators and executive to the troubles of the people they rule when they, being what the charitable call overworked and the uncharitable culpably inattentive, fail to notice them for themselves. Thus, for example, it had been *The Times* which roused the country to the appalling state of our armies in the Crimea. In this tradition were Ritchie Calder's *New Statesman* articles, in 1940, on the tragedies of the people of the East End of London at the beginning of the German air-raids. Even more in the same tradition was the Editor's descriptive article on conditions in the great 'shelter' in the Stepney fruit-market, conditions which were atrocious. This article reached Winston Churchill by way of Harold Laski and Lord Ismay. Shortly thereafter Herbert Morrison was appointed Home Secretary in the place of Sir John Anderson, and Morrison later told Kingsley Martin that Churchill kept asking him whether he had taken steps to clear up the matter of the Stepney shelter. In brilliant support of the writings on this subject, the paper published a supplement, a remarkable series of drawings called 'Shelter Life' by Xavier Kapp.

For nine months from mid-1940 the paper was deprived, at least in part, of Raymond Mortimer's services, while the Literary Editor was working at the Ministry of Information on the French programmes of the B.B.C. His place was taken by Cuthbert Worsley. Thereafter, although Mortimer's resignation from the Ministry had been caused by ill-health, he returned to the paper and carried on, with the help of Pritchett to write some of the 'Books in General' articles.

In the years immediately before the war Victoria Sackville-West as well as her brother Edward had been working for the paper. She wrote a long and consistently admirable series of articles on the countryside and on what she made into the art of living in it. These articles differed widely from Easter-brook's country writings for the *New Statesman;* he wrote as a farmer with advanced ideas, his work in that field being continued after the war in the *News Chronicle.* Miss Sackville-West wrote as a poet, the poet of *The Land.* It is representative of Kingsley Martin's sense of values that these articles were continued through the war, years of too much news and too little paper; for, again, we were not merely fighting to survive, we were fighting for a set of values, and among the most important of those values was the one expressed in Victoria Sackville-West's vision of our land.

The old, pacifist Kingsley Martin had by no means been entirely suppressed by the new and reluctantly belligerent one. When the outcry, led by the admass Press, for retaliations on Germany in kind for the bombing of our open cities began, the *New Statesman* argued and pleaded against it by every means in its power, in leaders, in London Diary, and even with satire by reproducing, for example, the bitter-comic suggestion that the belligerents should save their petrol and pilots by agreeing each to bomb his own cities; after all, the result would be much the same.

Hitler's attack, in 1941, on his Soviet ally, which came as such a spirit-raising relief to the whole nation, was doubly gratifying to the *New Statesman.* The Editor's refusal to take the common and too easy anti-Soviet line was vindicated at last, at least as an expedient policy. The *New Statesman* had long argued that, like it or not, a Soviet Alliance was the condition of victory over Fascism. Such an alliance would have prevented war. Without it, war had broken out; now the alliance had been forced upon us by the Nazis. It would make victory more probable; and it would make the task of turning the war from a mere nationalist brawl into a revolutionary crusade much easier. It turned a pious hope of victory in a nationalist war into a reasonable expectation of victory for Socialist Europe. But the temptation to indulge in optimism was resisted; there was no more point in over-estimating Russian strength, as the Communists at once began to do, than in under-estimating it, as the Right were doing. Aylmer Vallance's (unsigned) discussion of the odds in the Russo-German war was objective, cautious and very sober. He forecast that the German Panzer divisions would force their way deeply into Russian territory; he also foresaw that the quick and easy victory in Russia which was essential to the Germans, would evade them, was, in fact, a military impossibility. Finally, he forecast, with astonishing exactness, where, geographically, the turn in the tide would come.

The Editor, while twitting the Communists on their repeated and highly ridiculous policy-somersaults, did it lightly and with tact: after all, Communist influence in certain unions and in the People's Convention for what that was worth, was strong; no point in irritating our new patriots. The same light touch was used to comment on Right reactions: ' . . . Lord Davidson, the famous manager of Lord Baldwin's Conservative Party, usually comes into the Ministry wearing a pink rose. On Monday, it is said, he wore a red one.' And, as if to vindicate the *New Statesman*'s former and consistent Popular Front policy, Sagittarius wrote, in a concluding verse of her poem on the new situation:

> This strange but logical event
> Proves dead Geneva's argument
> And makes its truth self-evident
> To minds the most defective. . . .
> Faced with the common enemy
> Extremes must as allies agree
> For there is no security
> Unless it is collective.

The Editor and J. M. Keynes were soon worrying a new bone of contention in the shape of the Second Front contro-versy. The *New Statesman* looked forward to a Second Front from 1942 and urged this policy whenever it was appropriate to do so. Its Editor and contributors had good reason to know what they did not necessarily imply in what they wrote: that there were men at the top or very near it who still hoped to see the Nazis and the Communists destroy each other, while we merely defended ourselves or fought the Germans just enough to help make the odds between the two totalitarian belligerents more nearly level. Was it certain that our delay in invading Europe at some point was caused entirely by military considerations, or was there a political reason for it? The Editor hammered away at the arguments for a Second Front as soon as possible, and hinted of non-military reasons for our failure to concentrate on attacking the Nazis from our side while they were so dangerously engaged in the East, by writing of certain people, 'much influenced by an often unconscious fear of a Russian victory on the Continent'. Keynes was angry; he tried to convince Kingsley Martin that this 'lunatic frame of mind' was non-existent, was a figment of the editorial imagination. He was wrong and the Editor was right; he knew it at the time and, despite Keynes's hint that the agitation for a Second Front should be dropped for the time being, persisted in it.

The United States of President Roosevelt's New Deal was an ally very much to the *New Statesman*'s taste. Although Kingsley Martin was, during a visit to the United States in 1942, to remind his readers that America was very much a foreign country whose people happened to speak English, the fact remained that friendship between radical America and radical England was easier than between radical England and the rigid conservatism of Stalinized Communism. The warmth with which the paper spoke of the Soviet Union's sufferings and triumphs and of the Red Army's heroism in both failure and success has in it a touch of that excess, that self-consciousness with which we praise when we can the efforts of an associate with whom circumstances rather than inclination have united us and whom we are guiltily conscious of not unreservedly liking or trusting. With Roosevelt's America the editorial tone was easier, more natural. Harold Laski, who was writing much for the paper at this time, was a personal friend of both the President and of Felix Frankfurter, and he had other friends, as well as enemies, among the top Americans. Moreover, the President's latter-day Fabianism and his strong anti-imperialism were, the first in the old, the second in the new, *New Statesman* tradition.

It is true that as the paper became more definitely Socialist with the progress of the war, for a reason which will appear, its position was in a few respects—for example in the matter of economics—nearer to Communism than to New Deal 'Fabianism'. Yet it remained firmly hostile to the Idol State. Cole, Laski and the Editor himself, if they were Marxists, were far from being *étatistes* still. The *New Statesman* certainly found the idea of America's support for our cause more reassuring than the Soviet alliance, however admiring and respectful its tone when dealing with the splendours and miseries of the Red Army.

The paper, in the person of Aylmer Vallance, had been happier in its forecasts touching the Russo-German war than in its estimate of what would happen in the Pacific and the manner in which America would become involved as a belligerent. But then nobody seems to have expected Japan to join in the mad dance in quite the brilliant, dashing, treacherous and, to herself, fatal way which she chose. The *New Statesman*'s Far Eastern correspondent did, of course, see that with the Russians fighting desperately and with their backs to the wall outside Moscow, in the Ukraine and in the Don-Volga Basin, Japan had more freedom to strike where she chose. But its analysis of her position led to the conclusion that Japan would, as usual, 'move just as far as she judges she is able to without uniting those she threatens', and that the possibility—it was not quite a hope—of bringing her militarists to reason lay not with us but in Washington.

As a matter of fact *New Statesman* contributors had as much difficulty in making head or tail of what the Japanese were up to as did everybody else, until Dorothy Woodman's article analysing their policy over a period of nearly thirty years appeared, and suggested that a plan to drive the Western powers out of Asia had been consistently followed since the First World War. We have heard much, since 1950, from solemn pundits on the subject of the new Soviet diplomatic invention for deliberately confusing and finally demoralizing the opponent by blowing hot and cold alternately. There is, of course, nothing in the least new about this; it is as old as diplomacy, consisting as it does simply in a peacetime version of the sort of wartime treachery used by Frederick the Great with much advantage. Tojo used it in 1941: in December of that year one of H. N. Brailsford's leaders began:

> Like a grotesque divinity in one of her classical prints, Japan still postures with uplifted sword. Will it ever strike? No one can feel sure, but if it remains for ever a painted blade above a painted ocean, the prestige of the booster who wields it must sink out of sight. During the week-end the Premier, General Tojo, announced that he proposed to 'purge' the Western Democracies out of Asia and to 'crush' them if they resisted him. Simultaneously he asked for a renewal of the interrupted Washington talks.

Not only was the *New Statesman* less inclined to believe the Japanese trustworthy than the United States Government seemed to be; the paper was, so to speak, already at war with Japan: for many years it had supported the cause of China, and one of its persistent themes became the need and duty to support China as a democratic ally. At the time, of course, Chou En-lai and Chiang Kai-shek were on the same side, and both could reasonably be considered as trying to create a democratic republic in their country. At last came Pearl Harbour, which blasted the Americans into the war and thereby ensured the defeat of both Japan and her European allies. It was a week or two before this became apparent. In his first leader after the event Brailsford was very sober:

> America is now our belligerent ally in law as well as in sentiment. But our satisfaction over this immense addition to our military resources is overshadowed by the consciousness that we are comrades in disaster. From the standpoint of morals and politics Japan's treacherous attack may turn out to be in the long run one of the capital mistakes in world history, for it has mobilized the hesitating American people for total war. But we have to face the fact that as a military performance it revealed a deadly efficiency.

But this tone did not last. *New Statesman* editorials were soon taking the line that our pre-1941 faith in victory, held to despite the facts of the military situation, could now be replaced by a certainty of ultimate victory because of the military facts. The USSR, the USA and the British Commonwealth, in alliance, were simply not defeatable by any combination of powers, so that victory had become simply a question of time.

In 1942 Kingsley Martin went to the United States. He was able to go by air: flying the Atlantic was not then a commonplace. When it came to returning home, 'the supply of magic carpets had given out', as he wrote in the American Diary which replaced London Diary for that week, and he ultimately, after great difficulties and using all the influence he could muster, was allowed to recross the Atlantic, one of six civilians among 15,000 American soldiers, in the *Queen Mary*. Meanwhile, the points which he emphasized in his American Diary were American irritation, not all of it unreasonable, over our conduct in India; and, in contrast, the 'American Imperialism' of Henry Luce and his *Time* and *Life* editors.

American criticism of our Indian policy was so childish and ill-informed that Critic, the arch-anti-imperialist, found himself, although he could not defend it, at least making it clear that we could not walk out of the sub-continent just like that. He was even driven to retorting, as he reported in the Diary, that 'their objection to our not quitting India was only exceeded by their annoyance when we did quit Burma'. Nevertheless,

> To do any good the Englishman [officially in the U.S.] must be anti-imperialist. If he then discusses India as a factor in the war and frankly discusses not only Britain's shortcomings but those of Congress and the Muslims, and the complications of the situation, he will find Americans remarkably attentive and willing listeners.

The Editor was invited to the White House, decided that the talk and the occasion were off the record and must not be used as *New Statesman* copy, only to find that Mrs. Roosevelt had 'interviewed' him, in her syndicated column 'My Day'.

Anti-imperialist America was obviously a powerful ally in the *New Statesman*'s long strife on behalf of the peoples of India and the Colonies in their desire to be free of British tutelage. When it came to that other front of the paper's journalistic war, the battle for 'Underground' Europe, the case was very different. It was said of Canning that he was conservative at home and a radical abroad; Roosevelt was a radical at home and in the British Commonwealth, but, perhaps only expediently, a reactionary in Occupied Europe. It will be recalled that he maintained his relations with the government of Pétain and that he was obstinately hostile to General de Gaulle, and to most of the other European Governments-in-exile in Britain. Despite the fact that the President was much less wary of Communism on its native Russian heath than was Churchill, he was distrustful of the Resistance Movements in Europe which the British Government, under Socialist pressure, was beginning to help and encourage. A great deal of that pressure came from the *New Statesman*.

The *New Statesman*'s role as an agitator of European revolt and exponent of the policy of supporting that revolt even though this might seem to mean supporting Communist revolution in Europe, by no means excluded the Germans. The paper recognized the existence of a brave Resistance Movement inside Germany even if others ignored it, and insisted upon the distinction, at one time made by almost everybody but gradually forgotten by most, between Germans and Nazis. In this policy it was to fall foul of Lord Vansittart when it claimed that that nobleman's pamphlet *Black Record*—attacked in the paper by Brailsford as the most evil kind of propaganda which aimed to blacken a whole people—was being used, in translation, by Goebbels, Nazi Minister of Propaganda, to stiffen German resistance to the Democracies by showing them what their enemies really thought of them. This accusation, which was also made by *Reynolds News* on the authority of the Czech Government-in-exile, was challenged by Vansittart; and the Editor was asked to produce proof of it. Kingsley Martin was not free to divulge the source of his information, and when he pressed Edward Beneš to allow him to do so, Beneš denied having said anything of the kind. A withdrawal of the statement was published in the *New Statesman* and the row ended amicably, but this did not stop the paper from continuing to argue that it was as wrong as it was foolish to treat the whole German people *à la Vansittart,* in the same spirit as the Nazis treated the Jews.

The *New Statesman*'s argument was very simple: the Führer of the Germans was now the head of international Fascism; the only militant enemy of international Fascism had been and was and would be international Democratic Socialism; therefore our allies must be international Democratic Socialists. And we must help and encourage them to rise in revolt; in fact, we were doing so. Keynes, in a letter to Kingsley Martin, interpreted this to mean that the *New Statesman* was telling its readers that we, Britain, were encouraging Communist revolution, and he insisted that this was not true. It might be all right to say that we *should* be doing so, though he himself would not wish the *New Statesman* to do so. He hoped that it would not.

This hope was disappointed. As the war progressed, the *New Statesman*'s theme became more and more clearly that the outcome of the war could be, should be and perhaps would be, international Socialism. To some extent this was, no doubt, a rationalization of the Editor's wish to find some justification sufficiently great for so atrocious an affliction of the human race as the war which was being fought by so great a part of it. It was, as I have said, expressed in wholehearted support for the emancipation of colonial peoples, notably of India; and in support of the underground European revolution. The nature of our ally Stalin's régime was, no doubt, a difficulty; but with the entry of the United States into the war and Roosevelt's contacts with Stalin, this difficulty seemed no greater to the *New Statesman* than it did to F. D. Roosevelt himself. The American President, tolerant of the Left and strongly anti-Imperialist, was, for the *New Statesman, the* great man.

The *New Statesman*'s chief exponent of the European case became Dorothy Woodman, who was Secretary of the Union for Democratic Control, of which Kingsley Martin was the Chairman. Dorothy Woodman devoted the Union's principal energies to creating, in the cant phrase, a 'climate' propitious to post-war Socialism. The genuine anti-Fascists in the European Governments-in-exile became her friends and worked with her, and she had contacts with the Resistance groups all over Europe. It was this which enabled her to write, for the *New Statesman*, a series of articles, uniquely well informed, about our potential allies in Occupied Europe, Communist, Socialist, Liberal, and Catholic. The paper was the first to give real hard news concerning the activities of these heroic partisans, whose part in winning the war has since been recognized.

Probably the most important public consequence of this *New Statesman* campaign, based as it was on special knowledge, was to give support to those who were trying to switch Allied support in Yugoslavia from one group of partisans to another. At a time when, officially, we were still helping the Right-wing leader Mihailovich, the *New Statesman*, that is to say Miss Woodman and the Editor, were aware that this officer was not in fact fighting the Germans, and that the effective anti-Nazi and anti-Fascist leader was the man who became known as Tito. The aid we were getting to Mihailovich was being used, in fact, to fight Tito and prevent a Communist revolution triumphing in Yugoslavia. The knowledge of what was really happening reached readers of the *New Statesman* in a dramatic manner. Three of Tito's men who had been captured by the Germans had been put to work on the north Baltic wall, a Todt project. They contrived to escape, and from Scandinavia they were smuggled across to England where they made their way to the U.D.C. office. An interview with Kingsley Martin made a sensational article in the *New Statesman*, giving details of the progress of Tito's partisan forces. The article in the *New Statesman*, translated into Serbo-Croat, was distributed among the partisan fighters in the mountains of Yugoslavia, and when, in 1945, Kingsley Martin visited Tito's army, he discovered that there, as in India and in the Colonies, the *New Statesman* had a towering reputation as a champion of liberty.

Not only did the Dorothy Woodman articles give the paper a unique standing among European exiles and in the Resistance Movements themselves, it also resulted in the paper being considered as sufficiently Left in the Russian zone of the war to be engaged in ideological debate by

Pravda. In due course Russian approval of a journal or for that matter of an individual was to become rather like approval of a movement or a cause by the *Daily Express*, a grave handicap. But in the long run the Russians, too, were to be disappointed in their journalistic ally.

In the four years 1940-44, the policies which the *New Statesman* adopted on the Home Front, the Imperial Front and the European Front were worked together into a single coherent and perfectly clear policy of which they were the parts: the world war and its aftermath must be turned into a means towards the only end which could at once justify it (if anything could) and ensure that it would not happen again: international, ultimately global, Socialism.

This policy was given form as consistent, persuasive argument and appeal addressed to what was good and righteous in all men. What was evil and unrighteous was, no doubt, sometimes too little regarded, but the fault was at least a generous one. In the course of striving for the great cause as it emerged at last clearly from the confusion of the Thirties, Kingsley Martin transformed not indeed the character but what I may perhaps call the dominant mood of the *New Statesman*. From 1913 to 1930, under Clifford Sharp and Mostyn Lloyd, the *New Statesman* was a Fabian workshop. After the amalgamation with *The Nation* and the advent of Kingsley Martin, it was, for some years, unsure of its method, though never of its aims. But by 1944 that uncertainty had quite vanished: the *New Statesman* had become a pulpit. At the beginning of the war the preacher's congregation numbered nearly 200,000, for it is estimated that on average six people read every copy of the *New Statesman*; by the end of 1944, nearly half a million sat under him, for the weekly net sale had risen to 70,000.

12

The H-Era

THE world since 1946 has been dominated by the
repercussions of a single event: there are echoes which
do not wane with time, but wax; it is so with the echoes
of the atomic explosion over Hiroshima This event was less
important as a conclusion, the end of the world war, than as
a beginning, the sombre and terrifying start of the H-era, a
stage in man's history which was soon seen as likely to be the
shortest and last, ending with the destruction of civilization,
perhaps of the human race, possibly of all life on man's
planet. By religious persons whom science had derided,
profane knowledge had always been seen as of the Devil; it
now looked suddenly as if they might have been right after
all. In the long, black shadow cast by the tower of knowledge
without wisdom which the physicists had erected, it was
difficult to enjoy what would have been the triumph of many
New Statesman causes, the coming into power of a Labour
Government inspired by Socialism. A great event, long
prepared for, became a small matter in the dark context of
H-politics.

It has not been sufficiently clearly realized, and it has
never, I think been stated in so many words, that what the
making of the H-bomb, that tremendous achievement of the
human mind, and of its foul brood of lesser weapons has
accomplished is the wiping out of several thousand years of
human progress; progress from the animal to the fully human
status for man. It has reduced the human race to its former
and humiliating position of being completely at the mercy of
forces apt to crush it out of existence by accident. This fact—
that now as in palaeolithic times man exists precariously
under constant threat of extermination by natural forces—is

obscured by superficialities: we do not crouch, few and fearful, in caves, but swarm, many and arrogant, in skyscrapers; we do not fumble with sticks and stones, but wield thunderbolts like Jupiter. But there is one natural force over which we have acquired no power, our own base nature; and this one force, because of our intellectual advance, has become more dangerous and more terrible than the sum of all those natural forces which made the survival of our genus in its youth so improbable.

This has been and is present all the time to the minds of thoughtful men. The five years which followed the General Election of 1945, with all their promise of the application, at last, of new statesmanly theories to practical government, would, by the nineteenth-century Fabians or even by the Popular Frontists of the Thirties, have been relished as years of victory in the present and promise for the future: the war had ended, at least for the British Commonwealth, in a peaceful social revolution of the kind the *New Statesman* had long looked forward to. But, by one of the usual ironies of history, this had happened at a time when the differences between one system of government and another were reduced to insignificance by the overwhelming difference between man's physical power and his moral stature.

Happily, all men, including new statesmen, are able to adjust their sense of proportion to favour their peace of mind. For a few decades man had thought it possible to plan long ahead for the future of the human race; but this, after all, was something quite new and it was not difficult to revert, as we have all unwittingly done, to living for today and hoping that tomorrow's sun will rise as usual. Before the Bomb was dropped the *New Statesman* tone for this epoch was set in the editorial for 12 May 1945. A measure of optimism seemed justifiable; with the USSR seemingly in need of aid from the USA, and a still Rooseveltian United States in the mood to give such aid, an era of peace with democratic Capitalism modifying Communism and Communism modifying democratic Capitalism, seemed possible. At this date Kingsley Martin was in San Francisco for the inauguration of the United Nations, and the editorial, 'The End and the Beginning', was written by Aylmer Vallance, who concluded:

Though peace in the Far East has yet to be won, we have been vouchsafed in Europe an opportunity which may never recur to rebuild our all-but-lost civilization. Its foundation must be based firmly on the recognition of the essential unity of the working people of all nations. Their needs and desires—work and security and 'a dinner of herbs where love is'—are one and the same. The Captains and Kings have made, between them, a century of greed and aggression, hatred and blood. They may now depart.

Kingsley Martin would have done it better, with more recognition of the fact that the people make the captains and the kings and that they are, therefore, always with us: Roosevelt died; the Bomb fell on Hiroshima; it was revealed that Mr. Harry Truman—no captain he but an unsuccessful haberdasher, a 'little' man if ever there was one—was quite as capable of doing the kingly work as any heir to a thousand years of royalty and militarism.

While the *New Statesman* was busy trying to analyse for its readers the muddle created by the dissensions between the Allies in Europe and the Far East, and sorrowfully reproaching Winston Churchill for tarnishing his heroic name by the very shady manœuvres he was employing in the hope of defeating Labour in the election, that atrocious contrivance which was to make our tenure of the planet more precarious than it had been for 20,000 years was in the making.

Throughout the election campaign the *New Statesman* repeatedly claimed that the Tories were harming nobody but themselves by their snide tactics, by putting it about that Mr. Attlee took his orders from that sinister Bolshevik intellectual, Professor Harold Laski, and by allowing Lord Beaverbrook to expose his political ineptitude in public speaking as well as in his newspapers. The paper claimed that the people were taking this election seriously, that they had faced their responsibility for the reconstruction not only of Britain but of civilization in general. The fact is that the election had been lost and won before the war and during it by the people's accumulated anger over unemployment and the foreign policy which had led inevitably to war fought under unnecessary difficulties. Not even the Labour Party bosses, Herbert Morrison for example, properly understood what an important part the *New Statesman* had played in canalizing this anger into the current which won the election. The paper's influence, like that of the old *New Leader*, was on local intellectual leaders, on teachers, professional men, the activators of local movements whose influence was important. The *New Statesman* did not, it is true, do much electioneering for the Labour Party; it created Socialists not Labour men. But the natural choice of Socialists when it came to voting was the Labour Party. This had not always been so and it is not absolutely certain that it will necessarily remain true. But in 1945 a majority of people had realized that Capitalism had meant (and therefore probably must mean) poverty in the midst of plenty; and war. The total rout of the Tory and Liberal Right completely vindicated these claims. The country, as the paper announced, had voted for Socialism. A quarter of a century of new statesmanly propaganda had not been written in vain. And if it was foreseen that the men of the Labour Party, while perhaps up to their work at home would fall short abroad, the *New Statesman* kept its doubts to itself and saw, in Labour's victory, as much hope for Europe as for Britain and the Commonwealth.

The victory of British Socialism has been received with almost incredulous applause in every democracy except the United States. There, gratitude to Mr. Churchill and a nation-wide confidence in the benefits of capitalism have combined to make some sections of the press and public look warily at that silent revolution of which the election results were only the dramatic expression. But elsewhere the electoral landslide has been welcomed as proof of the astonishing vitality of British democracy. The formation of a Labour government with a strong Parliamentary majority brings a sudden ray of hope to those democratic forces—in Spain, Greece and Belgium for instance—which had come to associate the name of Britain with monarchist intrigue and ineffective Amgotry. The Empire, while condoling with the great war leader, is delighted to see that the old country still has some kick in it. The Russians are awaiting events. They correctly estimate that the election was fought on domestic issues. They suspend judgment, therefore, until they see whether British Socialism will extend its influence to

foreign policy. If, as we believe, that is Mr. Attlee's and
Mr. Bevin's firm determination, and if they will support an
International in which the internecine conflict of Socialist
and Communist can be gradually healed, there is reason to
hope that the Russians will collaborate in the reconstruction
of a united Europe. . . .

The idea of Messrs. Attlee and Bevin doing any such thing
as R. H. S. Crossman, who wrote the above, hoped, now
seems odd. But it was Kingsley Martin's view that if you have
in power a Government you can hope to influence (instead
of one you can only hope to weaken), it is always tactically
sound to assume that it will do the right thing, at the same
time hinting that it damned well better! Moreover, before he
became soured by Soviet intransigence and corrupted by the
Foreign Office, Bevin had seemed to be a new statesman in
his ideas of building up the backward countries and his
looking forward to World Government. Besides, at the time,
optimism was in place. It was blasted out of place when the
Bomb fell. The news of the destruction of Hiroshima was
handled by the Editor himself; it was treated, from the
beginning, as confronting the human race with a clear
choice: Destruction or World Government. Moreover,
Kingsley Martin made a point of the first importance when
writing that week's leader:

> Let us immediately cease using such misleading phrases as
> 'the choice before mankind'. For mankind means, today,
> Truman, Attlee, Stalin and a number of other important
> politicians, soldiers and experts in war and production. . . .
> The essential decisions must be made by very few people and
> made very soon.

That attribution of evil solely to captains and kings which
Vallance had been guilty of and which, I believe, the Editor
himself would have repudiated out of his experience of
uncaptainly, unkingly men, had now become perfectly
sound. In short, the implication of the above paragraph was
this: to master atomic energy was to emasculate democracy.
Governments disposing of nuclear energy became incom-
parably powerful; and their constituents, who, by the nature
of things, could have no direct control over this energy,

became weaker in relation to the executive than ever before. For, ultimately, the power of any people to prevent any government from becoming tyrannical lies in the threat of insurrection, even though democratic rights make this unnecessary. Insurrection can succeed only where there is not too great a discrepancy between the kind of weapons which a mob can get hold of and the kind in the hands of the army. But the executive has always suffered from one weakness: the soldiers are also the people and may go over to the people. Science, by making it possible for a small élite to replace numerous armies, has taken from the people its last strength, that of numbers.

Kingsley Martin's leader went on to support President Truman's suggestion that control of the new power should be internationalized; it should indeed, and its secrets should be given at once to the USSR. For otherwise, said the *New Statesman*, the USSR would, in a few years, discover them for herself and so arm the resentment which would meanwhile have been roused in her by the threat to her equality of power and status with the USA, a threat implicit in the American monopoly of the bomb.

Thus, in its forecasts, forebodings rather, touching the political consequences of atomic energy, the *New Statesman* was as nearly accurate as it is given to us to be. Yet, as we can see now, it was advocating policies which were simply not on; and the reason for this is very obvious. The state of physics at this stage of world history demanded a new kind of world, a world in which nations gave up their sovereignty, presented other nations with military secrets of the greatest importance. It was in the tradition of the *New Statesman* to see this and to state it. Moreover, as the Editor and his associates knew very well, the usual time-lag of at least a quarter of a century between political theorists and politicians in office, formerly merely exasperating, had now become hideously dangerous.

The *New Statesman* was less happy in its forecasts of the economic consequences of the new source of energy. Critic fell into the hands of an excessively optimistic scientific friend, and in London Diary published this enthusiast's opinion that 'most of the economic problems we discuss look

pretty sick now' and that 'this should end the problem of
Indian and Asiatic poverty'. The new source of energy has,
in fact, had no such consequences in the eighteen years which
have elapsed, and does not even look like solving anything:
it is probably true to say that the only people not disappointed with it are the soldier-scientists and the politicians.
The *New Statesman*, the Fabian, tradition was the 'Wellsian'
one of science as the great liberator, and it would take
another decade to make it possible not, indeed, to break
with this tradition, but at least to doubt what was after all
an article of Socialist faith. Still, some small doubts were
soon being allowed to show; and it is significant that they
originated in the Editor's conversation with an Indian friend
who, as Critic wrote in the London Diary,

> . . . is, I believe, in this matter typical of his countrymen.
> They still look at political action from a moral point of view,
> and sometimes recall that the British used to share this
> characteristic. To them the obliteration of a civilian
> population (who as they see certainly had less responsibility
> for the war than the citizens of a western democracy with
> some control of their government) is a moral outrage made
> worse by the fact that the Anglo-American ultimatum to
> Japan made no mention of this new weapon . . . but I am
> sufficiently old-fashioned myself to believe that the principles
> for which we say we were fighting were based on a long
> experience of human relations, and that to act as if the people
> of any country were vermin outside the scope of moral
> obligation is to begin the disintegration of our own society.

The *New Statesman* had never been in any way tied to the
Labour Party: it had formerly been to the Right of it; it had
moved far to the Left of it in the Thirties and it was still in
that position in the Forties. It supported the Government
consistently in the creation of the Welfare State; it could
hardly do otherwise since the policies in question were, for
the most part, modified new statesmanship. But what was
not possible and what would have been inconsistent with
new statesmanship, was to support the Government's
foreign policy as conducted by Ernest Bevin. Even before the
Editor found it necessary to give R. H. S. Crossman his head
in criticizing Bevin, the paper was reproaching the Labour

Government for its preoccupation, only apparently justified, with domestic affairs while a tremendous and unique opportunity was being missed in world affairs.

> Every newspaper office has a huge bundle of letters on the significance and morality of atomic bombing. As I look through those addressed to the editor of this journal this week, I see that a large number of people are just sick and horrified; that some pacifists have not yet realized that neutrality has little meaning if a bomb dropped in Brussels will shatter London; that many soldiers and mothers of soldiers (their letters lie in front of me) who had tried to believe that the allies only bombed military targets, are appalled by the hypocrisy of our denunciation of the Germans for their indiscriminate bombing. (It is not so long since Roosevelt himself sternly questioned both combatants on this subject!) There are also sensible if rather generalized letters about the necessity of an international World Order. I should judge that this mood of fear and protest will last for some months, and that on its tide statesmen, able to see beyond the irrelevancies of national politics, could create a world order. If they miss the tide, cynicism and apathy will follow and the daily troubles that arise from the effort to return to normalcy in a world that cannot be normal, will once again submerge our thoughts and sap our wills. The time for Mr. Attlee and Mr. Truman to act is now.

In a 'Wellsian' situation, a 'Wellsian' solution; just as the supranationalist is always up against the fact that patriotism is overwhelmingly respectable, so the true realist, that is to say the man who can see that we are confronted by a situation hitherto found only in imaginative fiction, is up against that kind of harassed small-mindedness which is called 'realism' in politics, and which is a combination of fear, mental laziness and expediency. When the Editor wrote the above paragraph he cannot have hoped that Messrs. Truman and Attlee would really do what was necessary. Still, the *New Statesman* did all in its power to emphasize the urgency of this business: like Luther, it could 'do no other'. Professor J. D. Bernal's article, 'New Frontiers of the Mind', was the first of several, others being contributed later by Professor Blackett, which dealt with the subject technically and from technical data drew social conclusions. It was the *New Statesman*'s Turnstile Press which published Blackett's *Political Consequences of the Atom Bomb*. London Diary hammered away at it; leaders reverted to it.

Meanwhile, the battle against Ernest Bevin's 'Toryism' abroad was started—by R. H. S. Crossman in the summer of 1945 when Bevin's first speech on Foreign Policy was '. . . greeted with some enthusiasm from the Opposition and received in silence by his supporters'. The silence did not last, since ' . . . the task of criticism, both well informed and constructive, was left entirely to the Labour benches'.

At this stage the paper, later to be accused of sabotaging the Labour Government because of its anti-Bevinism, was willing to hope for the best, or at least to seem to do so for tactical reasons. Crossman wrote that he detected in Bevin's speech the beginning of a workable philosophy such as the Tories never had. But was not this philosophy, amounting to a coherent foreign policy as Crossman went on to state it, Crossman's and not Bevin's? It seems to me that when he wrote, for example,

> . . . He knows that if we are to avoid becoming a mere appendage of American capitalism, we must do everything to restore the purchasing power and wage standards of Europe, and we must form with the peoples of Europe a common market, big enough to enable us to stand up together to the export drive which American business is planning in the near future. He knows, lastly, that in seeking to create this common European market, he must avoid antagonizing America, whose financial aid we need, and that we must work with Russia, ever suspicious of plans for an anti-Bolshevik *bloc*. This is the framework of hard unalterable fact, within which a Social Democratic foreign policy— for that is what any foreign policy of Mr. Bevin's will be— has to be constructed . . .

when Crossman wrote this, he was doubtless rather willing to hope that Mr. Bevin knew these things than believing that he did know them. For Crossman went on to detect a very undesirable subservience to American reactionary notions in the Foreign Secretary's references to the Balkan countries and above all to Greece, whose Communist revolution had been openly crushed by British troops in Churchill's time. There was a serious danger that Bevin would turn out to be as reactionary abroad as he was radical at home, and that he would antagonize Russia which, for the whole world's sake, we could not afford to do.

Foreign Secretaries are of two kinds: those who like foreigners and those who don't; those who do are not popular at home, but they get good results abroad; those who don't are popular at home, since they appeal to the easy and base chauvinism in all of us, but they are apt to be disastrous abroad. Bevin did not like foreigners. I believe that historians will conclude, in time, that his appointment to the Foreign Office was a serious blunder and that Crossman was perfectly right in the attacks which he was to make on him.

I have done my best to explain the reasons for the *New Statesman*'s more or less pro-Soviet line in the Thirties, a policy which, whatever has since been said, appears, on careful re-reading of the paper, to have been always and clearly conditional and which never excluded criticism of Stalinist excesses. The war and its immediate aftermath produced many new reasons, as well as feelings, for maintaining and affirming the same policy. Neither Kingsley Martin nor any of his contributors showed much liking for Soviet Communism as such. Unlike the Webbs, they never became converted to admiration of Communist imperialism. What they did have their minds and hearts set on was the hope for international Socialism, that hope which had coloured the paper's picture of the USSR during the war, especially the later part of the war. International Social Democracy in the Old World, co-operating with Capitalist Democracy in the New, that, surely, was the one hope of world order and therefore of salvation from the Bomb. This world order had become not merely desirable, it had become vital. It seems clearly to have been Kingsley Martin's idea and hope, a not unreasonable one until 1947, that just as the Western Democracies would, under the influence of friendship and co-operation with the Communist empire, move socially Left, so the Russians, under the influence of friendship and co-operation with the West, would move, socially, towards a measure of liberalism. Each great social system would thus learn to avoid the excesses inherent in it, and the ultimate result would be worldwide new statesmanship. For that is what it comes to.

As I say, this hope was not unreasonable in 1945 and 1946. The world had been shattered, we had to reconstruct it, we should welcome the chance to do it generously and sanely. There is an analogue: London had been shattered, we had to rebuild it, we had a chance to do so generously and sanely. In both cases that chance was missed, and in both cases for the same humiliating reason: interests vested in vicious traditions. And this was the more mortifying to new statesmen since, during the war, they, notably R. H. S. Crossman, had been allowed and in fact encouraged to use the B.B.C. to give every encouragement to the European Socialist revolution. Britain, turning reactionary with victory, failed to keep the promises which her Socialists had made in her name and with her blessing. But even on the plane of international politics as they had recently been practised, new statesmanly hope was not unreasonable; Attlee and his colleagues were soon showing in India that they could handle foreign affairs, or at least imperial affairs, with a breadth of mind, a generosity, an imaginative sympathy which transcended the nagging warnings of 'realists'; and that they knew how to choose the man for the job. The Americans had shown that they were able to understand and get on with Russian Communism if they allowed themselves to do so. The Russians, in Central Europe, were tolerating and working with non-Communist, even with Constitutional Monarchical, régimes. Clearly, there was a great deal of goodwill in the world, the war seemed to have shaken us into a better frame of mind towards our neighbours.

But the *New Statesman* also saw that this would not last and that what was immediately necessary was a lead. Britain could and should take that lead. The inability of the Labour Government to rise to this opportunity in Europe; the growing fear-induced aggressiveness of the Soviet Union confronted with the American Bomb; the aggressive response, perhaps in part induced by bomb-guilt, of the USA: these things were all connected and the *New Statesman* foresaw them. But until 1947 it continued to hope against foreboding, for it was not until then clear that these failures were inevitable. There are conditions in which too much intelligent pessimism is downright wicked. It is the duty of the dedicated preacher to give hope; he must certainly not create despondency by persistently crying that there is no hope.

There were other and associated reasons for the *New Statesman*'s post-war pro-Russianism. The *New Statesman* believed, and Kingsley Martin argued strongly and lucidly in the paper, that unless we remained firmly in alliance with the USSR, there could be no solution to the problem of Germany. He was, as events have demonstrated, quite right, but his need to believe in a rational solution to most problems made him overlook the fact that there was never any real goodwill on either side. American business interests proceeded to create the West German 'industrial miracle' both because it was profitable and because a successful capitalist Germany would be a bulwark against Communism. And Stalin never had any intention, as far as one can judge, of co-operating with the West. But the *New Statesman* believed, as I have said, that it might even be essential to mankind's survival that the three world dominating powers, the USSR, the USA and the British Commonwealth, understand one another and act in concert as friends, however critical of each other. Now, however much loose anti-American talk there might be in Britain (and anti-American chatter became, with Income Tax evasion chatter, the favourite indoor sports of the middle class for a time), there was never really any question of our American alliance. To put the matter at its lowest, we could not afford to quarrel with our bread-and-butter. It was at this level, for instance, that the *New Statesman* dealt with the matter of the American loan. G. D. H. Cole, writing in the paper, lamented it, but he did not come out strongly against accepting it. He lamented it because it must mean some measure of subservience, for even a Labour Government of Britain, to United States capital; but he did not suggest refusing it, because, like other new statesmen, he realized that the degree of continuing austerity this would have involved would certainly bring down the Government. But even on a higher level, that of mutual understanding and respect, there was never any danger of a serious quarrel let alone war with the United States. Unlike Bevin and Attlee, the *New Statesman* never had any fear of the USA retiring into isolation again. So that, on the Western side of the world, international relations needed no journalistic help. But it was very necessary indeed to make a special and deliberate effort to understand and be friends with the Russians; and to persuade the Americans to do likewise. American-British friendship was so solid that America and Britain could well afford to be critical, and at times downright abusive, of each other. Even such appalling *gaffes* as Anthony Eden's war on Egypt, or United States imperialism in Latin America, were not to do much damage to the alliance. But with Russia, touchy, remembering past wrongs, terribly stricken, deeply suspicious, the only safe, the only useful, the only completely sane attitude must be one of patient forbearance sustained until she, in her turn, showed some towards us. This was Christian charity; it was also plain sense: you did not provoke to violence a sullen, badly wounded and frightened giant, capable of crushing the life out of you even at the cost of his own. Capable, too, if soothed and befriended with sufficient understanding, of becoming at least a peaceable if still unfriendly neighbour.

In 1947 a winter of almost unprecedented severity, co-inciding with a famine in dollars, led to the breakdown of our power supply system because of shortage of fuel and the run-down state of much of the equipment. Power cuts had to be made, and Mr. Emanuel Shinwell, Minister of Fuel and Power, decided, with the agreement of his colleagues, that one of the unessential industries whose work could be suspended (in the event for a fortnight) was that of the periodical Press. As a result several hundred periodicals, including the entire trade and technical Press, had to cease publication. An attempt was made, in the House of Lords, to get the weekly journals 'of opinion' exempted from this ban. It failed, of course: no government loves its critics, and no democracy can discriminate in favour of intelligence though it may be forced to do so in favour of organized power—money, for example, or trade unionism. The *New Statesman*, the *Spectator* and others were, as the *New Statesman* recorded in a Supplement on this crisis published six months later, classed with 'aids to betting and pornography', and Kingsley Martin reprinted 'Lucio's' lament in the *Manchester Guardian*:

> Down with the highbrow sheets that cherish
> The deeper draughts from wisdom's vat;
> Let *Statesman* and *Spectator* perish
> Even as *Tit-Bits* and *Home Chat*.
> There is no dodging this fell hammer,
> Down fall our brightest and our best.
> *Peg's Paper* (merged, I find, with *Glamour*),
> Like the *Economist*, goes West. . . .

The Supplement published in August of 1947 simply brought together, for the record, as it were, the new states-manly writings which had appeared, during the crisis, in daily papers which had offered the hospitality of their space to certain of the weeklies. The *Daily Telegraph* offered space to the *New Statesman*, but by then a similar offer by the *News Chronicle* had been made and accepted, and *The Observer* also made room for the banned weeklies. Nor were these news-papers alone in thus signally recognizing the importance of the weekly press; there was also the B.B.C. At this time Kingsley Martin had long been well known to radio audi-ences, a fact to which the rapid rise in *New Statesman* circula-tion has sometimes been attributed. He was sometimes a member of that remarkable institution, the B.B.C. Brains Trust, which had made an impression on the country's social life. He was in a position to ask the B.B.C. to give the prin-cipal weekly journals of opinion a place on the air. The B.B.C. agreed. Each editor spoke for his paper, and there were round-table conferences between them. The experiment was so successful that the broadcasts did not cease with the raising of the ban: Kingsley Martin and Mr. Wilson Harris, then editor of *The Spectator*, continued to be heard on the air for the next six months.

An element in the *New Statesman*'s quarrel with Ernest Bevin was the Foreign Secretary's anti-Jewish and pro-Arab policy in Palestine. The paper pointed out that the main-tenance of order under the mandate in that unhappy country was costing us £100 millions a year. When Bevin tried to blame our failure there on the Americans, in a House of Commons attack on President Truman which, as R. H. S.

Crossman wrote in the *New Statesman*, 'should placate the most fervent critics of his American policy', Crossman wrote a characteristically lucid, terse and downright analysis of the Foreign Secretary's argument: it was true, as Bevin had argued, that America had strategic interests in the Near East; that her powerful and very large oil interests forced her to be pro-Arab; that the two million Jewish voters in New York alone forced her to pretend not to be pro-Arab and to equivocate in public. There was nothing to be said for America in this context. But what of it? The mandate was unworkable and it was time to say so, bluntly. Later, Crossman had to reproach Bevin for his rejection not only of our own Royal Commission's findings, but of the recommendations of the Anglo-American Committee on which he himself served, which investigated the Palestine problem.

The fuel crisis and the consequent publication ban were blessings in disguise for the *New Statesman*. For, as a result of them, the Editor and his principal colleagues, Crossman, Aylmer Vallance, H. N. Brailsford, V. S. Pritchett and Norman MacKenzie whose contribution was a miniature 'German Diary' on the parallel West German crisis, were read by millions instead of thousands, and the Editor, *qua* Editor of the *New Statesman* and not merely as a Brains Trustee, was heard by many more millions. In short, the paper was given a publicity boost which money could not have bought. The result was notable: true, the circulation had already been climbing steeply; but in 1945 it was still under 70,000, whereas during some weeks of 1947 it touched 90,000, the average for the year exceeding 84,000. During and immediately after the war, the Government supplied the men in all the Services with copies of the weeklies, and the *New Statesman*, like the rest, benefited from this. For some time, of course, the *New Statesman* had been making a profit; it now began to do more, it started to make 'real' money. But as nobody had ever regarded the paper as primarily, or even secondarily, a commercial undertaking the money was in due course reinvested in the paper.

The *New Statesman* criticism of a Government it was expected, at least by the Labour leaders, to support uncritically, was not confined to the Crossman-Bevin row. It was critical of the American loan negotiations, of the Bretton Woods agreement, of the Greek as well as the Palestine policy. At the end of the war the paper had seen the possibility of a United Europe under British leadership and with Russian friendship; its principal preoccupation became that of trying to make sure that the opportunity presented by this promise was not lost. In common with Mr. Henry Wallace and his followers in the United States, and incidentally with two-thirds of the United States people according to a Gallup Poll, the paper was distrustful of dollar imperialism, into which the originally imaginative and generous offer of General Marshall had been transformed. Yet it was very difficult to criticize this dollar imperialism, for it was inextricably confused with the genuine idealistic generosity of the American people.

Bedevilled by these ambiguities and confusions, the question of what I may perhaps call *N.S.*-U.S. relations, which were to become strained, was exceedingly involved. The late President Roosevelt's colleague, Henry Wallace, was a warm-hearted, rather simple-minded, Left-wing liberal. It was largely in his leadership of an American faction that the *New Statesman* saw hope of new statesmanship being applied on a worldwide basis. Kingsley Martin had met him when he was in America in 1942 and as a result of their talk, and of Kingsley Martin's subsequent interview with Luce of *Time* and *Life*, he wrote an article in the *New Statesman* (described by Keynes as an 'inspired analysis'), discussing the two possible post-war American policies, Luce's American Century and Wallace's Century of the Common Man. Wallace was detested by the American Right and even by the American Centre, and by these enemies his name was associated with the extreme Left of the British Labour Party whose outstanding personality in the House of Commons was Mr. K. Zilliacus, who was as critical of Ernest Bevin as Crossman himself. Bevin's excesses of anti-Communism made him a popular figure in America; he received, indeed, an embarrassing tribute in the form of cabled 'support' from a group of American Right-wingers, led by Luce the publisher, on which Critic commented:

Last week I expressed some regret at the weakness of the American Left, but the manifesto cabled by the American 'liberals' to Mr. Bevin makes me realize what vast accretions of strength they have recently had. Their message of greeting warmly endorsed the domestic and foreign policies of the Labour Government and gave a pledge to oppose ill-informed criticism of the British Government in the United States. There are several stars new to the liberal firmament amongst those who signed. For instance there was Bishop Manning whose last notable incursion into British affairs was to lead a crusade against allowing Bertrand Russell freedom to teach philosophy in New York City; perhaps in his new enthusiasm for liberalism he will invite Professor Laski to lecture. The Editor of the *Reader's Digest* has apparently come all over pro-Labour, and so has America's bitter radio critic, Hans von Kaltenborn. Mrs. Luce, whose last conversion was to Roman Catholicism, has followed with a warm embrace of British Socialism. Her husband, the publisher of *Time* and *Life*, also signed the manifesto. The current issue of *Time* gives earnest of its opposition to ill-informed criticism of the Labour government by asserting that Socialism must inevitably suppress democracy, and by taking the *Daily Express* to task for remaining so 'sensationally calm' in the face of Mr. Silkin's tyranny. This gallant group of liberals wish to express their solidarity with Mr. Bevin against the 'Wallace-Zilliacus Axis' which seeks 'a return to those Anglo-American policies of concessions and retreats which have already placed half of Europe and much of Northern Asia under Soviet domination'. Since no one can blame these retreats on Byrnes or Bevin it is obviously the policies of Roosevelt and Churchill which are condemned.

In late 1946 and early 1947 there had been much talk in America of a 'preventive war' whose object was to be the crippling of the USSR, thus checking the spread of Communism. This was one of the political imbecilities which the *New Statesman* set itself to expose and deplore. Britain's severe economic crisis, aggravated by the savage arctic winter, gave Americans the impression that Britain was done for; she could certainly no longer be relied on to hold the front line of capitalist democracy. Russia's own famine harvest of that year had weakened her; it might be a good moment to attack her. This was the sort of mad reasoning which seemed to *New Statesman* writers to be extremely dangerous, however complaisantly it might be accepted by most of our Press. And it accounts in some measure for that pro-Soviet and anti-American bias of which the paper was soon to be accused even by its friends.

This anti-Americanism amounted to pointing out that the USSR, if threatened and A-bombed, would necessarily invade and occupy Europe—there was no army strong enough to prevent her from doing so—and that to defeat her the United States would have to destroy every city, including Rome, Paris and probably London, which the Russians had been frightened or exasperated into occupying. Reluctant though Americans might be to accomplish this destruction, they would have had no real alternative.

Yet even in the United States the new statesmanship of the Forties and Fifties was not without friends and supporters. For, opposed to the idea of Luce's American Century (the name given to dollar imperialism), was, as Kingsley Martin had written, that of Henry Wallace's Century of the Common Man, a doctrine which, albeit attractive to the American people, was unable to compete in its influence on the United States Government with the *Time* and *Life* policy of dealing with 'Communist aggression' by an even more aggressive and indeed warlike anti-Communism. But neither by Wallace nor by the *New Statesman* was the case for the USSR at all easy to argue without apparent 'fellow travelling'. The Soviet Union made a major blunder by rejecting Marshall Aid; had she accepted it Congress would have refused the necessary funds, and the whole scheme would have fallen through, with the result that impoverished nations would not have been open to 'dollar imperialism'. But what was worse, she rejected the Baruch Plan for the international control of atomic energy; and this rejection seemed to Americans, and could only with great difficulty be presented as other than,

> The wanton sabotage of a wise and generous offer and final proof for those who wanted it of Russia's sinister intent to paralyse any action through the United Nations.

Thus Kingsley Martin, who went on to say that America was,

half unconsciously, taking over Britain's nineteenth-century role. But it was going to cost her every penny she could raise. And her methods were not ours. Senator Cabot Lodge declared that, 'We must modernize our approach . . . the old striped pants approach [in diplomacy] is as out of date as cavalry. . . '. Sagittarius pounced joyfully on this one:

America advances a suggestion
   On how diplomacy should be arrayed
For dealing with the vexed Near-Eastern question
   Now called the Anti-Communist Crusade.
Old diplomats wore quaint and changing fashions
   And made no hard-and-fast sartorial rule,
     They never paid attention
     To the dress for intervention
When keeping Russia out of Instanbul.

When Russia was both Orthodox and Holy
   She likewise was forbidden to encroach
And Western Powers came together slowly
   On the periwig and knee-breeches approach.
They made the same approach in peg-top trousers
   When diplomats wore watch-chains in festoons,
     A most successful series
     Wore sideburns and Dundrearies
And stays and fancy vests and pantaloons. . . .

They say Back, Back, Back to Godless Russia
   And bolster Greeks and Turks with guns and grants
     But though the stroke's a bold one
     The game is such an old one
Why don't the Yanks unpack their old striped pants?

The austerities of the times and the *New Statesman*'s support of the Government's tight-rein policies did not lead to the conclusion that because the paper was virtuous there should be no more cakes and ale. It was light-hearted where it could be. When Dr. Edith Summerskill at the Ministry of Food made her egregious remarks in the House on the relative merits of mousetrap and less common cheeses, C. E. M. Joad weighed in with a highly entertaining pseudo-scholarly analysis of taste in cheeses which led him to some severe conclusions concerning the limitations of the female mind. The *New Statesman* might recognize the economic advantages of factory cheddar; it was on the side of those who preferred Stilton and Camembert.

In 1947 Henry Wallace was invited to Britain as the *New Statesman*'s guest. What was to have been a private visit turned, vastly to the *New Statesman*'s advantage, into an international event. Nobody had expected that interest on the part of the daily and Sunday Press which wrought this transformation; nobody had expected the overwhelming concourse of people flocking to all the meetings which Wallace addressed. In London, the Albert Hall could have been thrice filled if the *New Statesman* could have got it. Wallace's success was nevertheless understandable: he was the man who thought that American money should be spent not simply in buying Old World armies and Old World political reactionary leaders to defend the cause of democratic progress and peace, but on raising the whole world's standard of living. The English found American aggressiveness as alarming as it was distasteful. Wallace's speeches in Britain, mildly and generously liberal by European standards, infuriated the Americans. And since the Conservatives in Opposition, the Bevinites in the Government, and the British Press were all equally afraid of offending the Americans, the reception of Wallace's speeches, and notably of his B.B.C. broadcast which, said some who may have been right at that, was written by Kingsley Martin, was a bad one. Critic commented:

The press has been a bit flummoxed to find that Henry Wallace was not at all anti-British and was quite prepared to admit that the Soviet Union is sometimes wrong, and that he had something clear and constructive to say. This doctrine is neither 'woolly' nor in the least 'anti-American'; it is merely a restatement of the New Dealers' remedy for which he and Roosevelt worked during the war. He urges that America's colossal surplus of wealth should be used in making friends for democracy (a market for the United States) by raising the standard of living everywhere instead of in bolstering up régimes merely because they are anti-Soviet. I was not surprised that Conservative newspapers should have attacked Wallace, but I must admit disappointment that the *Manchester Guardian* should not have troubled

to understand what he was saying and should have attacked
him for no reason that I could see, except that he had not
adequately attacked the Soviet Union. His object was to
state the alternative to Communism, to remind people that
ideologies are not stopped by bombs and to establish this
community of agreement between the British and the
large numbers of Americans who had not yet caught the
anti-Communist disease. . . .

The anti-Communist disease: the *New Statesman* was alone
in watching, uneasily, the development of this sickness, and
unique in forecasting McCarthyism, not, of course, by that
name, in an article by E. Penning Rowsell which recalled
the anti-Red terror of 1920 in the United States and which
demonstrated that the conditions for a repetition of the
disease in an even more virulent form were present.

In 1949 the paper was involved in a case, of what I may
call the classic type, in which an editor finds himself protect-
ing a contributor or the writer of a Letter to the Editor,
against the authorities. The Press has, as the watchdog of
liberty, civic duties which, although its freedom has been
established by two centuries of struggle in which many
editors have suffered terms of imprisonment and financial
ruin, may get editors into serious trouble.

In this case he had published a letter exposing the allegedly
pro-Fascist and anti-Semitic behaviour of the police in the
course of brawls provoked in Hackney and Dalston by the
organized louts of Sir Oswald Mosley's Union Movement.
The letter was signed 'John Hadlow', which was not the
writer's name. In the following week a paragraph in London
Diary made reference to it:

Several correspondents have written to suggest that a number
of the policemen in Dalston and other East London districts
were once members of the Palestine Police. Is this true?
If it is, it might explain such anti-Semitic discrimination on
the part of the police in the East End as was described in
this journal last week by Mr. Hadlow (the pseudonym of a
well-known police reporter). I notice that Arthur Koestler,
in his latest book *Promise and Fulfilment,* says that anti-Jewish
feeling reached 'scandalous proportions' in the Palestine
Police—scandalous, that is, even when we recall the nature

of the provocation in this least necessary of British wars. Koestler writes: 'With Black and Tan veterans in leading positions, riddled with former members of Mosley's Blackshirts, the Palestine Police was one of the most disreputable organizations in the British Commonwealth.' When the Palestine Police was wound up its members were offered employment in the Metropolitan Police. How many accepted? And how many were then drafted into East London districts?

John Hadlow's allegations gave rise to an enquiry by the Home Office, as a result of which the police were vindicated. But this is not the point: the Editor of the *New Statesman* had been asked to divulge the name of 'John Hadlow' and he had refused to do so. In a subsequent article he explained that this was not only his right but his duty.

. . . the only exception, we believe, is where the Official Secrets Act, or Parliamentary privilege is involved, and even here it may well on occasion be the duty of the editor to go to prison himself rather than break faith with the contributor.

This explanatory article had been made necessary by a discussion of the case in the House of Commons, in the course of which Members showed themselves strangely ignorant of what was meant by freedom of the Press.

If I now refer briefly to my own relations with the *New Statesman*, for which I began to write in 1949, it is because I can by so doing throw some light on the influence which the paper was apt to have on a writer's career; and on the editorial atmosphere in which he worked. I had written two articles without having any particular paper in mind. When I re-read them it occurred to me that they were new statesmanly. It was, however, without much hope that I sent them to the *New Statesman*, which had never been an easy paper to get into. I have not had many more agreeable moments in my working life than those when, opening the mail one morning, I found proofs of both articles for correction. I wrote more: I met the Editor, I met Aylmer Vallance and Norman MacKenzie. The only disadvantage I ever experienced from being a regular *New Statesman* contributor was that reviews of my books in the paper seemed to become less indulgent. On the other hand their sales increased. The other advantages were manifold: I received, sometimes from the Editor himself but constantly from Aylmer Vallance, patient help, sympathetic advice in improving or trying to improve my work; and, what was no less valuable, a firm rejection with a good reason why when I offered poor work. As for the effect of becoming a *New Statesman* writer, it was very surprising: from being obscure and very definitely 'struggling', I found my work being sought after by other editors, by publishers and by B.B.C. producers.

The *New Statesman*'s alarm at the first United States re-action to the news that the USSR had the atom bomb drove the paper into an intensification of its critical attitude towards the United States Government. The quarrel did not reach its crisis until the attack on the *New Statesman* by the *New Republic* when it dropped its support of Henry Wallace and ceased to be militantly left-wing. Kingsley Martin's reply was published in both the *New Republic* and the *New Statesman* and in part by *The Observer*. The trouble was the *New Statesman*'s fierce conviction that the State Department's policy in the Far East was wrong and very dangerous, a difference which became acute during the Korean War. The paper showed itself consistently friendly to the Chinese Communists, whereas America was deeply involved with Chiang Kai-shek and doing everything to strengthen the footing which this alliance gave her for her armies in Formosa. The Editor and men who thought as he did had been much less impressed, in their attitude to both Stalin and Mao Tse-tung, by George Orwell's *1984* than the rest of the thinking world. It is fair to say that they had been *too* little impressed by that sick vision of Communist Oligarchy carried to its logical conclusion. But they saw the 'Cure'—i.e United States intervention possibly in the form of a pre-ventive war—as worse than the disease. Thus the paper's hostility to the American militarist Right was intensified when, in 1950, the USA 'China Lobby' nearly succeeded, with the help of General MacArthur, in stampeding the Truman administration into undeclared war on the Chinese Communist Republic by getting a 'military mission' landed in Formosa. This move was defeated by the influence of Dean Acheson, but had it succeeded the British Left, even the official Left, Mr. Attlee's Labour Government which had recognized the Communist Government of China, would have been in opposition to the American Government in its Pacific but far from pacific policy. This contretemps was avoided in the event by everyone pretending that the war between North and South Korea was not a war between Russo-Chinese Communism and Western Democratic Capitalism. But the *New Statesman* remained urgently critical of Pentagon fire-eaters and Republican jingoism, too little critical of their Communist equivalents.

The *New Statesman*'s attitude in the Korean War was at first so strictly reasonable and impartial that it was certain to be unpopular. The unforgivable sin in a war situation is to be reasonable. The paper accepted the Security Council's decision that North Korea had, in fact, committed an act of aggression against South Korea. Only later did it come to the conclusion that this act of aggression had been provoked by South Korean aggressiveness. True, the South Korean American puppet Government of Syngman Rhee was even more corrupt than Chiang Kai-shek's, but this did not justify the North Korean Communists:

> For the first time a puppet Government, controlled and armed by one Great Power, had made war on the puppet Government of another Great Power. The Security Council on the evidence before it has condemned Northern Korea as an aggressor. In obtaining this verdict the United States was aided by the absence of Russia, which thereby in effect waived its power of veto. Jumping the legal gun by a matter of five hours, America announced its intention to protect Southern against Northern Korea and also formally declared its determination to prevent any attack on Formosa, at the same time warning the Kuomintang rump against continuing their blockade of Communist China. By this unilateral action in taking over Formosa, which should by universal consent be returned to China, the Americans have weakened the basis of legality on which they stand, and shown that the underlying issue in the Pacific is the rivalry of two Great Powers. Yet, as the Korean conflict was presented to them, Britain, and the other members of the

Security Council could see no alternative but to accept America's lead, however apprehensive they might be of its outcome.

Apprehension, the *New Statesman* believed, was very much in order. For:

> It is only too possible that the upshot of American action in Southern Korea will merely be to build what Mr. Acheson might properly call a 'position of weakness'—that is a strategic point which from a military point of view is hard to defend, which is based on no popular support, and which is just as vulnerable to the ideological attack of Communism as the present régime of Mr. Syngman Rhee.

It must be confessed that the language which the *New Statesman* chose to use and which Kingsley Martin both used and allowed in this and subsequent crises, does something to justify the accusation of unfair bias against America and in favour of the Communists.

> Instead of arguing the necessity of checking aggression and seeking a settlement at the same time, some American Imperialists now see before them a prospect of opposing Communism by force all over the world, and presumably of finally scoring a great military victory against China and the USSR.

Doubtless the persons referred to were correctly called Imperialists. But the word was too heavily charged, it had been too much abused by the Communists for the purpose of vituperation, and it would have been tactful to avoid it. I cannot find that Communist Imperialists were so called in the *New Statesman*. What, of course, drove the Editor to these extremes was fear of the influence of Americans like James Burnham whom he quoted as saying, ' . . . the third world war has begun, but when we make it a shooting war is a matter of expediency'.

Meanwhile, the real facts of the Korean situation were put before *New Statesman* readers in a perfectly impartial article by Dorothy Woodman whose knowledge of and popularity in the East, which she had visited with Kingsley Martin— she was particularly at home and liked in Burma—made her the *New Statesman*'s specialist in Far Eastern affairs. Miss

Woodman gave chapter and verse for the paper's assertion that the Korean War was a manifestation of the worldwide struggle for power between the two super-states. It also showed, however, that we had no real alternative to following America's lead but also no excuse for not understanding exactly what we were doing and why.

Because it is extremely difficult to recall, after ten years, precisely the mood of a war situation, it is not now easy to see why, albeit allowing for the occasional error of linguistic tact criticized above, even the *New Statesman*'s friends were becoming uneasy at what they considered its unfair bias against America in the world struggle. This, chosen as representative, does not strike one as partial:

> . . . that the Communists should pretend that they alone are anxious for peace when they are prepared to defend any breach of the peace provided that the aggression is Communist.
>
> Recognition of Communist motives, however, does not in the least excuse the Labour Executive statement that failure to secure the international control of atomic weapons has been solely due to the intransigence of the Russian leaders. This is as blatant an over-simplification—not to use a stronger word—as any in the Communist propaganda the executive is denouncing. . . .

And in the same number of the paper R. H. S. Crossman's 'How to Limit the War' was perfectly fair to both sides. And that, of course, was the trouble. Kingsley Martin and his colleagues made no tendentious moral distinction between the two contending immoralities.

The fact remains, however, that Kingsley Martin started the Peace with China Council which organized meetings all over the country and whose principal object was to ensure that General MacArthur should not be allowed to cross the Yalu River and get into war with Communist China. The Council and the *New Statesman* both held to the view that the North Koreans were the aggressors, but insisted that the sole duty of the United Nations was to halt them at the 38th Parallel and not to ignore the warnings of India's ambassador in Peking that if the U.N. armies advanced to the Korean frontier, then China would officially enter the war. Thus the *New Statesman* was a moderate supporter of moderate

American policy, but hostile to the Right extremism of Mac-Arthur and his admirers.

However, in February 1951, G. D. H. Cole wrote a remarkable, and for him very unusual, article in the paper, entitled 'As a Socialist sees It'. In this he said that he could not regard the invasion of South by North Korea as aggression, nor the 38th Parallel as a frontier. The war was a civil one and we ought not to be involved in it at all.

> Looking on the Korean War as a civil war I wanted the North to win. The Government of South Korea seemed to me to be a hopelessly reactionary puppet affair, which had no chance of survival without American support. And I could not contemplate any solution of the Korean question that would involve permanent American intervention on the Asian continent. I do not like Communism; but I like even less reactionary landlordism backed by foreign force against the will of the people . . .

The article was a fervent declaration of Socialist faith, and coming as it did from a man who had developed a very cool head out of the ardour of his youth, it was moving. It concluded:

> The duty of democratic Socialists is therefore to do what they can to get in between the rival pressure groups of world revolution and world capitalism. The 'third force' cannot now be a great armed Power: it can still, given the right lead from Britain, be a great force for clear thinking and plain common-sense. . . .

Cole's article was not, of course, *New Statesman* policy, which, as we have seen, was reluctant support for the United Nations position combined with restraint of General MacArthur, a policy which triumphed when, in fact, President Truman recalled and broke that great but dangerous soldier. But as Cole had written for the paper since its very early days and was associated with it in the minds of many, what he said was widely regarded as what the *New Statesman* wanted to advocate. The distinction between Cole's policy and the Editor's was overlooked and the paper regarded in America as virtually Communist.

Kingsley Martin's willingness to publish views which were

not those he himself had arrived at is probably one of the things which has led to the belief held in some quarters that he was too 'suggestible'. Listening to some of his old friends or associates talk, one gets the impression of him as a soul for which rival powers continually struggled, victory in the struggle being a measure of influence over the paper's policy. There were, throughout his editorial career, always influences at work on him, for he was an Editor ready to listen to other people's opinions and to modify his own when it seemed to him that they were more nearly right than himself. There is no merit whatever in rigidity of opinion, in refusal to accept that marvellously wise advice which Cromwell gave to the less flexible of his followers: 'Believe, in the bowels of Christ, that ye may be mistaken.' And it is true that sometimes two or more influences at work on the Editor were in conflict. But I do not believe that these voices, speaking respectively into his left and his right ears, did much more than externalize, embody his own 'voices', the voices of that unending inner debate which occupied his mind and spirit and which made him what he had become, one of the very few really great editors.

When it had become known that the USSR had, as the *New Statesman* had forewarned that she would, made the atom bomb, there was a second movement in the United States to begin a preventive war—that is, to destroy the USSR before she became strong enough to defend herself. It is quite possible that this is what the United States should have done; conceivably a worldwide *Pax Americana* could have been imposed. But the idea was extremely repulsive to the majority of Americans. Vyshinksy, for the Soviet Government, had offered an atomic disarmament pact with international inspection and destruction of stock-piles. Although this would have meant leaving the USSR, with her huge army, stronger than the Western Powers, this was the course favoured by the *New Statesman*. It was so favoured because the alternatives were immediate preventive war on the USSR, or, by way of compromise, manufacture of the H-bomb (called the Hell Bomb in the *New Statesman*) by the United States. The *New Statesman* was strongly against both these alternatives to the Vyshinsky pact. (So was David

Lilienthal, Chairman of the USA Atomic Energy Commission, who resigned in order to be free to urge the President to refuse to make the new bomb.) Crossman, writing the *New Statesman* leader just before Truman rejected Lilienthal's advice and decided to make the H-bomb, made another attack on Ernest Bevin:

> We have more than once stressed our view that the gravest mistake of British foreign policy since the war has been Mr. Bevin's failure to take up Mr. Vyshinsky's new proposals at Lake Success for atomic disarmament. Perhaps they are nothing but a trick of political warfare. But no one can know for certain whether they are or not until they have been put to the test in serious discussion. By sticking stubbornly to the Baruch proposals which were always impossible of acceptance by the Russians and which have now been completely out-dated by the Russian manufacture of A-Bombs, the Western Powers during the last six months have made it appear that they are determined to prevent even an attempt to reach an agreement. Such a position may conceivably have been tenable for the USA—before the revelation about the hydrogen bomb. For Britain, which is indefensible against atomic attack, it was always criminal folly.

New Statesman opposition to what it saw as the hysterical aggressiveness of the American Right never, of course, amounted to general anti-Americanism, but it began to be labelled as such; just as the paper's insistence on trying to take Communist 'peace propaganda' seriously (although never losing sight of the probability that it was nothing *but* propaganda) was soon being labelled pro-Communist.

Re-reading the paper after ten years the following criticism seems to me fair and valid. Socialism has always had two main streams: the source of one is the traditional revolutionary ideal of setting the people free; the source of the other is the Marxist economic ideal. In practice they are not, as Orwell was the first to make clear, easily reconcilable. In its policy attitudes from the Thirties to the end of the Fifties, the *New Statesman* tended too much to navigate the stream of Socialist Order, and neglected the stream of Socialist Freedom. In its dislike of Capitalist abuses it rather closed its eyes to Socialist abuses.

The outcome of the General Election of 1950, which put Labour back into office without an effective majority and which showed Britain equally divided on class lines, led the *New Statesman* to urge not that there had been too much Socialism between 1945 and 1950 but, in one sense, too little. The Cripps 'wage freeze' had operated too much against the interests of the workers. G. D. H. Cole, having analysed the cost-of-living index and tendency and shown that many people in the lower ranges of salary earners had expressed their discontent by voting Conservative; having warned, too, that although the manual workers were politically loyal to Labour, they too had their discontents, concluded:

> Rationally, the best solution would probably be to raise children's allowances and pensions and to grant substantial tax remissions in favour of the lower group of salaries. But it looks as if things have gone too far for such a solution to have a chance.

Salaries and wage rates would have to go up; and to pay for this while avoiding runaway inflation there would have to be not only greater output but also a profits 'squeeze'.

Although it was obviously more difficult for the *New Statesman* to remember that it was a journal of dissent when its 'own side' was in office, it had certainly not become complaisant and it had, as we have seen, remained very critical of the Labour Government's foreign policy. In the early 1950s, J. B. Priestley introduced a new note into the *New Statesman*, a note of something like weary contempt for all politicians whatever their party; by presenting himself as a victim of the powers that be, of what he was later to call Topside, he began that attack on the Establishment which has developed since into an attitude of mind and therefore become innocuous; he did his readers a valuable service, however, by demonstrating that the Establishment, Topside, was not really affected by the political beliefs of the men in office. He brought back into the paper something which had been lost, traditional radicalism, a picture of social and political life in which the citizen is clearly seen as standing distrustful of and ready to be opposed to authority whatever that authority calls itself. There was, in his writing for the

New Statesman at this time, a salty flavour of the old *Nation*, but with the urbanity of Gerald Barry's *Week-end Review* for which Priestley had written, which was very welcome and which, in an increasingly conformist world, was also of very great value and importance. It was also Priestley in the *New Statesman* who helped to break through the Iron Curtain by an Open Letter to Ilya Ehrenburg, who had attacked him for not attending the Communist-organized 'Congress for Peace' in Paris. At the time, this effort to talk into the closed world of Communist secretiveness had no consequences: they were to come later, when the old tyrant Stalin was dead and succeeded by a man with less inclination to play Big Brother.

Priestley's manner in the *New Statesman* did a very valuable job because it personalized and gave character to the dilemma which the paper was dealing with in the field of international politics; the dilemma of the Third Force man, nation or community caught between two conflicting Topsides both making unscrupulous use of the Admass, another of Priestley's brilliantly descriptive *New Statesman* neologisms. To be in the middle is to be regarded by both sides as the enemy. Whenever, on either side, a move was made which seemed to shift the world a little in the direction of democratic Socialism and away from the two extremes, the *New Statesman* became enthusiastic: it is in these outbursts of enthusiasm that the key to understanding the new statesmanship of the Fifties is to be found. The first of them was the warm front-page welcome given to the Marshall Aid offer and the praise of Ernest Bevin for his prompt acceptance of it and advocacy of the policy behind it. But it was in Henry Wallace's terms that the paper welcomed this policy. The second such occasion was when the *New Statesman* loudly applauded Tito's courageous break with Stalin. Here, the Editor thought, was the first move towards realization of what had become his own idea of what progress in politics might be: each country finding its own way to Socialism. Can Nikita Sergeivitch Khrushchev who, it would seem (as will appear), was among the paper's readers, have borrowed the notion from the *New Statesman*?

Part of the golden mean rule which new statesmen had

adopted entailed deprecating the use of violent and un-scrupulous propaganda. This reasonableness, too, is always hard to forgive. From time to time there crept into the paper a note of weariness with the idiots on both sides, a still more terrible sin. Worst of all there was a tendency, which hundred-percenters Left and Right found intolerably offensive, to take the mickey out of both sides. There were White Blimps and Red Blimps and they were both as ridiculous as they were dangerous. Thus, for example Critic:

> From a propaganda point of view the advantage of the Colorado beetle is that Colorado is in America. By declaring that Americans have been dropping their own peculiarly nasty brand of beetle on the pure soil of Eastern Germany, Soviet propaganda may hope to increase general anti-American feeling and persuade Germans that if the potato crop fails, it will not be the fault of the Communist government but a proof of Washington's malice or of New York's desire to sell insecticides! How many Germans believe it I don't know. They learnt to believe almost anything under the Goebbels' régime, so they may even today believe that the Americans would be foolish enough to drop from aircraft beetles which, being uninhibited by barbed-wire frontiers, and insufficiently indoctrinated in capitalist principles, cannot be relied upon to feed exclusively on Communist potatoes.

13

The Thaw?

IN 1951 two men joined the *New Statesman* who were to carry it into its third era: John Freeman and Jeremy Potter. This will be a convenient place in which to say something about the development of the paper's management.

As the *New Statesman*'s success under Kingsley Martin's editorship had made it into quite big business, the department of management as organized by John Roberts had given birth to sub-departments. Roberts, and Hewson the Company's Secretary, the two oldest inhabitants, had seen the enterprise grow from one which existed from hand to mouth on loans made by its directors, into a business with a turnover climbing towards the quarter-million mark. In 1951 John Roberts was Managing Director of the company; the Manager of the paper was Ernest Willison; the Advertisement Manager Jack Hoole. Although Roberts still kept the principal business decisions touching the *New Statesman* in his own hands, he was primarily concerned with re-investing *New Statesman* profits in two new, expansionist ventures: Turnstile Press, a book-publishing house which was a financial failure; and Ganymed Press, which was engaged in reproducing works of art by an unusually faithful process. This has been more successful, but it is no longer connected so closely with the *New Statesman*.

Ernest Willison was an old servant of the company. He had been trained as an engineer but, in 1926, at the age of thirty, he joined the *New Statesman*, so that he was with the paper during the last years of the Clifford Sharp era. His first job was to build up advertisement revenue, handling all the advertisements except those from publishers, which had always been treated as a separate department. It was Willison who made the *New Statesman* one of the few weekly papers which carry several pages of classified small advertisements; he thus brought into existence a sort of exchange and mart for intellectual eccentrics, new statesmanly cranks, and so ensured that the 'small ad.' pages are not the least entertaining reading in the paper. During the second German War he had to leave the paper to work at the Ministry of Supply, but in 1945 he rejoined it. He became a friend, and a great admirer, of Kingsley Martin. In 1947 he was made Manager of the paper; and in 1950 a Director of the company. Willison had some private means and when, at the end of the war, Edward Whitley, who had done so much, so quietly, to keep the *New Statesman* alive in its early years, died, Willison bought the greater part of his holding in the paper, thus becoming the biggest single shareholder in the old Statesman Company. He was a gentle, kindly and friendly man with a great gift of loyalty, and his influence in keeping the business and editorial sides of the paper working together in harmony was of the first importance. But his health was poor and declining, and in 1954 he died.

Jack Hoole had looked after the publishers' advertising in the *New Statesman* for thirty years, from 1920. He had, by 1951, become not only a 'well-known figure' but an institution in the publishing world. He was regarded as a sort of personification of the *New Statesman*, and an inexhaustible source of publishing gossip. By his own account he saw the Editor as the captain on the bridge, himself as fireman stoking the boilers. Hoole died in November 1951 and Jeremy Potter, who had joined the paper in February, took his place.

One of the minor reasons for the *New Statesman*'s financial soundness was the rather strict economy used by Kingsley Martin and John Roberts in the running of it. In the early Sharp era the *New Statesman* was considered to pay its writers rather well. Later it got a reputation for being mean. Writers on the one hand, and editors and publishers on the other, will never agree about what constitutes generosity in payment for the writer's work. Both Kingsley Martin and John Roberts had been very poor in their youth. Kingsley Martin, who could, of course, himself decide what writers were to be paid, was incapable of thinking that a man's first object in writing for his paper was money. He believed, and to a great extent rightly, that writers found in the *New Statesman* a means of publishing views and feelings which they were concerned to publish, and gained a cachet which was of use to them with other editors and with publishers. It remains true that he underestimated the rate at which the cost of living rose and with it the fees which a writer should be earning. It is unlikely, however, that he ever lost a writer through meanness. It is true that when Raymond Mortimer left the paper it was to do less work for much more pay; but it was more leisure Mortimer wanted rather than more money. The same was true of Cuthbert Worsley. In any case Martin's payments policy was not entirely his own. He was free to be generous, certainly, for he was the master; but the influence of Maynard Keynes on the Board encouraged his natural parsimony. Keynes, indeed, who had never believed that a weekly journal of opinion could possibly pay, was so surprised at Kingsley Martin's and John Roberts's success in making the *New Statesman* profitable that it seems to have quite gone to his head. He could not bear to see the profit margin reduced by increasing payments to writers, even though this simply meant paying more in taxes.

However, in his last years as Editor, Kingsley Martin became a more generous paymaster. Upon his retirement the rates paid by the paper were substantially increased and they are now appropriate to its business prosperity.

Potter, born in 1922, had gone from school straight into the Army and from the Army to Oxford. In 1948, when he was twenty-six, he got a job with the Medici Society, where he learnt something about printing and publishing, went on the road as a traveller, and was eventually made Sales Manager. He had a rather tenuous connection with the *New Statesman* in that he had been a friend, since childhood, of Mima Freeman who was assistant editor of the *Universities Quarterly*, published by Turnstile Press, a *New Statesman* enterprise; and that he had met John Roberts, whose Ganymed Prints competed with the Medici Society's. Roberts and Willison were at the time on the lookout for an heir to the *New Statesman* management; they picked Jeremy Potter. His first task in his new job, before Hoole's death, was business managing the *Universities Quarterly* and the *Political Quarterly* for Turnstile Press.

By 1953 Ernest Willison's declining health had made his work something of a burden and Potter was appointed his deputy, to lighten it. Thus when Willison died, Potter was ready to take his place. Meanwhile, things were happening at a higher level which were to affect his future with the company.

As John Roberts, with the management of the *New Statesman*'s everyday business delegated to subordinates, became more involved in expanding the Company's interests through Ganymed and Turnstile Press, he became less involved in expanding them by way of the *New Statesman* itself. His policy for the paper seems to have become one of leaving well enough alone. A point was reached at which he and the Editor were opposed to each other at Board meetings, with the result that the *New Statesman* was marking time instead of advancing. True, although the paper was running profitably the circulation declined sharply between 1951 and 1955, and nothing was done to help it by promotion, although the money was there, for advertisement revenue continued to rise sharply. New Directors, men of very high standing and ability in their professions, were invited to join the Board of the Company, but the problem was not solved until, in 1957, John Roberts decided—being then over sixty-five—to retire.

He had served the paper for forty-four years and moreover done more than any other man to get it firmly established on a business footing which is probably uniquely sound for this kind of publishing. He had started as little more than office-boy in a subsidized undertaking and he had ended as master of a business, in some measure created by himself, which was making large profits. To do this in the grocery or hardware trades is not remarkable; to have done it in the field of serious periodical publishing and with a journal openly critical of and even opposed to the very system by virtue of which it existed, was an astonishing achievement. For it should be remembered that Roberts had made possible the transformation

of the *New Statesman* from a venture in subsidized Fabian
propaganda into a financially independent paper without
ever asking its successive editors to compromise with the
world, the flesh, or the devil of commercialism.

Potter, meanwhile, and although the deadlock at Board
level prevented him from carrying out plans he had made,
was doing what he could to raise the *New Statesman*'s net sales
to the sort of figure which the Editor's success in broadening
its appeal without compromising its integrity had made
possible. In 1951, when he joined the paper, the average
weekly sale had been nearly 85,000. But a few months later
in 1951, the *New Statesman*, in common with other weeklies,
raised its price from 6*d*. to 9*d*. in order to keep up with the
exorbitant and rising cost of paper. The net sales fell by about
11,000. To me it has always been a source of surprise that so
small a sum as 3*d*. a week should have any influence whatever
on subscribers to a journal: granted that there are, among
New Statesman readers, people who are obliged to look at the
pennies—students, working-class intellectuals, professionals
in their salad days—yet it seems improbable that a sum of
13*s*. a year can make any difference nowadays. However, the
fact remains that the threepenny rise in price reduced the
paper's circulation to something under 74,000.

On the subject of the *New Statesman*'s readership, in 1955 a
survey of readership was carried out by the rough-and-ready
device of printing a questionnaire in the paper and asking
readers to answer it. I call this device rough and ready
because such a method cannot produce a statistically valid
'random' sample. Nevertheless the sample was very large;
more than 9,000 of the paper's 72,000 weekly purchasers
answered the appeal. Analysis of their answers revealed
53 per cent. to be under forty years of age, 24 per cent.
under thirty and only 11 per cent. sixty or more. Two out
of three *New Statesman* readers proved to be married and
more than half of these had young children. A third of the
readership was earning over £1,000 a year and there were
many surtax payers. This salary figure would now, of course,
be higher.

It seems that nearly 30 per cent. of *New Statesman* readers
are engaged in the Civil Service or Education, at various

levels including the top in both cases. This accounts for the paper's influence on ideas not only in the present but in preparing the future: 22 per cent. are in business, also at all levels, and 11 per cent. in the sciences either on the academic or the industrial side; 7 per cent. in the arts; and 5 per cent. are students. In the early Sixties, 23·5 per cent. of the paper's readership is overseas, and of this figure about 20 per cent. is in the United States and 10 per cent. in Canada. It is impossible to arrive at a political breakdown, but probably about 40 per cent. of readers are Left of centre, another 40 per cent. in the Centre, and the rest on the progressive flank of the Right. Most *New Statesman* readers read *The Times*, the *Daily Telegraph*, or *The Guardian*, and a majority of the House of Commons reads the paper. One very interesting point which emerged clearly was that readers remain faithful to the paper. More than 20 per cent. of the readership had been taking the *New Statesman* for twenty years, more than 50 per cent. for ten years.

In his *Study of History*, Arnold Toynbee shows that at the head of every civilization there is what he calls a 'creative minority', not necessarily office holders. That minority seems to me, in our civilization, to read the *New Statesman*.

So much for the quality of the readership. Its quantity continued to fall during the early Fifties. The man who must be held principally responsible for a paper's sales is the Editor, in that his policy and manner, the success or failure with which he gives expression to the paper's 'whatness', is what attracts or repels readers. But competition for attention is so ferocious that unless the management side of his paper succeeds in 'selling' him to new readers, his talent, even if it amounts to genius, will not, unsupported, hold circulation steady or rising. It was here that the effects of John Roberts's preoccupation with Company business other than that of the *New Statesman* itself, and his doubtless natural feeling that his forty-odd-years job of establishing the paper had been completed and well done, was felt. It is, perhaps, also possible to detect a shade of weariness, not quite of flagging, in the editing of the paper. For a quarter of a century Kingsley Martin had poured a very powerful current of energy into the *New Statesman*; it was at least possible that he was showing slight signs of exhaustion.

By 1954 sales had fallen below 69,000 a week. It was the year of Potter's appointment as Manager. They began to rise. By 1957, when John Roberts retired and Potter, at thirty-five, assumed all the responsibilities of management, they had recovered by 10,000 a week, and two years later again passed the 80,000 mark. Advertisement revenue did not closely follow the circulation graph. With a setback between 1949 and 1951, it rose fairly steadily throughout this period— some justification for John Roberts's apparent complacency —taking a great leap to top £90,000 in 1958-59 and £125,000 in 1960-61. Not the least of the management's tasks was to keep this figure rising in step with the rising costs of production. It will be recalled that the price of the *New Statesman* to its readers was 6*d*. in 1913. It is interesting to consider what it should be in 1963 if it had had to rise in step with the rising costs of producing the paper:

Between 1913 and 1963:	*Per cent.*
Writers' fees have risen	1,000
Editorial salaries	800
Office salaries generally	1,000
Printing costs (printer's wages, etc.)	1,200
Paper prices	600
(Actually more; the journal is now printed on much poorer paper than used to be the case. Paper of equal quality has risen by about 1,800 per cent)	
Freight costs, etc.	600
The cost of the *New Statesman* to the public	50

John Freeman joined the *New Statesman* some months after Potter had done so, upon resigning from the Labour Government. This statement will suffice to indicate that his career had already been a brilliant one. It is sketched in Chapter 14. Freeman's mentor in journalism and in the technique of extracting the right editorial decision out of a situation vexed by conflict of opinions was Aylmer Vallance, with whom he worked in harmony; the two men developed a warm mutual understanding which became a close friendship. A less strong-minded and decided character than Freeman's would have been in some danger from Vallance's almost excessive clear-sightedness in the judgment of political and social issues and personages. For Vallance's technical skill and inexhaustible goodwill were not supported by any such faith in causes or, indeed, in the destiny of mankind, as alone fits a man to control a serious newspaper or journal of opinion, at least in Britain. Vallance, in complete control of a paper, would have produced something like *Le Canard Enchainé*, which would hardly have been to the English taste. Freeman was never in any danger of such excessive detachment.

He learned the techniques of journalism and of producing a weekly paper from Vallance; but he remained unaffected by Vallance's political cynicism, and strongly attached to those principles which had led to his resignation from the Government. As the circumstances of that resignation have an important bearing on the *New Statesman*'s policy during the following years, something must be said about it here. Its origins go back some years.

Freeman had become a member of the Labour Government in 1946. He was a member of that group of young Labour men in the House of Commons which was called the Keep Left group, of which Richard Crossman was also a member, perhaps its most brilliant one. This group became important in 1948 when Aneurin Bevan, the leading Left-winger among the Party's leaders, albeit a ferocious anti-Communist, became restless and uneasy at what seemed to him the slow loss of Socialist emphasis and drive in the Government and in much of the Labour Party. There gathered round him, quite loosely and informally, a number of men, among them the best brains in the Party, who held strongly Socialist opinions and who wanted to see them realized in Socialist policies.

Came the Korean War; with Stafford Cripps's retirement and Gaitskell's succession, this war, with its demands on money for rearmament, began to have consequences for the budget. It was in the winter of 1950-51 that Hugh Gaitskell and the Cabinet decided that one way to save money for spending on arms was to make cuts in the Health Service. Bevan made it clear that he would not stand for this: partly, no doubt, his attitude was produced by the fact that the Health Service had been his work; but there was more in it than that. It seemed to him a poor kind of Socialism which penalized the indigent or relatively indigent sick in order to buy arms to fight in a dubious cause under American pressure. We have already seen what other Socialists, other new statesmen, thought of this cause: Kingsley Martin had espoused it very reluctantly and conditionally and because not to do so would have meant disavowing the United Nations as the one hope of an effective international authority; G. D. H. Cole (*see* Chapter 12) had written passionately against the war in the *New Statesman*. Moreover, it seemed to Bevan that if his general dissatisfaction with the way things were going in the Government was to lead to his resignation, the issue of Health Service cuts would be a good one to resign on, for it would readily be understood by the public and it would symbolize that shift to the Right which he deplored. In March 1951 Bevan sounded a few of the Left-wingers on whom he thought he could count; if he resigned, would they support him? John Freeman was one of the men Bevan counted on; he was right. When, in April 1951, Bevan did resign, Freeman resigned with him.

On two occasions in the past Kingsley Martin had asked him to join the *New Statesman*, but Freeman had had to refuse on the ground that he could not do so while continuing as a member of the Government. Kingsley Martin's own policy and the policy he was giving the *New Statesman* at this time was already essentially like that of Bevan and the Keep Left group. He seized the opportunity to invite Freeman on to the paper again, and this time his offer was accepted, although after some slight hesitation.

The partial coincidence of views which united Kingsley Martin with the men whom it is now convenient, if a shade misleading, to call the Bevanites can be traced to his lifelong distaste for heavy expenditure on armaments, except when this was obviously essential, a distaste shared by the whole body of English political dissenters, as I have shown, and very firmly grown into their traditions. The rationale of Bevan's largely emotional act of resignation, which had been given its clearest statement after discussion between him, John Freeman and Harold Wilson, was the correlation between Health Service cuts and the expansion of arms expenditure. Kingsley Martin could not but be sympathetic to a cause which made such a point of the first importance.

These events and ideas resulted in a state of affairs which was new in the *New Statesman*'s history. The Editor, although two men who had influence with him were more or less hostile to the Bevanites—Leonard Woolf because he thought them anti-American, tiresomely sectarian and anti-liberal, and Cole because he distrusted Bevan as a possible demagogue—was involved in the Leftist cause. Freeman had resigned from the Government to support it and would obviously continue to support it as a journalist; Crossman, the most brilliant political journalist in Britain, and long the *New Statesman*'s chief leader writer on Foreign Affairs, was of the same opinions. Norman MacKenzie had always been to the Left as a Labour Party man; Aylmer Vallance had, by this time, washed his hands of politics and did not care either way. In so far as Bevanism was a definite faction of the Party, it had to have a Foreign Policy if it was ever to make a bid for power. That policy was the *New Statesman*'s (that is Kingsley Martin's and Richard Crossman's) 'Co-existence',* so that there was yet another bond between the Left of the Parliamentary Labour Party and the *New Statesman*. In short, the paper became deeply involved in and for a time committed to a faction fight within the Labour Party. As a consequence it became partisan and contentious in its domestic political writing. What was the effect of this upon its readers? The paper does not seem to have lost or gained circulation as a result of it. It became the darling, once again, of the non-Communist Left; but it became anathema, as it had never quite been before, to the orthodox Labour men. It was accused of doing all in its power to discredit and bring down Hugh Gaitskell—incidentally a contributor from time to time. It is generally held that all this did the *New Statesman* some harm; it is difficult to see

* See p. 285 below.

how or why. It may, perhaps, have made it less influential with men who were not engaged in this struggle and who found it merely distasteful, judging it as a sweaty struggle for power among Labour Party leaders.

One can, I think, put a finger on the event which detached the *New Statesman* from Bevan; it was his espousal of the British H-bomb. The experienced Parliamentary politicians on the paper may have realized that no potential Foreign Minister could possibly, at this time, have deliberately divested himself of negotiating strength by repudiating this weapon; but the *New Statesman* of Kingsley Martin was not going to support a man who could make that famous 'naked-into-the-conference-room' speech. In that speech, Aneurin Bevan himself treated Bevanism with contempt. The paper could again withdraw to a point from which the prospect was wider and longer.

One of the greatest difficulties which Socialists had to contend with in the Fifties when the true nature of Stalinist Socialism had become clear to all, was that of supporting Communism in those parts of the world where, however undesirable Communism *à la Russe* might be, Communism untainted by pan-Slav nationalism was often vastly preferable to the political system or junta it was fighting against. This was nowhere truer than in China. Whatever services the Kuomintang had rendered in destroying the old corrupt imperialism of the last Manchus and in fighting militarist Japan, it had, by the Fifties, become not only corrupt but it had lost its effectiveness, the support of the people, and its independence (to the United States). On the other hand, the Chinese Communist leaders were admitted to be not only very able but dedicated men of unquestionable integrity. It was clear that the only hope of good government and of some rise in the living standard of the people was in the Communist Party. For years the *New Statesman* had published articles which made it as clear as in the nature of things it could be made to English readers, what was happening in China and why Socialists, and indeed even Liberals, must give their support to Mao Tse-tung. There was also a world-political reason for doing this: the Chinese Communist Army was powerful, growing, well trained, successful; it had its roots in the people and a following in the country of scores of millions. In the event of war with a Great Power, it would be supported by the Red Army of the USSR. If the American Government, backing Chiang Kai-shek under the sinister influence of the China lobby in Washington, became involved in a war with Communist China, then the third world war, the H-bomb war, would have started.

So the *New Statesman* was pro-Communist in China because that was the only sensible and humane thing to be. Nevertheless, in a London Diary paragraph in 1952 touching the final defeat of the Kuomintang, Critic used a form of words which was unfortunate:

> Thirty-two lucky people, some Communists, some fellow-travellers, others sympathetic persons, have left by plane for Peking through Prague and Moscow. The opportunity is too good to miss and they will be able, we may be sure, to tell us about the feelings of liberation among common people now that the Kuomintang has gone, about an administrative honesty and efficiency never before known in China and about the great constructive work that is proceeding in industry and agriculture. But I hope they won't stop there. They must tell us what the Chinese say about the million and a half 'enemies of the people' who, it is apparently admitted, have been executed since the revolution. Were these executions really necessary? Would it not have done to disarm obstinate followers of Chiang? They must also tell us whether it is true that children are being encouraged to inform on their parents. . . . I should also like to know what their hosts say when peace-loving visitors tell them that indiscriminate charges of war-mongering are not really a help to peace.

This should be, and should have been, read with the *New Statesman*'s Chinese record in mind. The support which it had given to the Communists in whom it saw the only hope of stable and honest government for China, had been balanced and critical. But the attitude, implied by this paragraph, to *people*, seemed to some readers an outrageous one. The Editor had come a long way since 1930 and this choice of words made it seem possible that he had not taken the best road. There is an assumption, or there seems to be, that a Socialist Government could be justified in taking life on a wholesale scale. Leonard Woolf's reaction, expressed in a brief and pointed letter, appeared in the following week.

> It would be useful and interesting if *Critic* could give some indication to them and to us under what circumstances the execution of 1½ million persons by a Government is 'really necessary'.

It is one of the weaknesses of the Left-wing intellectual, or for that matter of the Liberal, that he is obliged to believe a man's a man for a' that: but the history and traditions of, for example, China, have not produced the same kind of human animal as have the very different history and traditions of Europe. It would have been surprising had they done so. Kingsley Martin's apparent callousness in this instance may have been no more than an unusual piece of carelessness in the choice of words; but if it was not that, then it was nearer to the Chinese state of mind than Leonard Woolf's indignation. The Chinese attitude to individual human life was made clear when, in due course, Mao Tse-tung was to imply that China was the one country which could stand an H-war, since the loss of a hundred or two million people would be neither here nor there.

That the reproach should have come from Leonard Woolf was of particular interest to insiders: it was long assumed, rightly or wrongly, that Leonard Woolf was one of the few people whose influence with Kingsley Martin was strong. But having committed himself, the Editor preferred defending his position, although it was hardly tenable, to withdrawing with an excuse and apology. In the same number of the *New Statesman*, Critic first revised his figure—the number executed was nearer two million; and he specified that the victims were Chiang's soldiers and that they were classified by the Communists as bandits. He went on to defend himself:

> The Chinese are proud of killing bandits and these figures are a matter of boast not of regret. They are appallingly large but certainly much smaller than the number of deaths which would have occurred if an American-Kuomintang army had tried to liberate China. I hold to my opinion that Mao is to be criticised only for killing enemies he might have disarmed.

The episode was paralleled by a row between Kingsley Martin, on a visit to America, and the *Washington Post*. It will be recalled that in the Korean War the Chinese Communists, intervening on behalf of their North Korean clients with very considerable forces, accused the Americans, who with small contingents of other United Nations armies were fighting the war for their South Korean clients, of using 'germ warfare'. It is difficult to see why the accusation should have been regarded as outrageous; neither the United States nor any other Power has ever stated that it will not use bacteriological weapons and it is very well known that all the major Powers are engaged in research in this field: that is, they are preparing to use biological warfare. However, all America's friends were most indignant at the accusation and the *Washington Post*'s attack was provoked by the *New Statesman*'s suggestion that the charge should be investigated. Today, a decade later, nobody would dream of regarding any Government's simple denial of such a charge as sufficient to dispose of it.

Despite the *New Statesman*'s alleged bias, it had long since given up all those post-war hopes of seeing the USSR move towards democracy, the Democracies towards Socialism, and both towards a meeting-point in International Socialism with new statesmanly government on a global scale. Something else had to be substituted and out of this need R. H. S. Crossman developed that idea of a Third Force already referred to on the axiom that 'We have two enemies: Communism and anti-Communism'. This conclusion was reached when the USSR, restored to enough strength to resume her imperial progress, ceased pretending to co-operate with more or less democratic governments in central and western Europe, and engineered the installation of Communist Governments at her own beck and call in all the Balkan countries except those already governed by clients of the Western Democracies. The USSR in short followed Britain's example in Greece. The Third Force was to be composed of those countries which rejected both Communism *à la Russe* and Capitalism *à l'Americaine*. But negative opinions held in common make a weak bond. A positive lead and policy were required. The *New Statesman*, and notably

R. H. S. Crossman, first nagged the Labour Government to provide these, and later dealt harshly with Ernest Bevin when he failed to do so. Meanwhile, again in the *New Statesman*'s opinion, Marshall Aid 'with strings' was proving a disaster: it was, among other things, turning potential Third Force countries into Communist allies.

The surviving part of R. H. S. Crossman's *New Statesman* policy, after the original hope for some sort of collaboration with the USSR and of creating a Third Force had been lost, was that which is generally known now as the policy of Co-existence—Crossman's words were 'agreement to disagree'—which now seems to be the policy of both the Kremlin and of President Kennedy's Government. The reasoning which led to it was Crossman's, but it was also a typical example of Kingsley Martin's policy, so exasperating to many, of pointing with childlike candour at the emperor's nakedness. The differences between the Communists and the Capitalists were unresolvable, and all the more so in that they were also the differences between United States and Soviet Union nationalisms, in fact imperialisms. If the argument became violent civilization would be destroyed. So stop arguing; drop the subject; leave each other alone.

As, in the new nations of Africa, Asia and America which the *New Statesman* had played a part in creating, the cloven hoof of the politician began to appear, so that the sandals of the new statesmanly socialist idealist had to be discarded as a poor fit, the *New Statesman* undertook the task of persuading us that having been liberal with our former subjects, we must now be patient, understanding and tolerant if it seemed that they were not all angels. A famous journalistic friend of the Africans, Basil Davidson, had given up his connection with *The Times* to write for the *New Statesman*. He joined the staff of the paper and it was clear that a man of his status could only have done this in a senior post; Kingsley Martin needed in such a post a man who could be left in charge of the paper when he was away and whose policy was the same as the Editor's. But it quite soon became apparent that their opinions were not, in important respects, the same. Kingsley Martin's disappointment at what I think it fair to call Russian Communist Toryism, the extreme resistance of the

Communist Party to anything like Social Democracy, and the even keener disappointment of some of his friends and advisers, had made him very distrustful of Communism, however willing to work with it for world peace; Davidson had not undergone quite such a crisis of confidence and it was from this that the differences between him, in whom some saw Kingsley Martin's successor, and the Editor arose.

In the first half of the Fifties decade J. B. Priestley wrote a series of articles under the general heading of 'Thoughts in the Wilderness' which gave a lead into the new attitude to politics and politicians which was to be typical of the last years of the decade and seems to be fashionable now. It is not clear whether Priestley had been banished in mortification or had withdrawn in disgust into the wilderness from which he addressed us on the subject of our goings-on. These articles are those of a radical humanist turned stoic, but the stoicism would not stick; Priestley was too involved with the rest of us ever to give us up as a hopelessly bad job. It is interesting to compare these writings with the kind of thing, in the same commonsensical manner, which Arnold Bennett had formerly written for the *New Statesman*. Whereas Bennett's tone is that of a man who confidently expects his suggestions and criticisms to be adopted sooner or later and to produce happy results, Priestley's, on the whole, is not. Times had changed; the 'advances of science' had driven thoughtful men close to despair.

If Britain does make social progress and very often behave with political good sense, it is because her dissenters, a permanent, amorphous, continually recruited body of unorganised radicals, from time to time come together into an effective 'movement' set up by some originally small body of citizens who dedicate themselve to the accomplishment of a reform. These latter people, those who turn the negative motions of social or political discontents into positive movements towards change, are the good, responsible, highly 'civic' citizens admired by Hippolyte Taine and detested by professional politicians. In our time they have frequently and perhaps usually been new statesmen; for the *New Statesman* is, above all, Britain's organ of dissent.

These forward movements in which dissenters turn, as it

were, into asserters, happen about once in a decade. The one which started in 1957 in the *New Statesman* has become not simply of national, but of international, importance. It has driven the Labour Party into a series of crises of conscience and policy; it has changed the defence programme of the reviving Liberal Party; it has affected the foreign policy of the Conservative Government. It is known as C.N.D.

The movement began with Priestley's article in the *New Statesman*, 'Britain and the Nuclear Bomb'. The immediate inspiration of the article was twofold: Aneurin Bevan, speaking at the Labour Party Conference, made it quite clear that a Labour Government would cling to the H-bomb as obstinately as the Conservative Government. The second event was the successful launching of the Soviet satellite, followed by an immediate outbreak of what may fairly be called *satellitis*, producing a rise in temperature and signs of delirium.

There is no point in picking out to quote part of an article which contained every single argument which C.N.D. was, in due course, to use. Priestley, and Kingsley Martin was of exactly the same mind, said with deep conviction and impressive sincerity that we must give up our H-bomb, and he then gave the spiritual, social, political and military reasons. Although R. H. S. Crossman's Third Force notion was dead, in a sense Priestley revived it, for he saw Britain as leader of a group of Powers voluntarily repudiating the horror weapons, prepared to defend themselves if invaded, intent on persuading the USSR and the USA to refrain from destroying civilization and perhaps all life on earth. Priestley thought that Britain could do this only if she vested herself with great moral force by divesting herself of the most immoral kind of military force ever contrived. And would we really be giving up anything much? Britain, with the H-bomb, was thus depicted:

> In the poker game, where Britain still sits nervously fingering a few remaining chips, like a Treasury official playing with two drunk oil millionaires, the stakes have been doubled again.

The conclusion of the article was the kind of thing which

does, from time to time, make a powerful appeal to the British, or at least to the dissenters among them:

> The British of these times, so frequently hiding their decent, kind faces behind masks of sullen apathy or sour, cheap cynicism, often seem to be waiting for something better than party squabbles and appeals to their narrowest self-interest, something great and noble in its intention which would make them feel good again. And this might well be a declaration to the world that after a certain date one power able to engage in nuclear warfare will reject the evil thing for ever.

The response provoked is a matter of history. The beginning of it can be found in the *New Statesman* correspondence for the following week. It was the *New Statesman*'s Editor who presided over the first meeting of the movement in Canon Collins's house. But starting C.N.D. was not the only step taken by the paper to expose the danger which bomb-happy politicians and soldiers were playing with. In November 1957 appeared an article by Bertrand Russell taking the form of 'An Open Letter to Eisenhower and Khrushchev'.

When a publicist uses this device he may or may not hope or expect the addressees of his letter to read it; his real purpose is to say things which he believes should be publicly said to them and which he thinks many of his fellow citizens would like to say to them. Lord Russell's purpose, and the *New Statesman*'s, was to make sure that the most powerful men in the world should be publicly requested to behave like compassionate and decent human beings. He told them that they had a power for good or evil exceeding anything ever possessed before by any man or group of men.

> One thing only is required to dispel the darkness and enable the world to live again in a noon-day brightness of hope. The one thing necessary is that East and West should recognize their respective rights, admit that each must learn to live with the other and substitute argument for force in the attempt to spread their respective ideologies. It is not necessary that either side should abandon belief in its own creed. It is only necessary that it should abandon the attempt to spread its creed by force of arms.

If they would do this, Russell concluded,

> . . . the forces of sanity, released from their long bondage, would ensure for the years to come a life of vigour and achievement and joy surpassing anything known in even the happiest eras of the past.

The fact that this appeal came from the greatest living philosopher was, of course, very important, but it will be noticed that the article represents a link in the chain of the *New Statesman*'s consistent post-war policy. It was still maintaining that, to borrow a phrase, eating people is wrong; that it was necessary is still very apparent. But that we do, despite the cynics, progress, is manifest from the personal consequences for Lord Russell of the line he had determined to take: he was, in due course, when at over ninety he had taken his appeal out into the streets, only thrown into prison; Socrates, after all, was made to drink hemlock.

One month after the article appeared, the *New Statesman* acquired a new contributor: Nikita Sergeivitch Khrushchev. His article, occupying nearly two pages and entitled 'Nikita Khrushchev Replies to Bertrand Russell' was sent through the Soviet Embassy, where it was translated into English and forwarded to Kingsley Martin with a personal letter, still in Russian, from the Communist leader. It represented a 'scoop' of the kind rare even in the daily Press and unique in the history of the weekly Press. Yet the jump in sales for the week in question was not large, about 2,000. On the other hand, attention paid to the Khrushchev scoop by the daily Press was certainly equal to several thousand pounds worth of publicity.

The new contributor's style was gratifyingly new states-manly. He agreed with every major point made by Russell; he stated that war was by no means inevitable; he undertook, on behalf of the Soviet people, to do all in his power to avert it.

> We, Soviet people, engaged in building Communist society— a social system in which, alongside the achievement of material abundance for all, there will for the first time be the free development of man's spiritual wealth, in all its diversity—we understand particularly well your concern over

the criminal policy of militarism, which absurdly wastes society's material resources, which corrupts man morally and which leads to people being brought up in the spirit of fear and hate. It is impossible to be reconciled to such a prospect—all the more so when today the wonderful discoveries of science have given man such immense power over the forces of Nature. Now there really are no limits to the possibilities of transforming Nature's destructive forces, or of using natural resources to ensure the prosperity of all peoples, on the basis of friendly co-operation among the nations.

The sweetness and light were perhaps a little overdone; one could not forget that these words were rather widely separated from the deeds of the Government for which the author spoke, as its Chief. There was, too, one paragraph of anti-American snide propaganda:

> . . . no wonder millions of British people feel legitimate anxiety and disquiet over the establishment of [American] bases on the territory of their country.

Still, the article did reveal and clearly publish a spirit of goodwill; and that the Soviet Government had adopted or was willing to adopt the Crossman policy of agreeing to disagree.

The paper's leader that week, written jointly by Kingsley Martin and Paul Johnson, used the Khrushchev article to castigate the United States Secretary of State, John Foster Dulles, whose anti-Left intransigence was seen by the *New Statesman* as one of the most dangerous forces at work in the world. But as will appear, it was in vain that the paper pointed out to Dulles that ' . . . the object of diplomacy is not to authenticate virtues but to achieve settlements'.

Paul Johnson, who was becoming the paper's foreign leader specialist, had joined the paper in 1955, at the age of twenty-six. His *New Statesman* career began while he was living in Paris and working as deputy editor of *Réalités;* he acted, at that time (1954-55) as the *New Statesman*'s Paris correspondent. He had been educated at Stonyhurst and at Magdalen College, Oxford, where he read history; he had served two years in the Army, attaining the rank of captain.

His subsequent journalistic career in Paris lasted three and a half years, and his transfer to the staff of the *New Statesman* followed R. H. S. Crossman's withdrawal. Crossman had decided to take the chance of teaching Socialist ideas to a larger if less receptive public, that of the *Daily Mirror*.

Although Lord Russell's Open Letter had been addressed to Eisenhower as well as Khrushchev, his American addressee was really John Foster Dulles, the man who determined United States foreign policy. Dulles took time to make up his mind to go into the *New Statesman* ring against the formidable Russian; not until early February 1958 was the United States Secretary of State added to the list of *New Statesman* contributors.

Meanwhile, the campaign for Britain's unilateral nuclear disarmament (C.N.D.) was being hotted up. Paul Johnson's leaders were curt and trenchant arguments against the pending, subsequently signed, agreement to allow the United States to establish rocket bases in Britain. An entertaining letter to the Editor, on this subject, will serve to express the *New Statesman* reader's reaction to Khrushchev as a contributor.

> Let me be the first to say it. Mr. Khrushchev's letter in reply to Bertrand Russell is all a fiendish plot. The mere fact that it was delivered in time to be published in the last edition of the *New Statesman* shows the underhand cunning of the man, and is a deliberate attempt to rob us of the promised American rocket bases on our soil. We must arm, arm, arm, arm, arm. For the Russians must be taught that the only way to end war is to have it.
>
> SPIKE MILLIGAN

Johnson, in a leader, characterized the Rocket Base agreement as a 'suicide pact'. The enemy of new statesmanly sense was Dulles.

> To quote Mr. Dulles' own words, America is engaged in a world contest against 'materialistic atheism'—thus becoming the first country to conduct its foreign policy on a religious basis since Spain under Philip II. . . . But you cannot be good if you are dead.

Johnson, whose mentor on the paper seemed to be John

Freeman rather than the Editor himself, was restoring a touch of the cold Sharpian astringency to its comments.

It may have been the paper's persistent attacks on him which stung Foster Dulles into following N. S. Khrushchev into journalism. His contribution appeared on 8 February. It was introduced in a leader which described it as 'honest, consistent, and extremely revealing of the man and his mind'. No doubt it was all this; it was, to the ordinary intelligent *New Statesman* reader, also very alarming. Khrushchev, following Russell, had written,

> It is not necessary that either side should abandon belief in its own creed; it is only necessary that it should abandon the attempt to spread its creed by force of arms.

Good, sound, new statesmanship, if the writer meant it, which after all he may well have done, not being a lunatic. Dulles's answer was to point out that the Soviet Communist Party had never repudiated the open and deliberate basing of the Communist creed on force and not on law, and as he was able to quote the case of the suppression of the Hungarian revolution by the Red Army he had a good case. He spoilt it by rhetoric, by presenting the American case as that of right against might. As a new statesmanly journalist he could not compare with Mr. Khrushchev. Had they been exiled and obliged to earn their livings, the Russian might have been worth a job on the *New Statesman*, while the American would have done better to apply to the BBC. But a second article by Mr. Khrushchev in which he resumed the entire history and policy of the USSR showed that as a permanent contributor he would have needed a lot of firm editing: for his contribution occupied five pages of the *New Statesman*, at least two and a half of which were tedious.

Had the Editor been anxious to retire and write that big book which gossip writers always believe is what editors want to do, he might have thought this a good moment. There could hardly have been a better 'curtain' for any editor than this capturing of the two most powerful men in the world as his contributors. In other respects, too, the paper was at the zenith of its second epoch; circulation, at about 78,000, was rising on a steady curve, and advertisement revenue, on

which expansion depended, was on the way to passing the
£90,000 mark for the first time. But if others, rather
maliciously, expected Kingsley Martin to bow himself out
at this point, the idea did not cross his mind nor that of his
readers nor even that of his colleagues. It is quite clear that
he was still very much a man dedicated to the responsibility
which his own talent and his own conscience had in some
sort created.

In 1957 there occurred an event which can be interpreted as a remarkable and unusual kind of tribute to the
New Statesman and its Editor. True, the tribute might be
considered a back-handed one, since it involved an attempt
to take the paper out of his hands by financial force. But that
in itself bears witness to the impression he made on the
principal men of his time in very diverse walks of life. The
righteous are not without enemies. The event was an
attempt to 'take-over' the *New Statesman* by a piece of financial
manipulation.

The late Aneurin Bevan is said to have disliked the Editor
of the *New Statesman;* his dislike was in no way modified by
the paper's Bevanite policy; he considered Kingsley Martin
insufficiently militant and uncompromising, a curious
judgment for a man who had himself compromised so
thoroughly in the end; he disliked him for being a middle-
class intellectual; and as the guiding spirit behind the
propagandist *Tribune* he was, perhaps, annoyed by the *New
Stateman*'s intellectual detachment and influence with people
who were failing to take and read *Tribune*.

It happened that one of Bevan's friends was the property
financier Howard Samuel. This singular man had made
several million pounds out of dealing in property in
London in the post-war years, a circumstance which should,
in the ordinary way, have made him a staunch Conservative.
But Samuel called himself a Socialist and he had intellectual
yearnings. He bought the publishing house of MacGibbon
& Kee, and he was *Tribune*'s backer. It is said that when he
set out to try to buy control of the *New Statesman* it was in
order to please Bevan. That Bevan knew of his manœuvres
is certain; as it is that he disapproved of them.

As a legacy of the *New Statesman—Nation* amalgamation,

the company which publishes the paper is the Statesman & Nation Publishing Company—61 per cent. of its shares were owned by the Statesman Publishing Co.; 36 per cent. by the Nation Proprietary Co. Of the three, the only active company was the Statesman & Nation Publishing Co., whose directors run the paper. But as majority shareholder in that company, the Statesman Publishing Co. is theoretically the boss and its directors could, for example, legally dismiss the Board and management of the Statesman & Nation Publishing Co. Ultimate control is therefore in the hands of the Statesman Publishing Co.'s shareholders and directors; but there was some overlapping of the two Boards; for example, John Roberts was at once Managing Director of the active Company and Chairman of the other one.

But there was a further complication: ordinary shares in the Statesman Publishing Co. carry no voting rights. Management shares, which do, were originally issued in the proportion of one to ten ordinary shares. Only 438 of these 8s. management shares were ever issued, and their owners are the legal bosses of the *New Statesman*. As the Company's shares have normally changed hands at par, it was theoretically possible to get control of this very influential weekly and of the flourishing Company which published it and, in the process, turned over about £200,000 a year, for the sum of £88.

But Howard Samuel's problem was not so simple as this makes it look. Some of these management shares were owned by Kingsley Martin, others by the Roberts and the Willison families; that is to say, they were not for sale. The rest were distributed among the other directors and among the heirs of the *New Statesman*'s original backers.

Samuel first moved to buy the Nation Proprietary Co.: 43 per cent. of its shares were held by the Joseph Rowntree Social Service Trust and 14 per cent. by Lawrence Cadbury who was at that time the principal proprietor of the *News Chronicle* and a director of the Bank of England. The £1 shares were not considered particularly good value at par; the Company's only income was from dividends paid by the Statesman & Nation Publishing Co., and these were limited since the Company did not exist to make money but to publish and expand the *New Statesman*. In June 1957 the Trust, and Cadbury, accepted an offer of £3 a share from Samuel, who thus acquired 6,835 shares. The *New Statesman* directors and management were given no prior notice of the fact that one-third control of the paper was about to pass from a charitable Trust and a Bank of England director to a real-estate tycoon. Samuel sought next to nominate two Nation Proprietary directors to serve on the Statesman & Nation Publishing Board. This was refused. For some years the Statesman Company's directors had·been thinking of forming a Trust for the Company's management shares; the time had obviously come to form it. Samuel took this as a move deliberately made to thwart him. Why he should have been indignant at this is not clear, but he was; one wonders what on earth he expected to happen. There were sharp exchanges between his solicitors and the Company's. Meanwhile, Samuel was buying more Nation Proprietary shares and succeeded in getting 65 per cent. of them. The owners of the remaining 35 per cent., Lord Keynes's Trustees, Lord Simon of Wythenshawe, Lord Stamp, and the heirs, respectively, of two former *Nation* editors, Harold Wright and Sir Hubert Henderson, refused to sell. In August 1958 the following appeared in the *New Statesman*:

> In view of speculative comments that have been made about the control of the *New Statesman* it seems appropriate to explain briefly the constitution of this journal.
>
> The policy of the *New Statesman* is exclusively in the hands of the Editor, who is responsible to the Statesman & Nation Publishing Company. This Company is owned by the Statesman Publishing Company and the Nation Proprietary Company, the majority of its shares being held by the Statesman Publishing Company.
>
> Ultimate control of the *New Statesman* therefore rests with the holders of management shares in the Statesman Publishing Company. Nearly 90 per cent. of these shares are held by the directors of that Company. Each director has recently signed a covenant agreeing (a) to ensure that the policy and characteristics of the *New Statesman* remain unaltered, and (b) to relinquish his shares on ceasing to be a director, in order that they may be transferred to a successor. The names of this Board, which has become in effect a

self-perpetuating trust, are Gerald Gardiner, Q.C. (Chairman), G. D. H. Cole, John Freeman, David Low, Kingsley Martin, John Roberts and Sir Charles Snow.

Meanwhile, the subject of the Editor's retirement was in the air. *The Observer* printed a canard that he was about to retire and make room for John Freeman; this was publicly denied, and *The Observer* was forced to apologize. The most that can be said is that at this time the reasons for his retirement were beginning to come into existence.

When Kingsley Martin made up his mind to go, his retirement, like the past thirty years of his life, was given to the *New Statesman*. For there is no point in pretending that he wanted to go; he felt no flagging, no weariness such as might have afflicted some men after three decades of immensely successful but exhausting editing in a period of violent events, and a man does not give up a lifework into some other man's hands without regret, and this was especially the case here, for Kingsley Martin and the *New Statesman* were inseparable, the paper had become Joan to his Darby. But since, for ten years, he had had it in mind that he would have to find a successor with an inside knowledge of the paper as well as all the other necessary qualities, and since that man was quite obviously John Freeman; and since John Freeman, having made one name for himself as a politician and now another as a television interviewer, was being besieged with offers of important posts and was, in any case, not the man to go on being Number 2 for much longer, however much he looked forward to editing the paper, Martin realised that he would have to go sooner rather than later, or possibly lose the very successor he himself had picked and favoured. John Freeman was not the only candidate: Norman MacKenzie had never, as it were, entered himself for the editorial stakes; but R. H. S. Crossman made no secret of the fact that he wanted the job, or of his belief that the *New Statesman* would, in the new and third phase of its career which was beginning, be best served by him. But Kingsley Martin had made up his mind that if the *New Statesman* must move with the times and undertake a new task of social service in completely changed conditions, then the man to control it was Freeman. If this view was to prevail, he himself must go soon.

Freeman had, of course, frequently been left in charge of the paper ever since the death of Aylmer Vallance, whenever the Editor was away. Kingsley Martin spent a considerable part of each of his later years as Editor in foreign travel; he enjoyed visiting other countries, seeing their rulers and their anti-rulers. In the Far East particularly, and elsewhere in what had been parts of the Commonwealth, he was by no means just another journalist; he was very much Mr. Kingsley Martin who had helped the country to its independence and must be treated as an honoured friend. Moreover this gratitude even survived the critical writings in the *New Statesman* which journalistic integrity might produce after one of the Editor's visits. There was nothing in journalism he did better than convey, either in a Diary or an article, his foreign impressions. While he was away Freeman loyally kept the paper to the course Martin had given, even though this was not the course he might have laid down himself. But with his other commitments, which he could not neglect while his future with the *New Statesman* remained unsettled, he had, in a sense, less to give the paper than it needed.

The problem was solved by Kingsley Martin's retirement; he would continue to serve the paper as a reporter at large. So closely had he been associated with it that there were some who almost expected either Kingsley Martin or the *New Statesman* to vanish into thin air when their marriage was dissolved. As for his monument as a great Editor, perhaps the greatest of our time, it is, of course, the *New Statesman*, 1930-60. I have been examining it for several years. I do not believe that more than half a dozen men have, in my lifetime, served us, the community, in our aspirations towards the good life as loyally and as well as Kingsley Martin.

14

The Third Epoch

THERE is a member of the *New Statesman* staff of whom I have said little although he had served the paper for eighteen years at the time of Kingsley Martin's retirement. I have kept him until now despite the fact that he had written every feature of the paper except Books in General; despite the fact that London Diary probably owed more to him than to anyone but Critic himself; and despite the fact that his contribution even to such extra-mural works as Kingsley Martin's *Life* of Harold Laski was important. This omission has been deliberate for a twofold reason: if the whatness of the *New Statesman* was ever represented by one person, that person was Norman MacKenzie; and because of this his service as representative of the paper's second epoch in carrying over its traditions and ensuring continuity of feeling and judgment into the third epoch, was of the first importance during the first year or two of John Freeman's editorship.

To give an idea of the nature of MacKenzie's importance to the *New Statesman* and of his services to it, I will use an analogue with the world of the theatre: there are actors who become great by being always themselves; there are others who so sink themselves into their roles that they serve playwrights and literature better than they serve their own egos, their own personalities. They are very rarely as much noticed and applauded as the other kind; but they make great plays. In the manner of such an actor entering whole-heartedly into a role and suppressing himself in so doing, MacKenzie sunk himself in the *New Statesman*. He did not intend to. Born in London in 1921, he was at the London School of Economics, studying Government under Harold Laski when Kingsley Martin, hearing him speak in a debate, discovered him. During the war Mac-Kenzie served for a while in the R.A.F., was invalided out, and returned to the L.S.E. to take his degree in government. Harold Laski considered him the most brilliant pupil he had ever had. His aim in life was to teach. But having been offered a post on the *New Statesman* and spent a day with Kingsley Martin at the Editor's cottage in Essex, MacKenzie, like Kingsley Martin before him, put aside the idea of teaching and joined the *New Statesman* in the summer of 1943.

Like most *New Statesman* men MacKenzie has travelled widely. From time to time he has reverted to his original intention; thus, from August 1947 until October 1948 he was on leave from the *New Statesman* and teaching at the Sarah Lawrence College in New York State. He received a Rockefeller Grant and travelled all over the United States. In 1950, and again in 1956, he was back in America for the paper. In 1959 he again had a long sabbatical leave which, at the invitation of the Social Science Research Council for Australia, he spent in Australia studying the status of women in that country; his *Women in Australia* appeared in 1962. He has travelled in Europe, parts of the Near East and South Africa. He has all the new statesmanly distrust of both capitalism and communism, and its faith in Socialism, of which he has written a short history. He has the new statesmanly non-conformist conscience, the application, the Fabian method (he has written Fabian pamphlets). He is a member of the Labour Party and was twice a Labour candidate for Parliament. Mackenzie had an especially 'authentic' brand of new statesmanship whose value was recognized by his colleagues.

But if the link with the Kingsley Martin era which MacKenzie helped to provide was valuable to the continuity of new statesmanly feeling, it might also be regarded as a constraining bond. For it was of the utmost importance that the still dissenting voice of the *New Statesman* be raised in present, not in past, controversy. The greatest danger run by a journal which has enjoyed a long sustained success is the feeling that a formula which has accomplished so much for a quarter of a century will do even more in half a century. And it continues to fight battles which have been lost and won. This is congenial to its faithful ageing readers, who have reached the time of life when they, themselves, tend to keep fighting old battles, and to live in the past; but it clearly offers nothing to the rising generations and it will fall upon evil days. It will wake up one morning to find that all its readers have died. This happened to *The Athenaeum*; and it is not that the journal in such a case fails to deal with the new problems as they arise; it is that it fails to adjust to the new spirit in which problems are dealt with. The matter of the editorial pages of, for example, the *New Statesman* itself during Kingsley Martin's last several years was up to date; the manner, the state of mind, were less so. A weekly which has shown absolutely extraordinary power not only of survival but of continuous success is *Punch*; a stock joke is the complaint that *Punch* is not what it was. It is because *Punch* is never what it was that its success has been unbroken. But with the arrival of John Freeman in the editorial chair it was not likely that the *New Statesman* would go on believing that the Thirties and Forties were, in some sort, still with us.

That Kingsley Martin himself had been looking forward into the new epoch is apparent from the fact that of the three major staff changes which were manifestations of what the new Editor's approach to his problem would be, the appointment of Anthony Howard had been planned and indeed decided on by Kingsley Martin, although it was implemented by John Freeman. Howard was a *Guardian* man and a very young man, and not until his appointment had the *New Statesman* ever employed a professional parliamentary correspondent with no axe to grind and who was, as Howard is, *persona grata* with all parties, so that he has access to information from all sides. Equally significant was the appointment of another young man as Literary Editor, Karl Miller; and of a third, Karl Meyer, as Washington correspondent with almost as much space as Howard at his disposal.

But the appointment of these three young men was by no means the whole story. Kingsley Martin's *New Statesman* was a product of passionate commitment to causes; therefore, having assurance and a received text, it preached. The *New Statesman* of John Freeman was, as was soon apparent. a product of scepticism and enquiry. The whole history of the attempts to install Socialism during the past thirty years is all the explanation of the change that is required. And those who are Socialists, or who wish to lead opinion in a scientific approach to politics—that is, in new statesmanship —have now got to start by making a new analysis which takes into account the world we actually have, like it or not. The Editor's thinking on these lines is just as apparent in the use of men like Peter Townsend and Professor Richard Titmuss in the *New Statesman*, as in the appointment of young and independent journalists to key positions. No man of sense can be sure of anything in the Sixties; and no text is still accepted other than by very old-fashioned people set in their ways and rejecting new thinking, such as Communists, orthodox Roman Catholics, Fascists, and in general the old. But the paper has no cult of youth. It is obvious that the Editor attaches importance to, for example, the writings of J. B. Priestley and Malcolm Muggeridge, and the reason is manifest; neither man is young and neither is a conventional Socialist; both are real anti-humbug evangelists who, like John Freeman himself, wish to look at and see the world as it is and not as some of us pretend it is.

It is of passing interest that by 1960 the *New Statesman* was able to take its revenge on richer organs of the Press by taking men like Howard from them instead of training men for them. The *Guardian* provided good training for the kind of journalist the times called for. As a Liberal newspaper in a community whose political Liberals were more or less disenfranchised by the power of the two major Party machines, it supported a Party which was in no danger of having to govern, yet its long tradition of serious political and social journalism saved it from the danger of irresponsibility. Its writers were free to develop a detached, highly critical, and exceptionally intelligent style in their approach to politics; and an occasional touch of contempt or derision was allowable. The *Guardian* had, in fact, itself become almost a journal of dissent, so that Howard, in transferring to the

New Statesman, was not obliged to change the point of view from which he wrote. The danger which he and the Editor have now to contend with is what I may perhaps call the 'French' danger. Deriding politicians in the manner of, say, Bernard Levin in his *Spectator* articles during the late Fifties, is great fun; and since we have to blame somebody for the ills we are heir to and no longer believe in the Devil, it is difficult to feel that there is anything wrong in making savage fun of them all. But self-indulgence, and indulgence of the reader, in this fashion can lead, as in France, to a breakdown in the Parliamentary system. The danger of this happening in the *New Statesman* is very small, for the Editor, having himself worked among politicians, believes them, rightly or wrongly, to be more industrious and honourable than the cynics give them credit for. He has, too, a new kind of political concern which has little to do with Parliament; he believes, or so it seems to me, that the centres and levers of power are now right outside Parliament so that Parliament is becoming an empty charade. And to some extent he therefore believes that the task of the *New Statesman* now, since it believes that people should have real democratic control over their own affairs, must be to try to identify these centres of real power and then to consider how they can best be controlled.

The situation which the *New Statesman* faces, politically though not socially, in 1963 is in some ways more like the situation it faced in 1913 than in 1931. The reader may need reminding that when the paper was started what the Webbs and Clifford Sharp had in mind was the possibility of persuading the 'natural' ruling classes of Britain, in the Conservative or the Liberal parties, to accept increasing measures of Socialism on its merits as the modern, scientific way of organizing and governing a country. Only later did this aim change to that of supporting and educating a specifically Socialist Party with a programme of introducing Socialism *en bloc*. It does not seem to me that the change was made with much enthusiasm at first, but the chances of getting Fabian Socialism embodied in a series of Acts of Parliament by a non-violent revolutionary party seemed fairly good.

With the advent of Kingsley Martin the *New Statesman* substituted a spirit of preaching for a spirit of teaching. It became much less unfriendly to the idea of revolution even accompanied by violence, although it never conceived of this as being at all necessary in Britain, where the Labour Party, kept Left by its intellectuals, was to accomplish Socialism. The paper, it is true, soon found itself running well ahead of the Labour Party and for ever turning round to see where that somewhat sluggish body had got to and to urge it to get a move on. There can be no doubt that from 1930 to about 1947 this was a perfectly reasonable policy and also that it was the policy of goodwill; it was not impossible of achievement, or would not have been had not the USSR constituted so massive an obstacle in the way of world Socialism. But under the assaults of its two enemies, the National Communism of Russia and the Capitalism *à outrance* of the United States, democratic Socialist parties everywhere suffered nothing but a long series of disastrous setbacks (except in Scandinavia); or they became, as in France, exclusively middle class, academic and ineffectual. But meanwhile, and rather oddly in the circumstances, the original Fabian—and new statesmanly—idea of converting the old middle-class parties to Socialism was having a considerable success, unnoticed as such.

In 1963 the possibility of any single revolutionary party introducing democratic Socialism *en bloc* has become remote. Consequently the situation which Kingsley Martin and the *New Statesman* he recreated were facing and dealing with for the decade and a half following 1930 no longer exists. The situation which faces John Freeman and the *New Statesman* which he, in his turn, will have to recreate, is very different. The difference is a derivative of Socialism's failures and successes during the paper's Second Epoch. The failures have almost all been caused by the one single but overwhelming disaster already referred to and unforeseen by Karl Marx or anyone else: the adoption of Socialist ideas in Russia and the coming into being of the USSR. Had Socialism been first introduced by a sophisticated, technologically advanced country, say the Germany of 1913 with its powerful and well-educated Social Democratic Party, strongly backed by the German working class, I believe we should by now have been much farther advanced towards a rational system of world government and a decent standard of living over a much greater part of the world. Its introduction by an intellectual and fanatical élite in a semi-barbarous land barely free of serfdom and with a political tradition of tyranny which had never been broken; a country which was socially, politically, economically and technologically backward and which was in any case in a state of collapse, this was a disaster. It ensured that all the abuses of tyranny would follow, though they might be given new names from the jargon of Socialist literature. Nothing could have so well served the cause of anti-Socialist reaction as the Russian Revolution and its long and terrible aftermath; for these events made it reasonable and necessary, once the truth was fully known, to be anti-Communist and therefore to some extent anti-Socialist. The Socialists everywhere could easily be tarred with the same brush as the Communists, and they were obliged to waste energy and weaken their own position in forever repudiating Russian Communism.

But Russia has been the bane of new statesmanly Socialism since long before the October Revolution. Readers may recall that Clifford Sharp could not find it in his heart to blame the German working class, and the German Social Democrats, for rallying to the German upper and middle classes in the face of the Russian threat. The *New Statesman* was not afraid to say that the German Socialists were bound to defend their civilization against the Russian barbarians who were our allies. It seems that if the great and noble idea of Socialist working-class solidarity transcending frontiers and rising above patriotism was a dismal failure in the event, it is because Russia was involved in the war. It is not absolutely inconceivable that had this not been so, then French and German Socialism might have brought the war to an early end by fraternization.

It should not be forgotten that even in the United States there was a strong Socialist movement in 1913. It discredited itself to a considerable extent by having recourse to violence; the I.W.W., the 'wobblies', were too nearly anarchists of the old nihilist kind ever to succeed in a land where English ideas of law prevailed. But, again, it was the excesses of the Russian Revolution which enabled the American Right to, as it were, paint the Reds black and rouse the whole national feeling of America against Socialism.

The failures of Socialism have done much to change the situation which political journalism has to deal with; its successes have done no less. The new statesmanship of Kingsley Martin had its triumph, but, alas! in the dark shadow of the H-bomb, in 1945-50. And perhaps its greatest triumph was in the emancipation of India. The *New Statesman*, and new statesmanly ideas, played an enormously important part in educating the political Labour movement up to the idea that India could and should be freed. We have forgotten with what passionate conviction by what formidably able men this was declared to be impossible, wicked, certain to result in massacre, chaos, anarchy. In, for example, *Last Essays*, pubished in 1930, Lord Birkenhead, who had been Secretary of State for India for four and a half years, published two essays proving that India could not be ready even for limited Dominion status until perhaps some time in the 'remote future'; in support he quoted authorites as diverse as Lord Russell* and the Aga Khan, who believed that India could not be prepared for Parliamentary self-government for 'several centuries'. It is true that Lord Birkenhead was consistently wrong in every prophecy and political judgment he ever made, but, still, one is not, I suppose, Lord Chancellor for nothing and he was considered to be a man of outstanding intellectual power. He was wrong, and the 'irresponsible' idealistic new statesmen were right. India had her massacre, but it did not lead to chaos; she has shown herself not only capable of stable government but of possessing a remarkable moral authority in world affairs. This was a triumph for new statesmanship. But it would be possible to argue that any repetition of this triumph is not only improbable for some considerable time, but perhaps even unnecessary. And this, if it turns out to be so, is, ironically enough, because of the parallel success of the older, the Webbian, new statesmanship. For the fact

* Not, of course, Bertrand Russell.

is that the older, the middle-class, political parties, have been converted to a measure of Socialism, or at least New Dealism. It is true that they still make free-enterprise noises and that the Conservatives chip away bits of the Labour Party's Welfare State when they can do so without much danger either to the edifice itself or to their vote-worthiness with the electorate. The Conservatives have the immense political advantage of having no principles and no policy. When, during the 1914-18 War, Clémenceau was asked to state his war policy, he replied that it was to wage war. The Conservatives' policy is to govern, and whatever is politically expedient becomes Conservatism. This is so successful in maintaining them in office that it has made an impression on the present Labour Party leaders, and it now seems improbable that, if they again get into office, they will repeat the performance of introducing a large measure of further Socialism *en bloc*.

And this is why I say that the situation facing the present *New Statesman* is more like that which faced Sharp in 1913 than that which faced Kingsley Martin in 1931. The Labour Party now looks like a Liberal Party of reform rather than a Socialist Party of revolution. The working class, relatively prosperous, has more to lose and will therefore become politically very cautious. The Conservative and the reviving Liberal parties have both accepted certain originally Fabian ideas as not only inevitable but positively good. The problem for the Socialist is therefore to persuade all or any of these parties to take increasing measures of Democratic Socialism into their programmes on rational and scientific grounds, and not for emotional, doctrinaire and revolutionary reasons. It will not matter to the sophisticated *New Statesman* of the Sixties what the political parties choose to call their acts, how they choose to cling in words and appearances to their old images. What will matter is what is done, not what is said. Doubtless the paper will continue to support the Labour Party as the one most likely to be persuadable and least hampered by its past or by involvement with irresponsible commercial and selfish industrial interests.

In practice all this must mean that the *New Statesman* of

the next decade must be as different from Kingsley Martin's as his was different from Sharp's. Of the men who will make it over, the key ones are Socialists, but their Socialism transcends Labour politics as did that of the Webbs. I think it might be put like this: Kingsley Martin's *New Statesman* approached the social and political problem emotionally, sometimes passionately, angrily, even 'artistically', feeling its way forward. John Freeman's *New Statesman* is more likely to be 'grown-up', at once less 'likeable'; and less exasperating. It must, surely, be more rational, penetrating, 'scientific'; more sceptical, more enquiring, and ruthlessly anti-humbug. In a sense, it will be going back to its roots. Its cry of dissent will be sustained, but worded otherwise: it will not cry, 'You are wicked!' but, rather, 'You are mistaken!' It will be against the Establishment, but it will not regard that nexus of interests which Priestley calls Topside as the Devil. It will remain capable of anger, but it will have its temper under firm control.

In another and important respect the paper is in a different and stronger position. It has means. Pleading, argument and preaching from doctrine may be the only methods open to an editor whose paper has no money. A richer paper can afford the Fabian method of thorough research followed by factual presentation. It is no longer reduced to saying, 'You must believe us because you know us to be trustworthy men of goodwill.' It can afford to say, instead, 'Here are the irrefutable facts of the case.' When Kingsley Martin took over the *New Statesman* it had a circulation of 12,000 and an advertising revenue of £7,000; it was losing money. The paper which John Freeman took over had a circulation in the upper 70,000s and an advertising revenue of not much under £100,000. In 1963 the circulation is rising into the 90,000s and I have no doubt that the revenue is following the same course upwards. What is equally important, Jeremy Potter's managerial policy and that of the Board is not to spend money on developing auxiliary businesses but on improving and strengthening the *New Statesman*. With care and good management, which seem assured, the paper will be able to afford the kind of scientific journalism which the times call for.

On the side of literature and the arts a fresh beginning has also been made, with the appointment of Karl Miller as Literary Editor. Miller was a pupil of Dr. Leavis, and he is a great respecter of his old tutor. He began his working life in the Treasury; but he wrote reviews for the *Spectator*, gave up the Civil Service for literature, became Literary Editor of the *Spectator*. His ability became apparent to watchful editors, manifest in the literary pages he was editing. He was known, moreover, to be an undoctrinaire Socialist.

It will be remembered that Walter Allen was not enjoying the executive side of Literary Editorship. He and John Freeman agreed together that Allen's talents were not being best used in that office. Freeman had long been seeking to secure Miller for the paper from the *Spectator* and in April 1961 he succeeded in making the change.

Miller is not one of the extreme, didactic 'academics' in literary criticism, not one of its puritans. But he does believe that Dr. Leavis and his followers have set up a new kind of integrity in literary criticism and have done a major service to the art of writing, and reset high standards which should be respected and referred to. He is young, thirty, and very much a man of his generation. This means that he has his limitations; for all I know they may be advantages in the time before us. Desmond MacCarthy and Raymond Mortimer were (Mortimer still is, of course) men of broad, European culture, as 'French' as they were English, and belonging to that order of men whose standards were in the classical literatures and who tended to believe that Paris is the foster-mother of every first-class brain in the modern Western world. Such Englishmen were, and are, as much at home in both the literatures and the countries of France, Italy, Germany and even Spain, as in their own. Karl Miller has a touch of the new insularity which is also to be found in the whole generation of younger creative writers. Perhaps that is not quite correct: he is not insular in the sense that Kingsley Amis is insular; but as a specialist in literature he looks West and is at home in the American idiom. He would not be happy to see our literary culture shrinking within the limits of our own shores. But he is 'insular' enough to be able to understand the present condition of English writing; it enables him to value the wealth of talent which the grammar-school revolution has produced in Britain and to avoid making a cult of literature as the preserve of an élite. This insularity—I personally use the word as a pejorative, but it could perfectly well be shown to mean 'purging' or 'intensification'—is matched by the present insularity of our Socialism. Both are products of the 'proletarianization' I have mentioned. The ideal of a working-class international has failed: the workers of the world have not united; they have, on the contrary, continued to heave bricks at each other on the ground that the other chap is a bloody foreigner. The cultural international has likewise failed and if Karl Miller is tending to make his half of the *New Statesman* take less interest in Europe and more in America, it is to some extent because that is what all our writers are doing: in so far as 'Europeanism' has been affected as a badge of cultural virtue by too many second-rate writers, they are probably right.

A similar change is occurring in the paper as a whole, although the Editor is a man of broad European sympathies with at least as much in common with the Raymond Mortimer point of view as with that of the new Little Englanders. But there is even more and better reason to shift emphasis from Europe to America in political, than in literary, criticism. The lazy conservatism of President Eisenhower, the social and political backwardness of the Republican Party, the dangerously fanatical capitalist-puritanism of J. Foster Dulles, inhibited this movement and made the *New Statesman* perhaps rather carpingly critical of the United States. The election of President Kennedy changed all that. And it seems quite clear that the timing of the new Editor's appointment has, like that of Kingsley Martin's appointment thirty years before, been made to match the beginning of a new political era. In the first epoch of the *New Statesman*'s life the centre of the world was Paris; there were more powerful countries than France, but none with her world-influence. In the second epoch the centre shifted to London in so far as it could be found anywhere at all. For this was a time of Troubles, a chaos. Europe had lost her nerve, at least for the time being and what looks like nerve is really the obstinacy, the guts if you like, of two or three very old men. In the Third Epoch the centre of power for the Western world must lie in Washington. American art, letters and politics must become of more importance than they were in the past.

Thus one of John Freeman's first acts of reorganization was to go to America and choose a man to be the paper's staff writer on the United States. He appointed Karl Meyer. His articles are very different, and in a way which is significant, from those famous articles which S. K. Ratcliffe contributed to the paper from America: to re-read some of these and then one or two of Meyer's is to realize at a glance what has happened to the world in the last fifty years: Ratcliffe writes from the periphery of a world to its centre; Meyer from the centre to the periphery. That is an exaggeration, but it makes my point.

Norman MacKenzie's decision, about eighteen months after John Freeman had taken over the paper, to return to his first love and, when a very good opportunity was offered in the United States, go back to teaching, will put the full weight of ensuring the paper's 'spiritual' continuity with its past on to John Freeman's shoulders. Its movement into the future is assured not only by the appointments he has made, but by the fact that his number two on the *New Statesman* is Paul Johnson, whose work has already been referred to and who is by now an old *New Statesman* hand despite his youth. His approach to the problems which the state of the world presents to serious journalists is 'scientific'. The eye that he casts upon the political and social scene is cold; but the anger which animates some of his writing shows that his heart is not as cold as his eye. His method, for example in the long features which he has written for the *New Statesman* (notably on South America), is to find out the facts, set them down tersely, and draw conclusions from them in the light of reason. He does not plead; nor does he preach; *il constate*. The method can be devastating; but it is difficult and even dangerous to use, for the user may discredit himself by a single serious mistake. A journalist who writes emotionally is much harder to fault. Johnson's other dangerous quality is wit: the English reader enjoys humour, especially, alas! whimsical humour; but he does not much care for wit. But Johnson is learning, and at least he does not pander to that special taste of the upper-class English for being 'satirized' by people careful to use only the most expensive whips, the most rare scorpions: when he is nasty he is really nasty.

It will be remembered that when the *New Statesman* was founded it was predicted by the know-alls that the Webbs would continually interfere with their editor. They did not; and since that time *New Statesman* Boards of Directors have been remarkable for allowing Editors a free hand and even for paying up, out of their own pockets in the old days, when this led the paper into expensive trouble. Maynard Keynes seems to have been the only director who tried to take a hand in the paper's editorial policy, but for years Kingsley Martin managed this situation with great skill, in such a way that he could take advantage of Keynes's positive contribution while retaining absolute control in his own hands; so far as I can discover, not once did Keynes's sometimes angry interferences alter the paper's course in the slightest degree.

For about half the paper's life the Manager and Editor were not directors. Then both Roberts and Kingsley Martin became directors. Both John Freeman and Jeremy Potter are now directors. Moreover, the Board has an exceptionally distinguished Chairman. Gerald Gardiner, Q.C., who became a director of the Company in 1953, was elected Chairman on G. D. H. Cole's death in 1959. He is also Chairman of the 'in effect self-perpetuating trust', the Statesman Publishing Co. which, by owning the management shares, protects the paper from financial raiders like the late Howard Samuel. For any journal, but more especially for any dissenting journal constantly engaged in criticizing men and institutions as it is bound to be, to have a great lawyer of liberal and humane views at the head of its Board-room table, and such an experienced newspaper publisher as Sir Leslie Plummer among the directors, are obvious and very great advantages.

What of means? The enormous change in the Company's financial position has been described. J. A. Morgan, the

Company's Secretary, is himself an old new statesman, having become Wilfred Hewson's assistant in 1946, and he succeeded him in 1953; his principal contributions have been in improving the Company's generous Pensions Scheme and introducing mechanization into its accounting. The large turnover he has to handle depends to a great extent, of course, on the success of the advertisement departments. In 1913 advertisement revenue was and seemed likely to remain so insignificant that Sharp told the Board that an advertisement representative would not earn his keep. Roberts changed all that. The General Advertisement Manager since 1958 has been W. A. Doody; his principal contribution has been to secure a healthy share of the new 'prestige' advertising for the *New Statesman*. Now, as in the past, publishers' advertising is a separate responsibility; it has been in the hands of Michael Roberts since 1954. The job is one for a diplomat. Publishers expect their books to be reviewed—they will probably forgive anything but silence—but they are the only manufacturers who have to put up with seeing their goods criticized, sometimes derided or even savaged, in the papers which also carry their advertisements. One of the principal incarnations of new statesmanship in the special rather than the general sense is Marion Fleisher, who has been secretary and assistant to the Manager for twenty years. Long service has been the rule rather than the exception on the *New Statesman*; it has contributed to the maintenance of the paper's traditions.

As to the man who leads the *New Statesman* and its company of old and new servants into the third epoch of its life, John Freeman, who is forty-eight, comes of the upper middle class and he received, at Westminster School and Brasenose College, Oxford, the conventional professional education of that class. Thus his background is that of, for example, R. H. S. Crossman and Aylmer Vallance, and utterly different from that of Kingsley Martin.

Freeman was always, since boyhood, interested in politics and always on the Left. What is, however, singular and significant, is that, unlike most other clever young men of the middle class but with Left leanings, he never for a moment or at any time paid homage to Communism. In the period of his extremest 'Leftism' he doubtless admired Lenin, and he certainly admired Trotsky whose political oecumenicalism attracted him. But, when everyone else was adulating Stalin, and later when Stalin had become the Western world's Uncle Joe, Freeman was implacably hostile to a tyrant whose villainy, not publicly admitted by the Russians until 1959, he was always convinced of. The villainy of which he held Stalin guilty was the perversion of Socialism so as to make a lie of what Freeman believed and believes essentially true. Such independence of mind in a man of his class and strong Socialist opinions is rare.

In 1937, when Freeman came down from Oxford, a fashionable thing for bright young men if they wished to make their fortune was to go into advertising. So he did that, and stayed in it for three years. It is very easy for a man who has read Greats to write advertising copy: Freeman himself claims that it is rather like writing Latin verse. But when the war broke out he did not wait to be called to the colours: any kind of civilian life seemed to him to have become, in the circumstances, quite 'unreal'; 'real' life had shifted its centre, it had become military. He volunteered, and became a guardsman in the Coldstream. He was on active service from 1940 to 1945. He was commissioned, he served in the Western Desert, through the Italian campaign, and into north-west Europe, and he ended the war with the rank of major.

In 1945, at which time he was with the Army in Germany, he was approached by the Labour Party and asked to stand for Parliament. He demurred; he did not want a parliamentary career; he held strong Left-wing views but he did not believe himself suited for active political life. His Labour Party contacts persisted; the Party was in need of Service men of his stamp for its list of candidates, and there was still a shortage. With many doubts he agreed to fight an election for them, principally because he was asked to fight in a Tory Party stronghold and there seemed no serious danger of his being elected. Thus he reckoned that he would be serving the Party, which had to fight hopeless constituencies as well as the other kind, while running very little risk of becoming an M.P. This did not mean that he could allow his candidature to be a mere formality: he fought the campaign in Watford as hard as he could, doing his best. It was with consternation that he learned of his election: he had been so sure of defeat that he had returned to Germany and got himself a permanent job with the Control Commission before the results of the polling, delayed in that war year, had been announced. He had thus become a professional politician *malgré lui*.

He did not like parliament; as he had foreseen, he detested the life, and he now holds that his ten years as an M.P. and a Minister were worse than his five years as a soldier. But it was quite impossible, since he was in for it, not to do his best; equally impossible that he should fail to be picked out by the leaders for swift promotion. By 1946 he was first P.P.S. to the Minister for War, then Financial Secretary to the War Office, finally Under-Secretary of State for War. In 1947 he led the United Kingdom Defence Mission to Burma. On his return he became Parliamentary Secretary to the Minister of Supply, in which office he remained until 1951.

The circumstances in which he resigned from office and joined the *New Statesman* have, since they were part of the great Bevanite Schism, been already described. In 1953 he announced that he would not stand for re-election to Parliament. His long *corvée* for the Labour Party ended in 1955. His service to the cause of political and social reform espoused in his youth, could now be given in much broader terms. It is inevitable that a man who has become a 'star' of the more serious side of television should often be the subject of conversation, and a question very often asked and rarely answered is why did he, who seemed clearly bound for the highest office, give up politics as he did? The answer is perfectly clear and simple—Parliament was not to his taste.

Epilogue

RIGHTLY or wrongly I derived new statesmanship, and therefore the *New Statesman*, from that sense of responsibility towards 'the people' (one might almost write simply 'people') and not merely towards the nation, which distinguishes a small but important section of the English upper and middle classes. I showed how this sense of social, as distinct from political, responsibility made a tremendous impression on Hippolyte Taine who studied the English as an anthropologist studies primitive tribesmen and was probably the most intelligent and sensitive foreigner ever to do so. Political Socialism became the expression, and the Labour Party the rather blunt instrument, of that social conscience. Since the strength of the Labour Party lay in a working class deeply suspicious of 'intellectuals', and in Trade Union bosses whose interest too often lay in fostering such suspicion, that entailed compromises which were sometimes crippling. Yet it is as well that they were made, for the 'intellectuals' and the Labour Party are still, albeit uneasily, in partnership, whereas elsewhere, for example in France and in Italy, the working class has come to look not to Social Democracy but to Communism for its leadership, and the erstwhile purity of Communist ideas has been permanently fouled by Stalinism.

But as I have already suggested, we can no longer look forward to an electoral victory for Fabian Socialism, for new statesmanship in alliance with Labour, as the Day on which Acts of Parliament will set all right. The position now seems to be, once again, that all three political parties will be open to receive measures of Socialism, which will not be so called, into their programmes; and no political party will henceforth, as far as I can see—which is perhaps not very far—plan to install Socialism *en bloc*. It seems quite likely, moreover, that the British Trade Union movement will, like so much else in our lives, become increasingly Americanized: that is, reduce and even drop its political activity and concentrate upon direct negotiation with the managers of industry, themselves long since converted to at least some measures of economic Socialism, in improving the lot of its members. Does all this mean an entirely new role for the social conscience in general, and for the *New Statesman* in particular? I think not: for, as Norman Mac-Kenzie showed in a typically thorough and 'dedicated' piece of writing which introduced a series of articles by Professor Titmuss in 1962, Britain is still two nations and the task of making it one remains.

The activity of the social conscience which found (and still has) its expression in the *New Statesman*, began in the parish, expanded to the constituency, the nation, the Empire, the Commonwealth. It is possible that one day there will be only people, not 'the people'. For the time being all that has happened is that the social problems which faced the Webbs in 1913 face the present *New Statesman* almost all over the world while they have become less acute at home. The many are still poor; but at least now we know why; and the majority are still destitute. We, at home, grumble at our social lot and we live in hideous danger from the abuse of our own scientific cleverness. Yet it is true that in Europe and in North America and in all the white countries of the Commonwealth, Fabian Socialism, new statesmanship (under a score of fancy names), has done something of what it set out to do. The people of those countries live better and more nearly under justice in 1963 than they did in 1913. Moreover, in all the new countries whose people are not white and who were under colonial rule, with the black spot exception of South Africa, native governments are in office, new statesmanship has provided them with an ideal, and the fact that they fall short of it, being human, does not mean that they and their people would not be infinitely worse off without it. They have, and they recognize it in their very special attitude to Kingsley Martin, a debt not only towards the general notion of new statesmanship, but towards the *New Statesman* itself.

In 1913 the task of the *New Statesman* was conceived of as nation-wide. It is now worldwide. And in a world where the English language is becoming, has already to some extent become, the *lingua franca*, the future of new statesmanship may well be even greater than its past.

Index

The abbreviation *N.S.* for *New Statesman* is used throughout.

Germany—*cont.*
194; effects of Nazism on, 201; and the Sudeten-Deutsch, 209-10; the Resistance Movement in, 235-6
Gill, Eric, 112, 113
Glover, Edward, 206
Gollancz, Victor, 134, 186
Gould, Gerald, 38, 59, 95
Graves, Robert, 129, 130
Great Britain, her position in the Thirties, 173, 178; assists Franco, 194; her failure to take the lead, 249-50; her friendship with U.S., 250-1
Great War, 1939-45: the *N.S.* and its conduct, 215-16; its early days, 217-18; the Second Front Controversy, 230-1
Grey, Sir Edward, 11, 46, 49, 50, 56
Guedalla, Philip, 96
Guild Socialism, 11-12, 48, 94n.
Gwynne, H. A., 102

'Hadlow, John', 259
Harben, Henry, 16
Harrison, Frederic, 9
H-bomb, effect of its manufacture, 239-40, 241, 243, 244-7, 249; manufactured by U.S.S.R., 266; America and, 266-7; Bevan espouses, 281, 287; Priestley and, 287
Henderson, H. D., 119, 126-7
Hewart, Lord Chief Justice, 103-5
Hewitt, C. R., 144-5
Hewson, Wilfrid, 271, 312
Hiroshima, 239, 243-5
Hitler, Adolf, 148, 152; the *N.S.* and his aggression, 180-1, 218-19; attacks Russia, 229-30
Hoare, Sir Samuel, 189
Hobson, J. A., 47, 101
Hogben, Lancelot, 212, 213-14
Hogg, Mr., 18
Hoole, Jack, 271, 272
Hoover, President, 147 and n.
Horrabin, J. F., 212, 213-14
Howard, Anthony, 300, 301-2
Huddleston, Sisley, 43
Huxley, Aldous, 204
Hyams, Edward, John Freeman on, viii-x; his relations with the *N.S.*, 260-1

India, the *N.S.* and, 135, 225-7, 305; the policy criticized by U.S., 234-5; the Labour Government and, 249, 305
Isaacs, Godfrey, 25
Isherwood, Christopher, 129, 132, 221
Italy, her aggression in Abyssinia, 152-4, 177; her territorial ambitions, 177; rise of the workers in, 193-4; assists Franco, 194

Japan, and Manchuria, 141-2, 146, 150, 151, 177; her attack on America, 232-4
Joad, C. E. M., 150, 154, 228, 257
Johnson, Paul, 290-2, 310-11
Jowitt, W. A., K.C., 103-4

Kapp, Xavier, 228
Keeling, Frederick, 33, 44, 48, 50
Keep Left Group, 278-9
Kennedy, President, 309
Keynes, J. M., Baron, 108, 136, 236, 273; Martin and, 110, 115, 118, 125, 140, 311; and a merger with the *N.S.* 119, 120-1; advocates a revenue tariff, 126, 137-8; and the May's Report, 139; his Peace Policy, 208-10; and Shaw's wartime letter to the *N.S.*, 219-21; his dislike of Brailsford, 226-7; and the Second Front, 230-1
Khrushchev, Nikita, 131, 269; his reply to Russell, 289-92
Koestler, Arthur, 259-60; and Leftism in the Thirties, 106, 107, 130, 131
Korean War, 261, 262-5, 278-9, 284
Kreuger, Ivar, 89, 126

Labour Party, the *N.S.* and, xii-xiii, 87, 106-8, 125, 280, 303; the Fabian Society and, 9; and peace in 1914, 50; Cole and, 93; in the Thirties, 127, 137, 139-40; Martin and, 139; defection of its leaders, 139-40; and Churchill, 216, 222; its weakness in office, 223; in power, 1945, 239; and the General Election, 241-2; its failure in Europe, 249, 315; and the H-bomb, 287; its present character, 306
Lambert, Constant, 124
Laski, Harold, 101, 134, 168, 204, 228; his friendship with Martin, 110, 201; reviews Wells, 148; his wartime policy, 222, 231, 232; and MacKenzie, 299
Lawrence, D. H., 34, 35, 37, 96
League of Nations, 176, 181, 185; fails to stop aggression, 142, 147, 150, 151, 153-4, 177; its rea weakness, 177-8
Leavis, Dr., 308
Le Bas, Sir Hedley, and the *N.S.* circulation, 81-2
Lee of Fareham, Lord, Sharp and, 83-4
Lees-Smith, H. B., 117